IMAGES
of America

CLAYTON

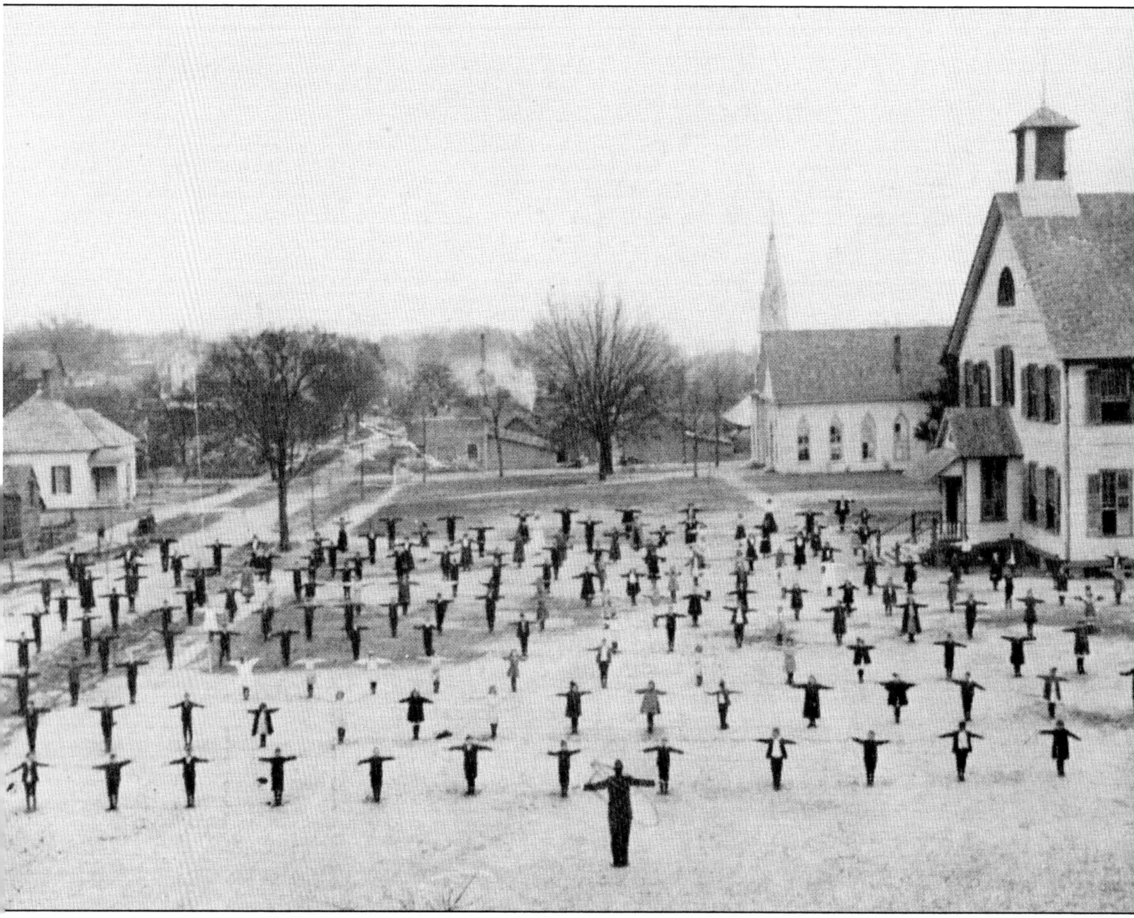

This photograph from 1909 showing Clayton High School students during morning calisthenics illustrates school leaders' commitment to students' physical as well as intellectual development. The classroom building (right foreground), completed in 1901, was first used as a private school and, in 1909, became a nine-month public school after voters approved a special tax. (Courtesy of John T. Talton's *Illustrated Handbook of Clayton, North Carolina, and Vicinity*, 1909.)

ON THE COVER: Blacksmith and machinist Colon Hamilton (left) is shown around 1920 in his Main Street shop with customer Ashley Horne II. W. E. Hamilton started the business as a wagon factory in 1897, and his sons Colon and James took over by 1904. (Courtesy of Hocutt-Ellington Memorial Library.)

IMAGES
of America

CLAYTON

Pamela Lipscomb Baumgartner
and K. Todd Johnson

ARCADIA
PUBLISHING

ISBN 978-0-7385-6743-3

Published by Arcadia Publishing
Charleston, South Carolina

Printed in the United States of America

Library of Congress Catalog Card Number: 2008929801

For all general information contact Arcadia Publishing at:
Telephone 843-853-2070
Fax 843-853-0044
E-mail sales@arcadiapublishing.com
For customer service and orders:
Toll-Free 1-888-313-2665

Visit us on the Internet at www.arcadiapublishing.com

Contents

ACKNOWLEDGMENTS

Individuals and organizations who have contributed photographs to this work are acknowledged herein, but several others merit special recognition:

The warm and enthusiastic support of Betty Coats, director of the Hocutt-Ellington Memorial Library, and the library's staff and board of trustees, whose efforts to preserve Clayton's history have been so vital through the years.

The late John T. Talton's Clayton handbooks from 1909, 1936, and 1961 have provided a tremendous wealth of historical information that otherwise would have been lost.

The late Virginia Lee Satterfield spent decades and untold hours poring over old newspapers (including eye-straining microfilm) and other records to provide at researchers' fingertips a treasure trove of primary source materials on Clayton's history.

The Priddy Foundation of Wichita Falls, Texas, and many local individuals and businesses showed generosity, allowing the library to purchase equipment and software necessary to make digitization of historical collections an ongoing part of its program.

The Friends of the Library sponsored this project as well as a digitization project to provide access to Clayton's history via the Internet.

Steve Biggs, Angela Tousey, and other staff of the Town of Clayton, together with Thomas Lipscomb IV and information technology specialists at the firm VC3, offered technical and logistical support in the digitization process.

Finally, thanks to all the individuals, families, organizations, and institutions who have shared their history with the library so that generations to come can know the story of this special place called Clayton.

Unless otherwise noted, images included in this book are from the 1909 and 1936 editions of John T. Talton's *Handbook of Clayton and Vicinity* or from the photograph collections in the Virginia Lee Satterfield History Room of the Hocutt-Ellington Memorial Library in Clayton.

INTRODUCTION

The earliest recorded history of the Clayton area is found in the journal of English surveyor John Lawson, who made a reconnaissance survey of Carolina in 1701 to explore development possibilities for the eight Lords Proprietors. As Lawson crossed the fall line between the Piedmont and Coastal Plain, he encountered the Iroquoian-speaking Tuscarora, who controlled the Neuse-Pamlico region and held a monopoly on trade between Piedmont tribes and Europeans along the coast. Conflicts between colonists and the Tuscarora led to a brutal war between 1711 and 1714, and the defeated natives were banished from the colony. The British crown purchased seven of the proprietors' interests in 1729, and European settlers soon began taking up lands there, some bringing African and Native American slaves.

In 1746, the colonial assembly created Johnston County from Craven to more effectively govern new settlers. The creation of Dobbs County from Johnston County in 1758 placed the Clayton area in the center of Johnston, and a new courthouse was built on William Hinton's plantation. It was there at Hinton's Quarter that a tax revolt took place in the summer of 1768, as backwoodsmen known as Regulators attempted to take over the county court by force. A mob armed with clubs repulsed the Regulators that same day and reclaimed power for the local ruling elite.

When Wake County was carved out of Johnston County in 1771, the seat of government moved farther east to John Smith's plantation, chartered as Smithfield in 1777. Etheldred Gregory eventually acquired the Hinton property and operated a tavern, Gregory's Ordinary, for travelers between Hillsboro and Tarboro until the building burned in 1809. The federal government established short-lived post offices nearby at Whitley's (1829–1834) and Pineville (1832–1836) in present Wilders Township and at Gulley's Store (1845–1856) near the old courthouse site.

By the 19th century, the planter families of William and John Hinton, John and Reuben Sanders, John and Samuel Smith, Aaron and Drury Vinson, John McCullers and others settled along the upper Neuse River to raise livestock, corn, and other products to turn into cash in Fayetteville, Petersburg, Norfolk, and other market towns. Cotton became an important cash crop following the advent of Eli Whitney's gin in the early 1800s. The area's abundant pine forests also afforded some landowners opportunities to capitalize on the naval stores industry for which eastern North Carolina was so well known. Most families, however, were of sturdy yeoman stock, and their farming was primarily for subsistence.

The North Carolina Railroad Company's decision to build a rail line from Goldsboro to Charlotte in the 1850s would forever change the local landscape. The route through Johnston County ran along the Raleigh–New Bern Stage Road, where Isaac and Sarah Stallings operated an inn and way station. About 1853, the first leg opened between Goldsboro and Raleigh, and the company located a wood-fueling stop on the Stallings property near present O'Neil and Front Streets. The widow Sarah Stallings sold lots around the station to William Sanders, who built a hotel; to Jule Nichols and W. W. Cox, who built stores; to Troy Bunn, who established a turpentine distillery; and to Wesley Hicks, who opened a bar room. Manufactured goods from the north became increasingly plentiful with the railroad's advent, and within a generation, items such as the spinning wheel and hand loom became relics of the past. Occupations such as tanner and cooper also became obsolete. In 1856, the federal government closed the Gulley's Store post office and opened a new facility near Stallings Station, naming it Clayton. A bill was introduced in the state legislature, although it did not receive a second reading, to incorporate the Town of Clayton in 1859. Ten years later, on April 12, 1869, Clayton finally received a charter.

Some sources attribute the town's name to U.S. senator John Middleton Clayton of Delaware. Others say antebellum school teacher William B. Jones named the town. Oral tradition handed down by descendants of a pioneer bright leaf tobacco producer in Person County suggests a humbler inspiration. John Draper Clayton, according to family tradition, frequently set up camp nearby while traveling through eastern North Carolina selling his tobacco in the antebellum years. He achieved notoriety when 100 pounds of his leaf tobacco sold for an astounding $40 on the Danville market. As a great-granddaughter wrote, he also enjoyed the distinction of having a town in Johnston County named in his honor. Lending the story credence is the nearby unincorporated 1840s village of Roxboro, the name of "Forty Dollar John" Clayton's hometown.

The Civil War of 1861–1865 brought sweeping changes. Clayton's young men answered the Confederacy's call to arms and formed a company of volunteers, the Clayton Yellow Jackets, in the spring of 1861. On April 12, 1865, local residents heard cannons and gunfire from a skirmish at the eastern edge of town between the remnants of Confederate general Joseph E. Johnston's army and advancing Union troops under Gen. William T. Sherman. Later that night, near the Clayton depot, the surrender of Raleigh was negotiated between Sherman and commissioners sent by Gov. Zebulon B. Vance.

Following the war, a scarcity of food and money resulted in a vicious crop lien system that transformed the Clayton area's long-standing subsistence-based farming economy to one dependent on cash crops—primarily cotton. Some prospered, but many struggled under the new order. Resourceful men such as Ashley Horne, William H. McCullers, and John G. Barbour were able to accumulate fortunes dealing in agricultural implements and supplies, and serving as bankers for those who needed cash or credit. These men also acquired extensive farming interests and, by 1900, banking institutions and lucrative manufacturing plants producing cotton textiles and cottonseed oil. J. Arch Vinson capitalized on virgin timber supplies and made a fortune in lumber. Efforts to make Clayton a bright leaf tobacco market in the first decade of the 20th century were not so successful, as competition from established markets proved too great. Tobacco still became the economic salvation of many struggling local farmers after cotton prices fell sharply.

By the dawn of the 20th century, it had become obvious that Clayton was no ordinary small town. A local news correspondent proclaimed in the August 9, 1890, edition of the *Smithfield Herald*, "Clayton is a blessed little place and boasts of being the wealthiest town of its size in the United States." This bold claim was reiterated in a Raleigh *Evening Times* feature on April 22, 1907. The headline read, "Clayton, North Carolina. The Wealthiest City for its Size in the World." The writer cited "United States statistics" (presumably based on Dun and Bradstreet reports). "This thriving little city" he added, "stands fourth, financially, of all the cities in the United States." Ashley Horne led the way, with business interests stretching across North Carolina.

Clayton was also recognized, in the words of the 1890 writer, as a "high bred little town." Laura Elizabeth Lee Battle's memoir, *Forget-Me-Nots of the Civil War* (1909), describes a racetrack on the outskirts of Clayton, complete with grandstand, erected for a state horseracing tournament in 1869. Competitors in regal costumes and throngs of visitors came from near and far. The columns of the *Smithfield Herald* and the short-lived *Clayton Bud* (1883–1887) abound with accounts of musical performances, speeches, debates, and social events "of a high order" in the late 19th century. Clayton's private academy, known variously as the Clayton Institute, the Clayton Academy, the Utopian Institute, and, in the 20th century, the Clayton High School, was perhaps the greatest source of local pride. The Utopian Institute produced several high achievers from the Horne and Ellington families, including Dartmouth College professor Dr. Herman H. Horne, University of Chicago professor and U.S. ambassador William E. Dodd, Southern Baptist Convention leader and college president Dr. John E. White, internationally renowned architect Douglas Ellington, and pioneer aviator Lt. Eric Ellington.

Clayton joined other progressive communities across North Carolina in 1899 in opening a liquor dispensary to control the alcoholic beverage trade. Further evidence of the town's forward-thinking "New South" spirit could be seen in the following developments during the beginning of the 20th century: Ashley Horne's Bank of Clayton (1899) and Clayton Cotton Mills (1900); A. J. Barbour's Clayton Cotton Oil Mill (1903) and Liberty Cotton Mill (1907); a municipal sewage system (1903); the Clayton Telephone Company (1907); the Clayton Building and Loan Association (1908); two newspapers, the short-lived *Clayton Enterprise* (1909) and the *Clayton News* (1911); a movie theater (1910); a waterworks (1912); and electric lights (1913). In 1910, the town's population was counted at 1,441, making it the largest municipality in Johnston County.

Clayton's success in business and agriculture peaked following World War I. According to the U.S. Census Bureau, the town's population actually declined slightly between 1910 and 1920 to 1,423. By 1925, there were two cotton mills, a cottonseed oil mill, two lumber mills, two fertilizer plants, and two ice plants, all together employing about 1,000 people. An agricultural depression that began in the early 1920s wiped out most of the Ashley Horne family's fortune in 1927. Other families saw their holdings depleted or gone altogether as crop prices plummeted, and both of the town's banks closed during the Great Depression. It was not until after World War II that the area's economy rebounded.

As in any community, Clayton's uniqueness was embodied in its people and in their schools, churches, social clubs, service organizations, and local government. A northern educator named Henry Winton opened an academy in Roxboro prior to 1853, followed by Prof. William B. Jones, who established the Clayton Institute in 1856. This school and its successors—the Clayton Academy, the Clayton Utopian Institute, and the Clayton High School—served white students until state funding for public high schools caused most private academies to close by around 1910. Quinton Mials and his wife, Lillie, opened a school for local African Americans about 1889. This public school, known as the Clayton Negro School, was named the William Mason Cooper High School in 1940.

Baptists of both races worshipped at the Johnston Liberty Meeting House on John McCullers's plantation beginning in 1811. In 1859, Methodists organized inside the town limits, followed in 1870 by former slaves from Johnston Liberty, who established a separate Baptist congregation in town. Johnston Liberty's remaining members relocated to town in the 1880s, changing their name to the Clayton Baptist Church. Subsequent churches included Clayton Primitive Baptist (founded in 1900), Everett's Chapel Free Will Baptist (1903), Mount Vernon Christian (1910), St. Augustine African Methodist Episcopal (1910), St. Joseph's Catholic (1910), Clayton (later North Clayton) Christian (1920), Clayton Church of God (1930), and Clayton Pentecostal Holiness (1931).

Clayton was the only town in Johnston County with a lodge for the prohibitionist Good Templars in the 1870s as well as for the Knights of Pythias, organized in 1903. Other clubs and service organizations dating before 1946 include the Granite Masonic Lodge (1865), the African American Odd Fellows Lodge (pre-1883), the white Odd Fellows Lodge (1897), the Star of Bethlehem Masonic Lodge, the Halcyon Book Club (1912), the Junior Order of United American Mechanics (1916), the Woodmen of the World (1917), the 20th Century Mother's Club (later known as the Woman's Club of Clayton) (1918), the American Legion (1919), the Clayton Rotary Club (1925), the Music Club (1927), the Junior Woman's Club (1928), the Felecia Book Club (1928), the Parmi-Nous Club (1944), and the Community Club (1945); the latter two clubs were African American.

Following World War II, efforts were made to rebuild the town's industrial base, but it was quickly becoming a bedroom community for the burgeoning state capital, where government and service industry jobs were more plentiful. Local promoters continued to push for industrial development and, by the 1970s, were successful in recruiting several major players such as Champion Products, Oneida Molded Plastics, Miles-Cutter Laboratories, Data General, and Natvar. The completion of Interstate 40 through the Clayton and Cleveland areas in the late 1980s opened a floodgate of residential and commercial development, assisted greatly by Johnston County's comparatively low property taxes. The town of Clayton alone has seen a population of 4,000 in 1980 grow to an estimated 17,000 in 2007. The number of residents within a 6-mile radius reportedly grew from 17,000 in 1990 to 40,000 in 2006.

One

Businesses and Industries

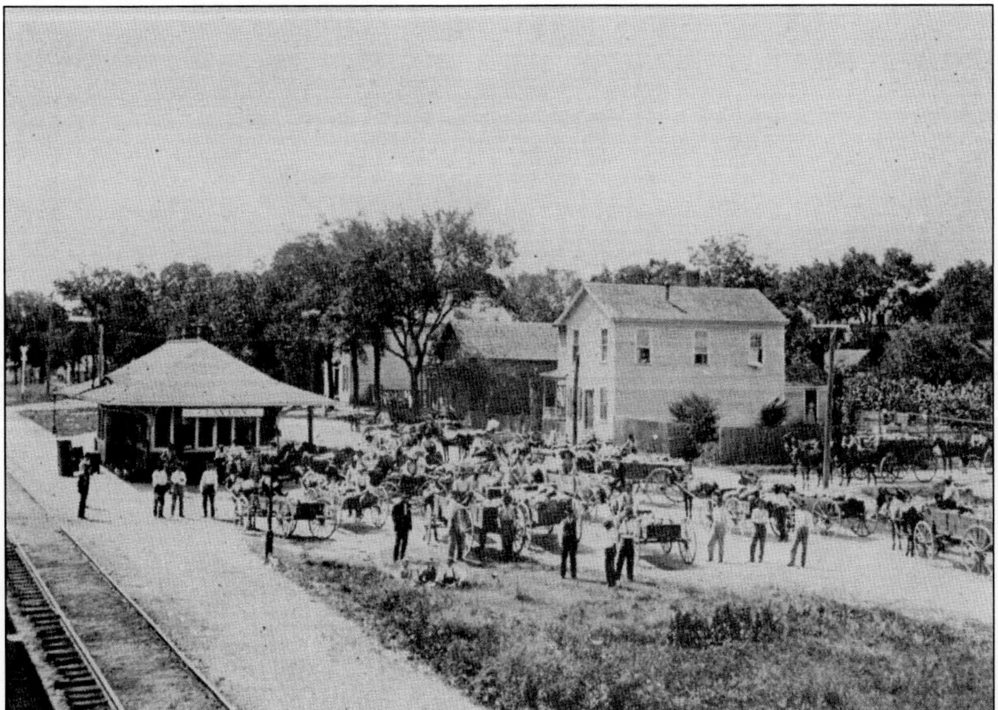

The railroad depot was the epicenter of Clayton in the days before automobiles and highways. This 1909 scene shows watermelon-laden wagons waiting for the train. News accounts indicate 95 carloads of watermelons were shipped out in 1907, with 105 going out in 1908. Truck farming, though not as lucrative as tobacco, offered farmers an alternative to low-priced cotton.

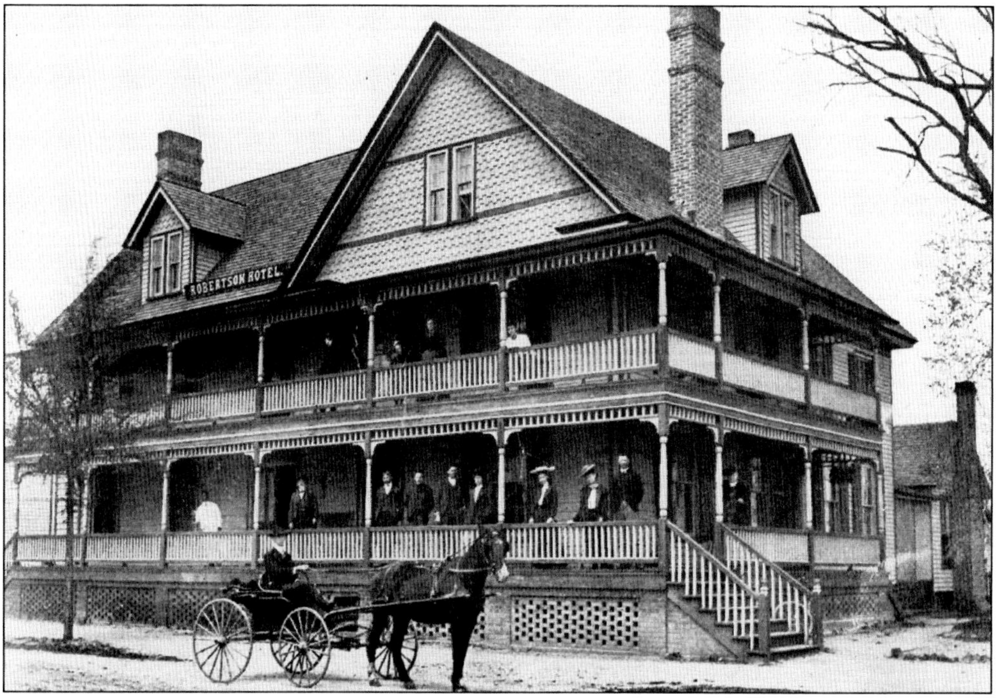

The Robertson Hotel, shown in 1904, was located on Front Street across from the depot. Dr. James B. and Julia Robertson operated the hotel from 1886 until 1906, when Heze Pool and his wife, Lily, took over management. Roy Robertson is in the buggy. From left to right on the porch are (first floor) Hal Rand, Dr. Robertson, J. F. Miller, Ralph Parkinson, Sam White, Nellie Pool, Lelia Shore Thomas, Claudia Mitchell, Will McCullers, and Julia Robertson; (second floor) Mr. and Mrs. Whitmore, Minnie Whitmore, and Pearl Robertson.

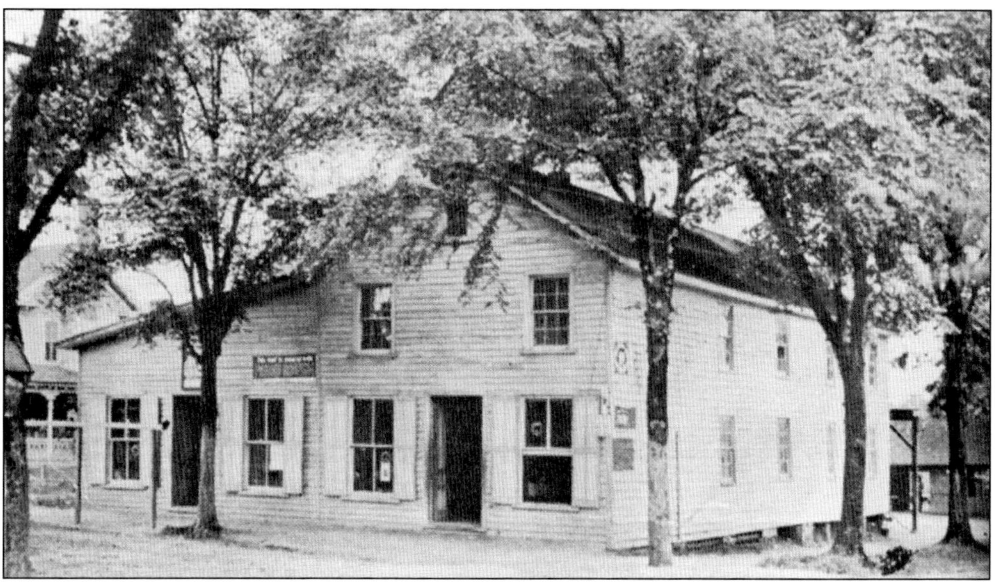

Brothers John I. and Luther Barnes operated the firm J. I. Barnes and Brother, a lumber and hardware business, shown on the corner of Second and Church Streets in 1909. This building was previously home to J. E. Page's Clayton Buggy and Wagon Works.

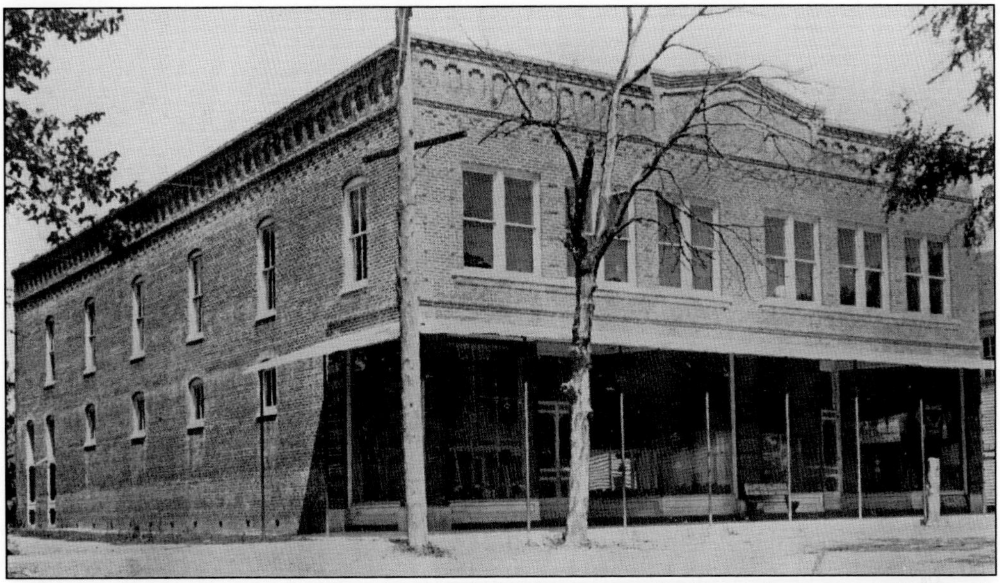

In 1906, Ashley Horne and Son completed this large store building, shown in 1909, beside the Horne mansion at the corner of Main and Lombard Streets. The business included dry-goods and grocery departments, cotton buyers, general merchandise, furniture, buggies, and gentlemen's furnishings. R. B. Whitley of Wendell purchased the business after the Horne company's bankruptcy in 1927, and Whitley's daughter and son-in-law, Rachel and William R. Peele, ran the business. The building is still standing, although the upper story was removed and the building was completely remodeled following a fire in the 1950s.

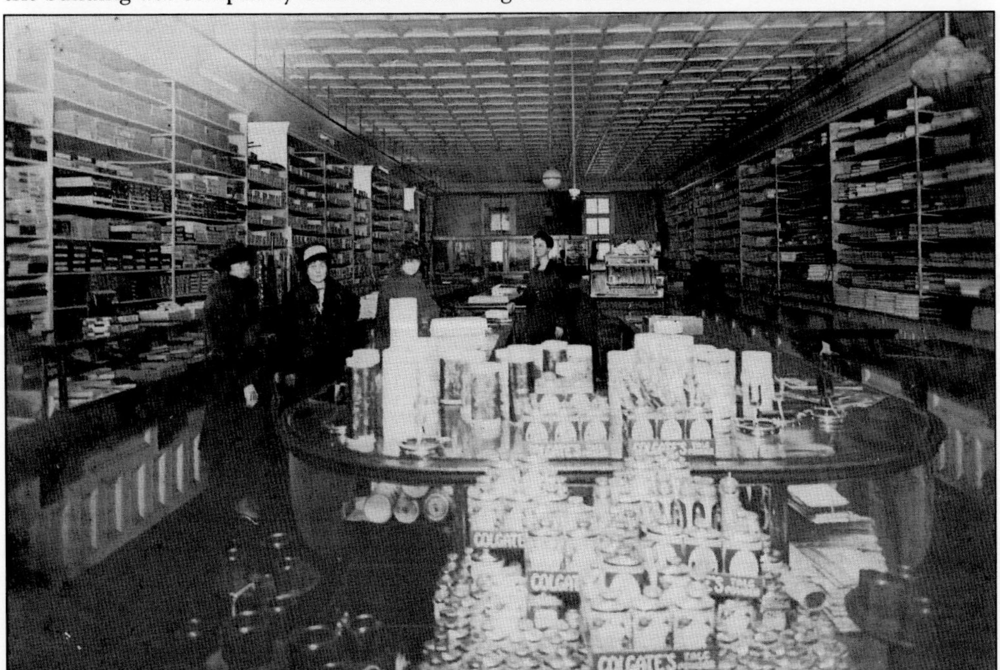

This interior view of the Horne store around 1910 shows the dry-goods department where ladies could purchase items such as clothing, fabric, sewing articles, perfumes, and powders.

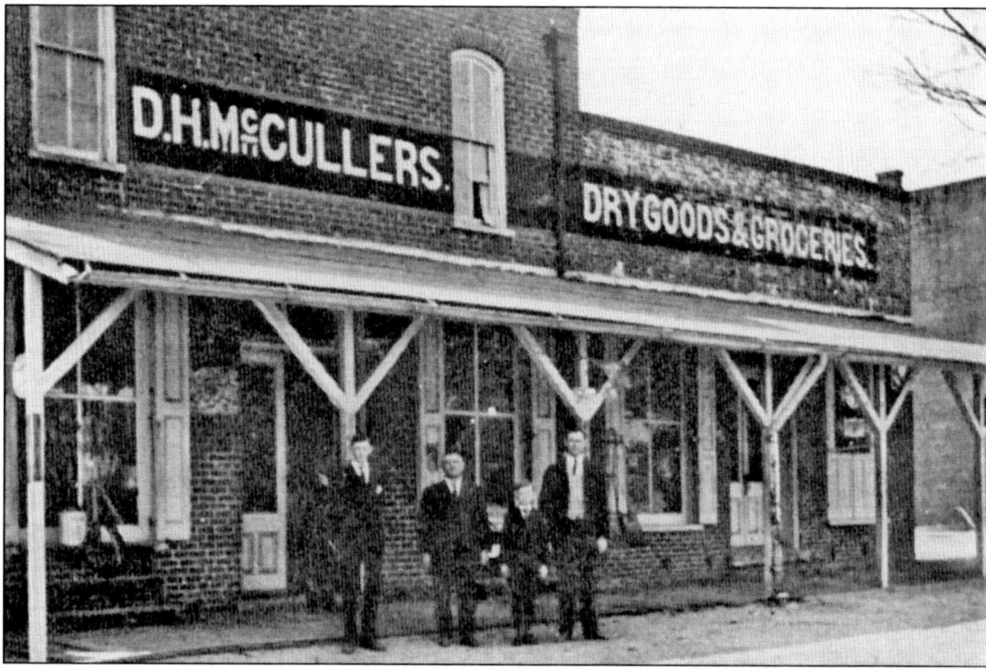

The D. H. McCullers Company, shown in 1909, was successor to a longtime family business established in 1869 by W. H. McCullers. This brick store, located on First Street, was built in 1887 and was the first brick store in Clayton. Standing in front from left to right are Bruce Pool, Jesse Hillard, Willard D. McCullers (son of D. H. McCullers), and Jim Williamson.

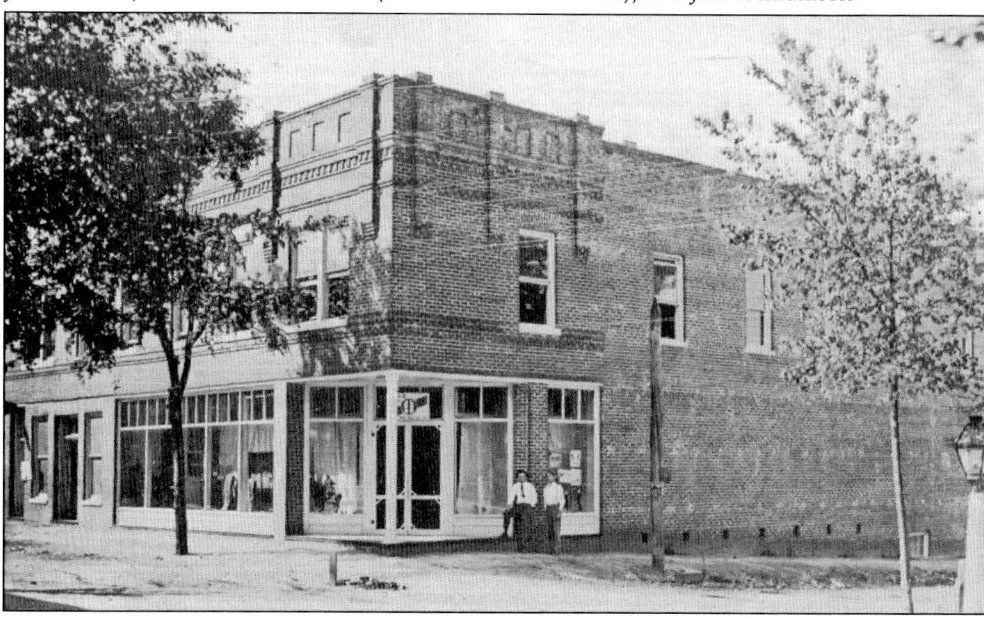

The J. G. Barbour and Sons building, completed in 1904, is shown here in 1909. The firm began in 1856 on the Barbour farm near Swift Creek and moved to Main Street in Clayton in 1881. John G. Barbour gave sons Julian and David interest in the store in 1888. After the death of Julian in 1911 and David in 1917, Julian's sons—Dwight, Swade, and Roger—operated the business. The business closed in 1976.

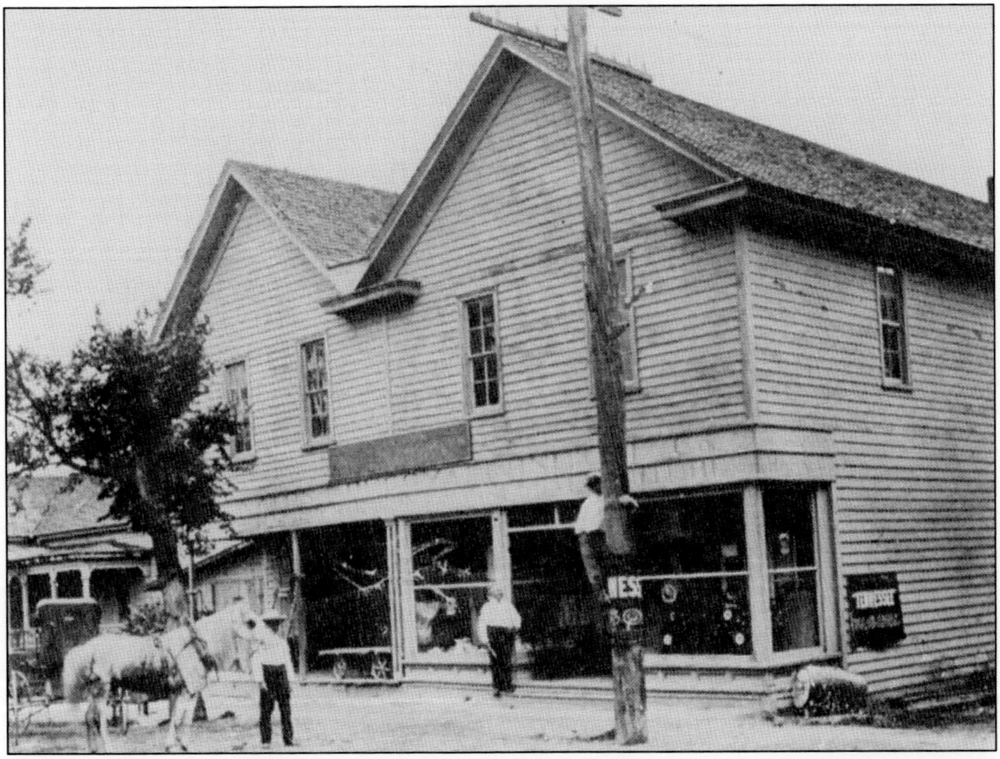

Clayton Buggy and Furniture was in business by 1904 and was housed in the building formerly used by J. G. Barbour and Sons. The building had been moved down Main Street to make room for the new brick Barbour building. The business was chartered in January 1907 by A. J. Barbour, D. W. Barbour, W. A. Barnes, B. M. Robertson, L. F. Austin, Charles W. Horne, and L. Gregory.

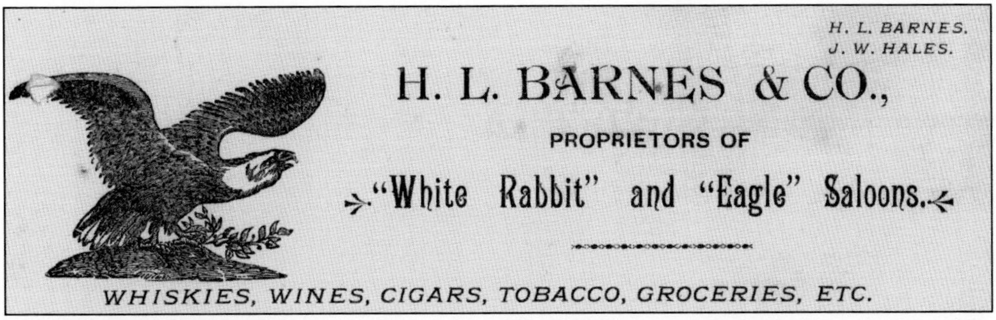

H. L. Barnes and J. W. Hales operated the White Rabbit and Eagle Saloons before 1899, when Clayton leaders secured legislative approval of a town-operated dispensary. (Courtesy of Carey Barbour.)

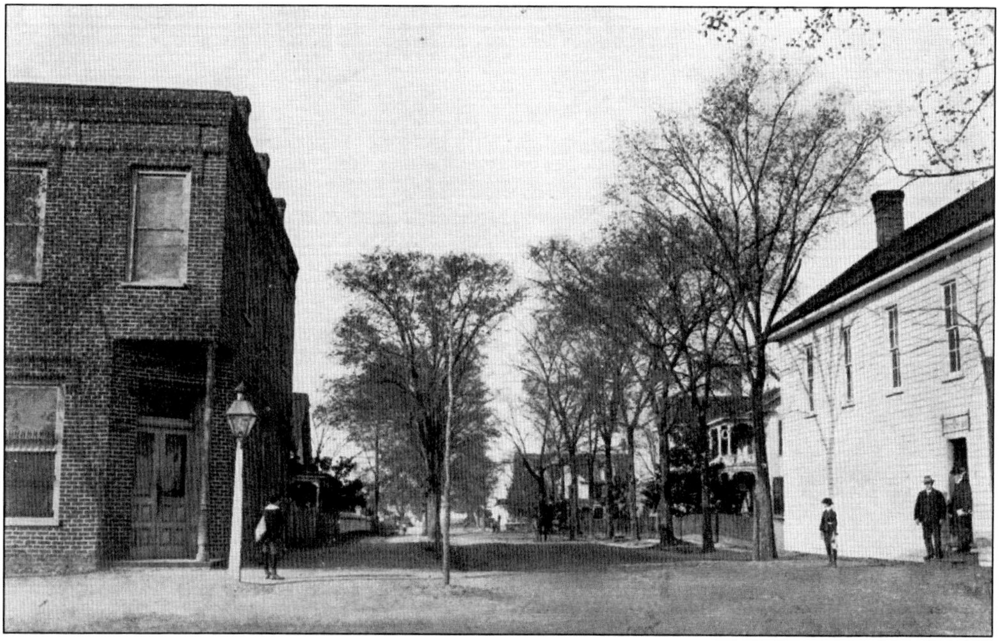

The corner of Fayetteville and First Streets was a busy place in 1904. The Bank of Clayton building (left) was used as a meeting place for the Masons, Pythians, and other clubs. The post office (right) was destroyed by fire about 1909. The Clayton High School dormitory can be seen on the back right.

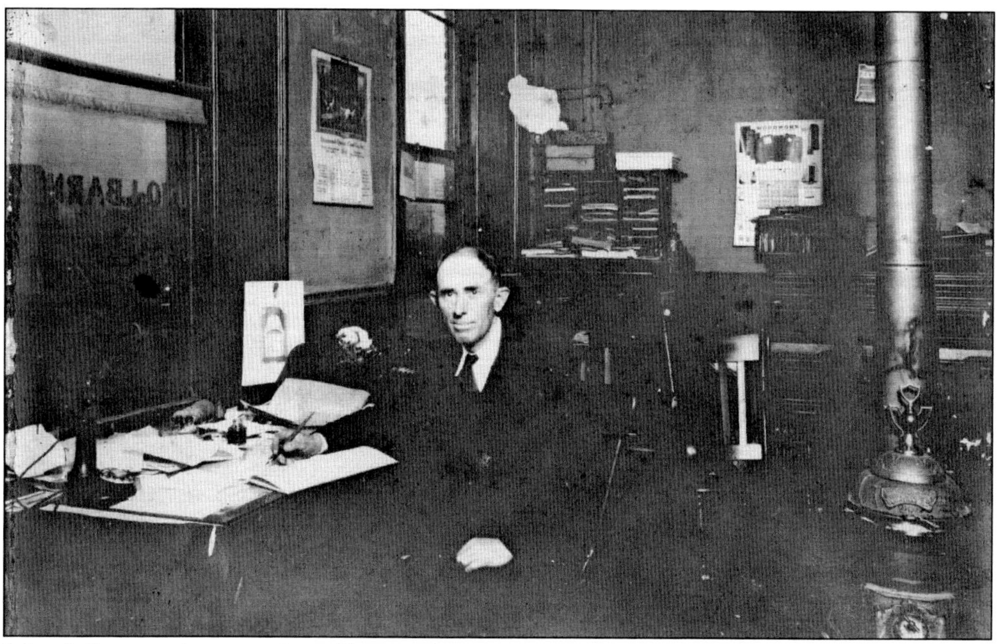

John I. Barnes, shown in his office in the 1920s, was an undertaker and dealer in building materials and coal. By the 1930s, he operated an ambulance service. Before going into business on his own, Barnes was a cotton weigher for Ashley Horne and Son, beginning in 1902. (Courtesy of John I. and Jane Barnes.)

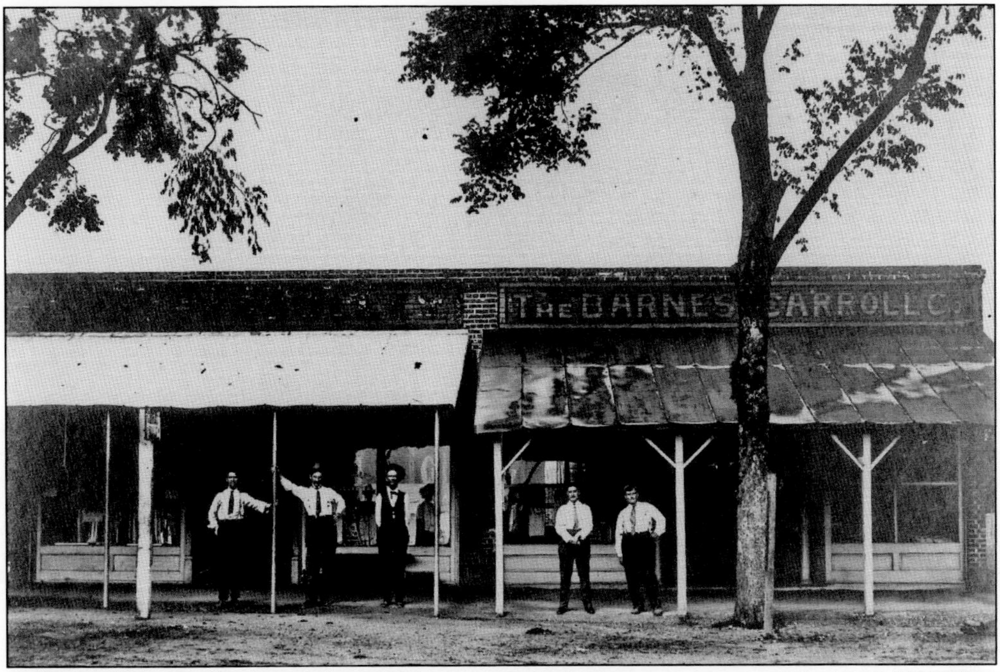

Gulley and Gulley, shown at left in 1909, was a men's clothing store operated by Mark G. Gulley, his son Charles, and cousin Riley Ray Gulley. The Barnes and Carroll Company was a dry-goods and notions store operated by Joe T. Barnes and Tom Carroll.

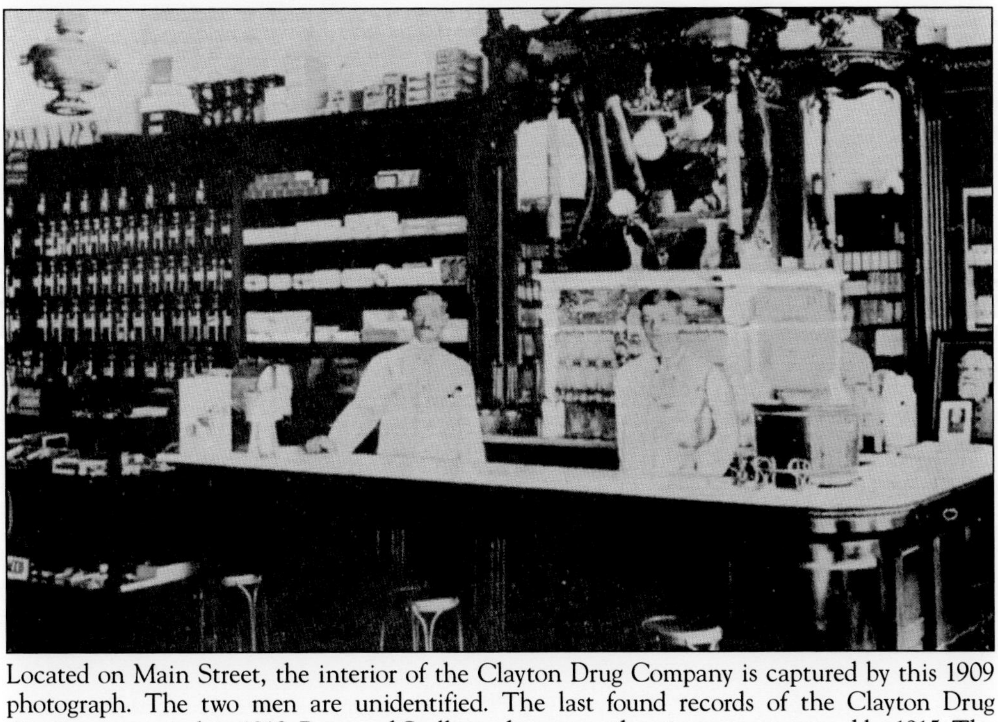

Located on Main Street, the interior of the Clayton Drug Company is captured by this 1909 photograph. The two men are unidentified. The last found records of the Clayton Drug Company were in late 1913. Pope and Stallings drugstore advertisements appeared by 1915. The Beddingfield brothers, C. H. and Edgar, bought the Pope and Stallings business in 1919.

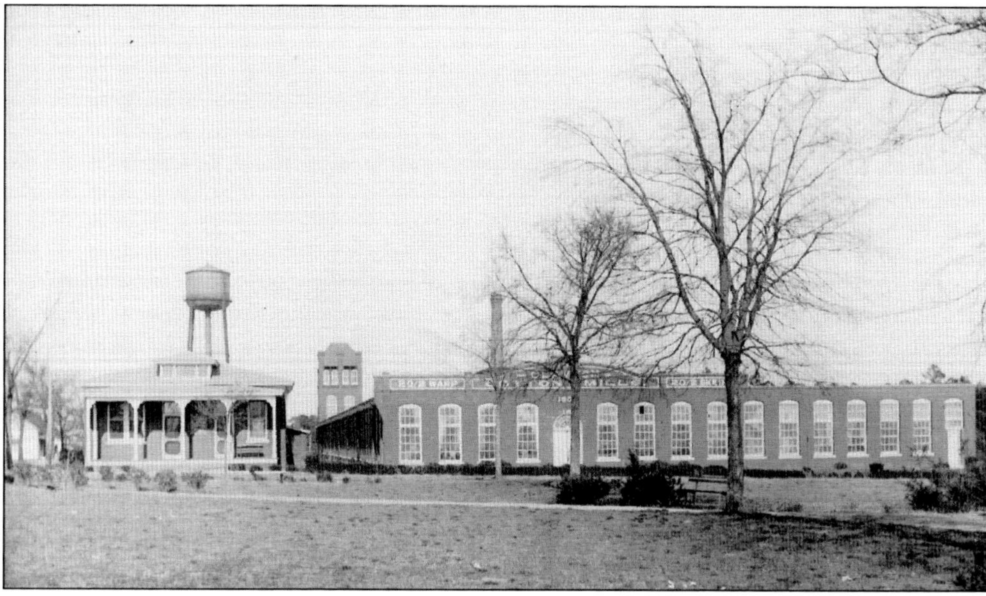

The Clayton Cotton Mill was built on a 100-acre tract of land purchased from the Dodd family in April 1900. The building was constructed under the supervision of George W. Ellis. The steam engine was turned on August 12, 1901. In 1909, officers were Ashley Horne (president), J. M. Turley (secretary and treasurer), and A. S. White (superintendent).

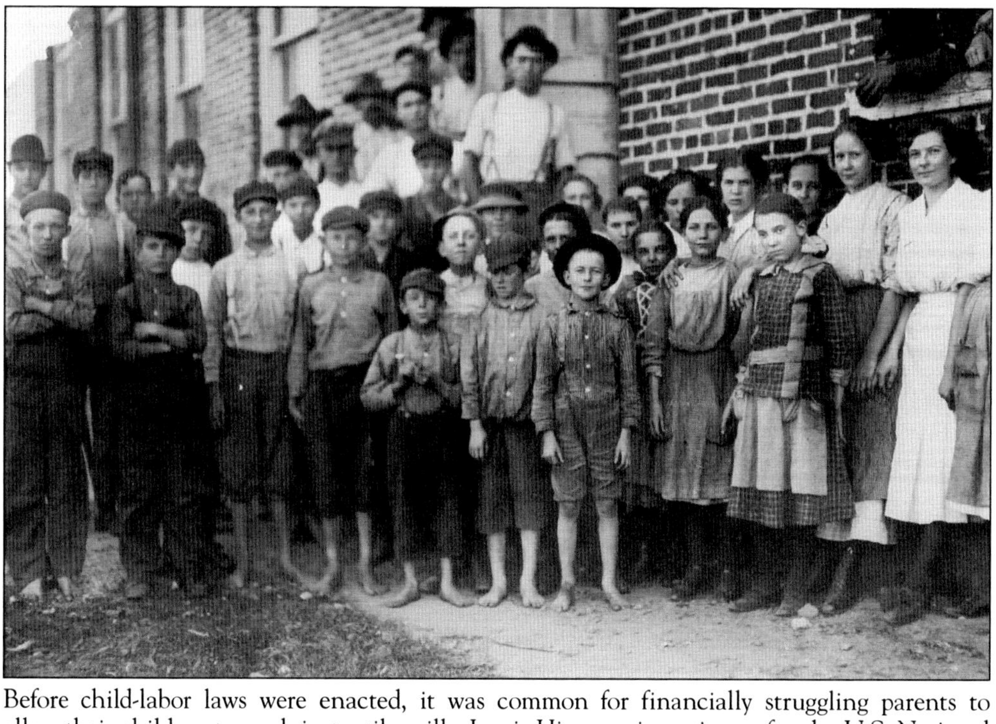

Before child-labor laws were enacted, it was common for financially struggling parents to allow their children to work in textile mills. Lewis Hine, an investigator for the U.S. National Child Labor Committee, visited Clayton in 1912 and photographed these young workers at the Clayton Cotton Mill. (Courtesy of the Library of Congress Prints and Photographs Division, Washington, D.C.)

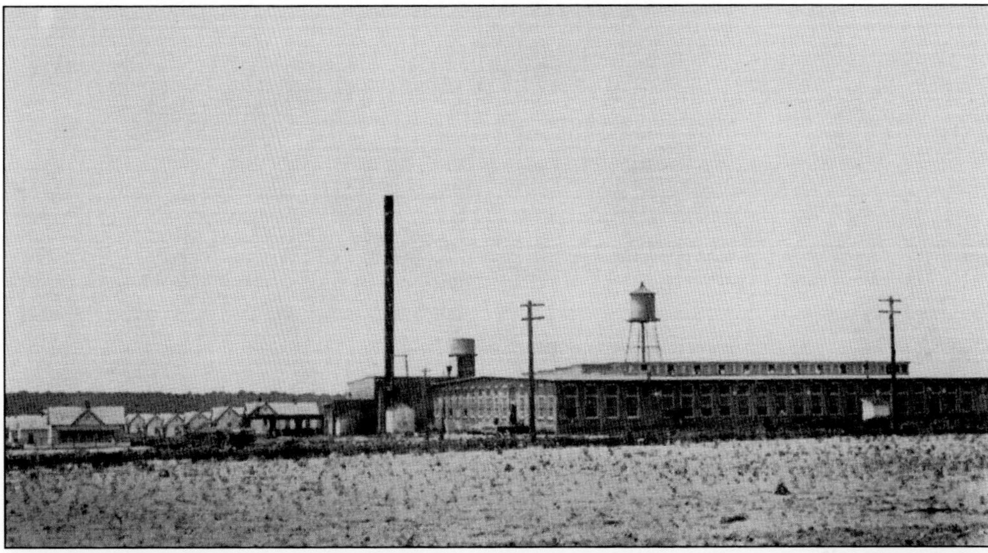

A. J. Barbour's Liberty Cotton Mill began making yarn at this location in 1908 (pictured in 1909). In 1927, the property was leased to Rockfish Mills. Brothers Dwight and Swade Barbour purchased the plant in 1932, changing the name to the Bartex Spinning Company. Norwich Mills of New York acquired the mill in 1946, and in 1980, Champion Products converted the yarn-manufacturing facility to a retail distribution center.

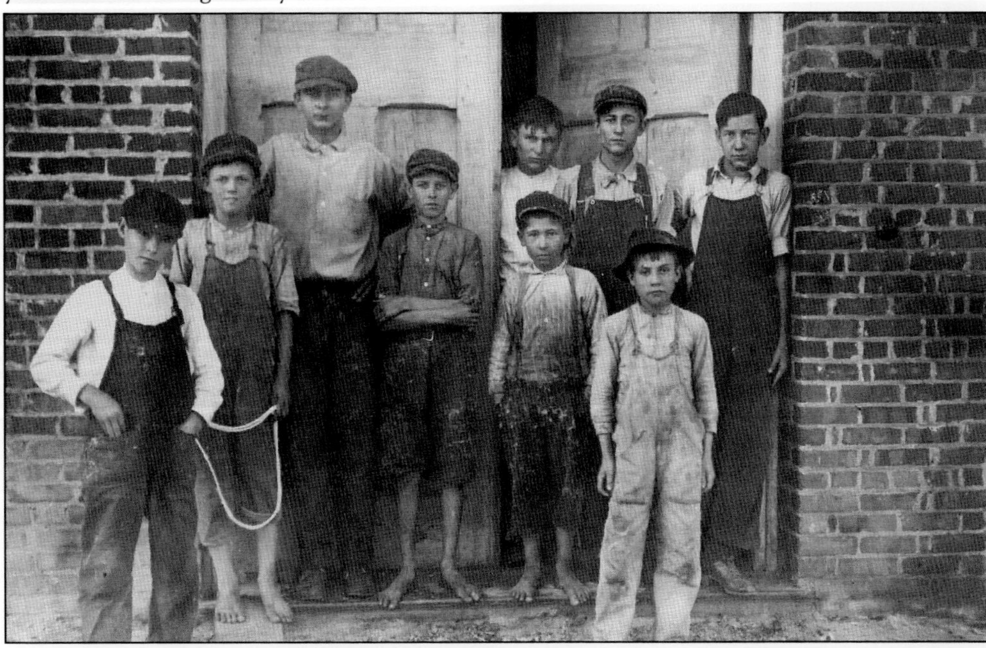

U.S. National Child Labor Committee investigator Lewis Hine photographed these young men at the Liberty Cotton Mill in mid-morning, October 29, 1912. "I saw a few very young spinners, one apparently ten years old," Hine wrote, "but could not get them out." Four years later, Hine's work resulted in the passage of the first federal child-labor law, although it was soon overturned by the U.S. Supreme Court. By World War II, American children no longer worked outside the home or family farm. (Courtesy of the Library of Congress Prints and Photographs Division, Washington, D.C.)

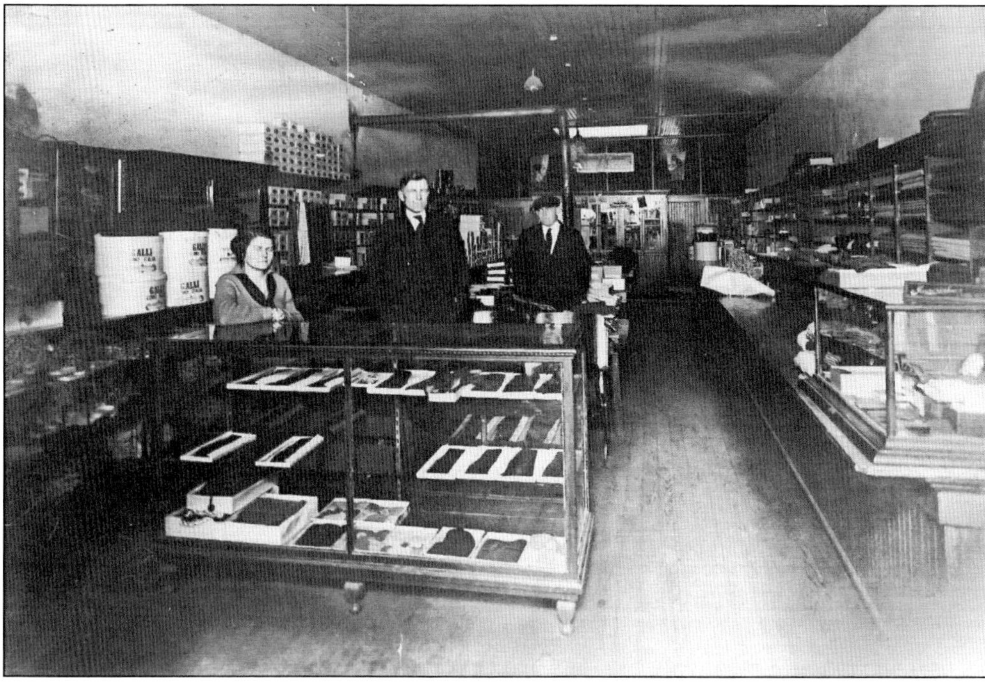

Joe R. Hinnant and Company employees are seen inside the store in this 1909 photograph. This business, located on Main Street, was a dry-goods, grocery, and general merchandise store. Pictured from left to right are Carrie Austin, Joe Hinnant (owner), and Roger Barbour (customer).

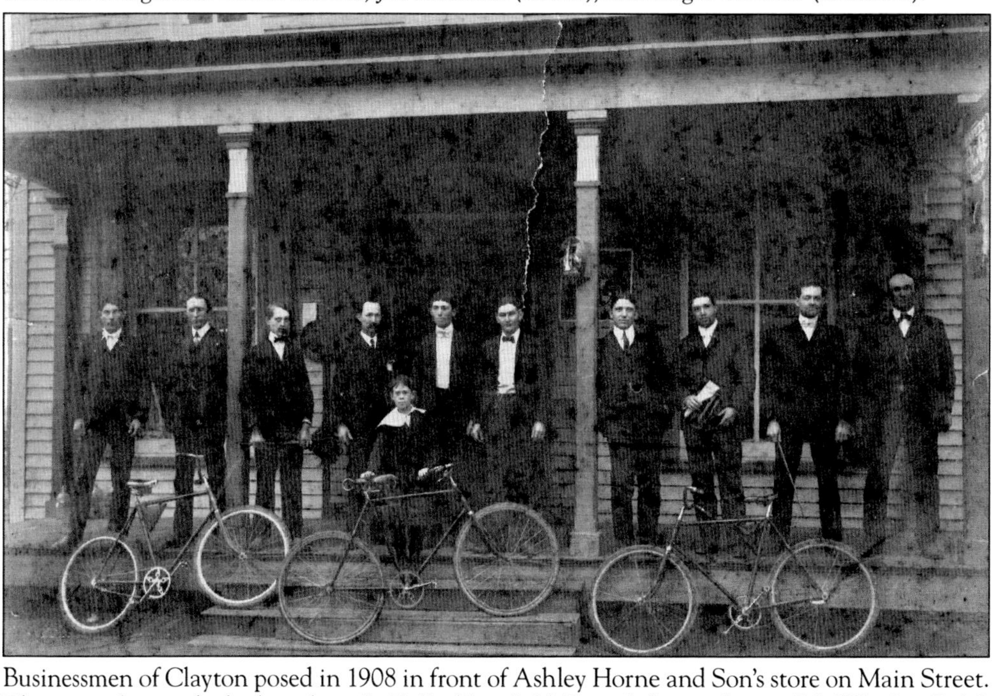

Businessmen of Clayton posed in 1908 in front of Ashley Horne and Son's store on Main Street. The young boy with the bicycle is C. H. Beddingfield. From left to right are Fab Whitley, B. M. Robertson, Jesse C. Ellis, O. G. Smith, John I. Barnes, L. H. Champion, John T. Talton, Charles W. Horne, W. I. Whitley, and John Arch Vinson.

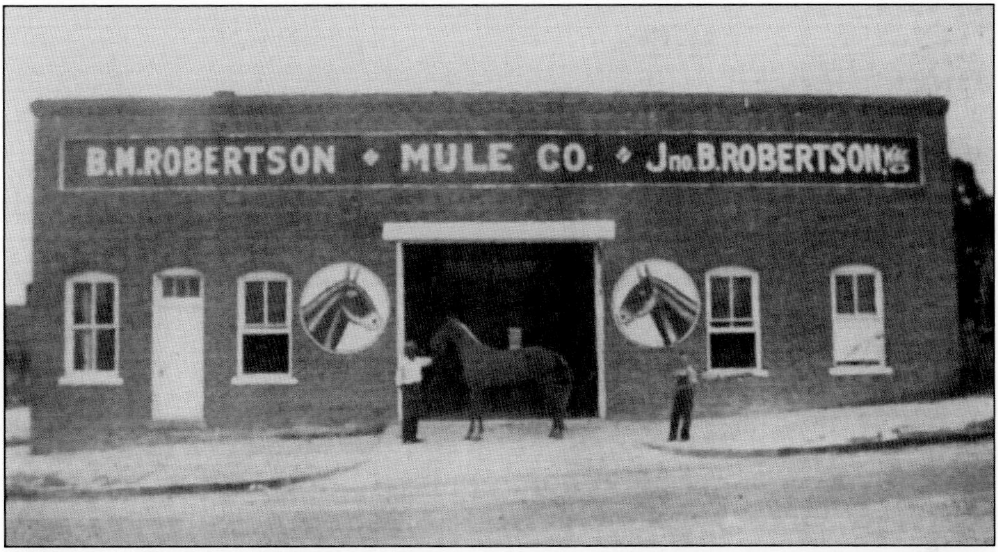

Battle Moore Robertson started in the livestock business in 1895. This brick building on Lombard Street was built in 1914 and could handle 50 mules at a time. Most of the mules were bought in Richmond, Atlanta, or Tennessee and were then shipped to Clayton by train. Sons John B. and Sam Robertson continued the business after their father's death in 1929.

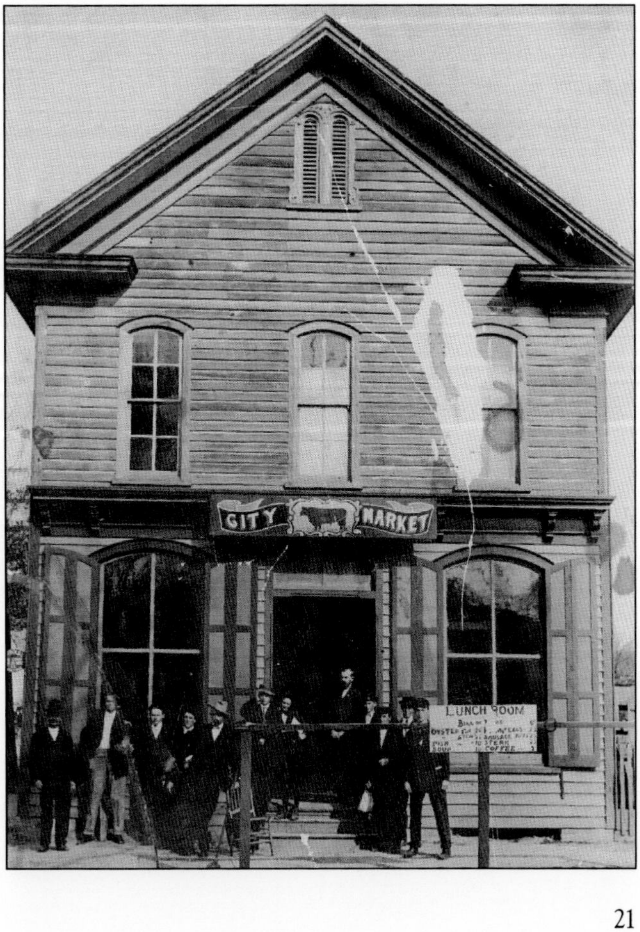

Zeb B. Jones ran the City Market and Lunch Room at the corner of Church and Main Streets when this picture was taken in 1910. Shown from left to right are H. W. Mitchell, Herbert Coats, Perrin Gower, Elmo Gattis, H. O. "Hal" Ellis, Clifford Hamilton, unidentified, Zeb Jones, unidentified, Linwood Beddingfield, Wilkes Barnes, and Dewitt Johnson. (Courtesy of the Mildred Jones Hill family.)

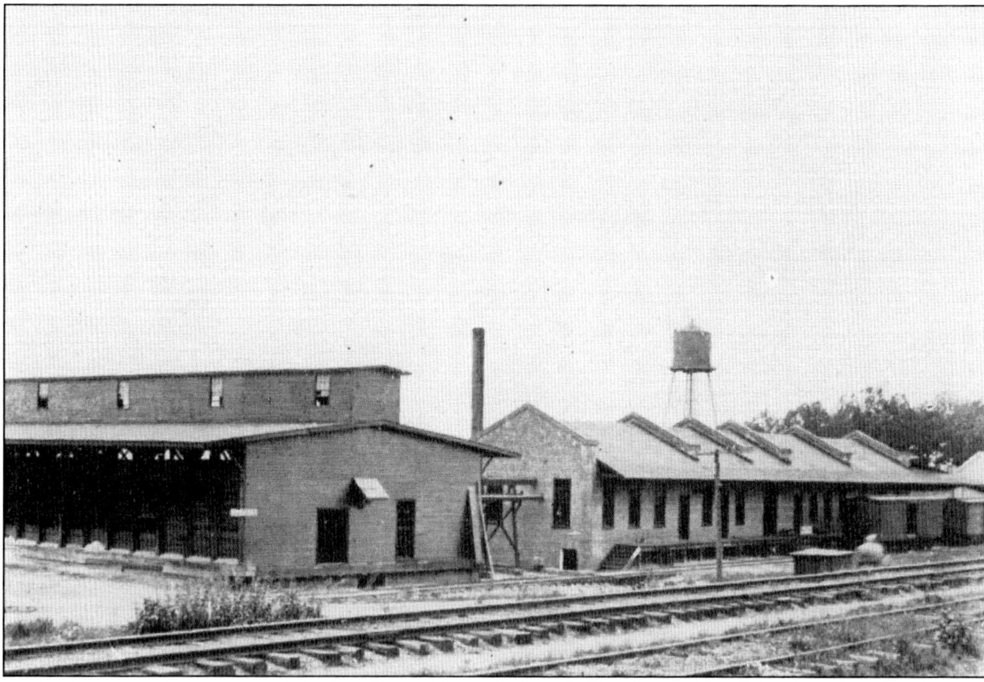

The Clayton Oil Mill was incorporated in 1901 with A. Julian Barbour as president. The corporation manufactured and sold cotton seed products and fertilizers, and also operated a cotton gin.

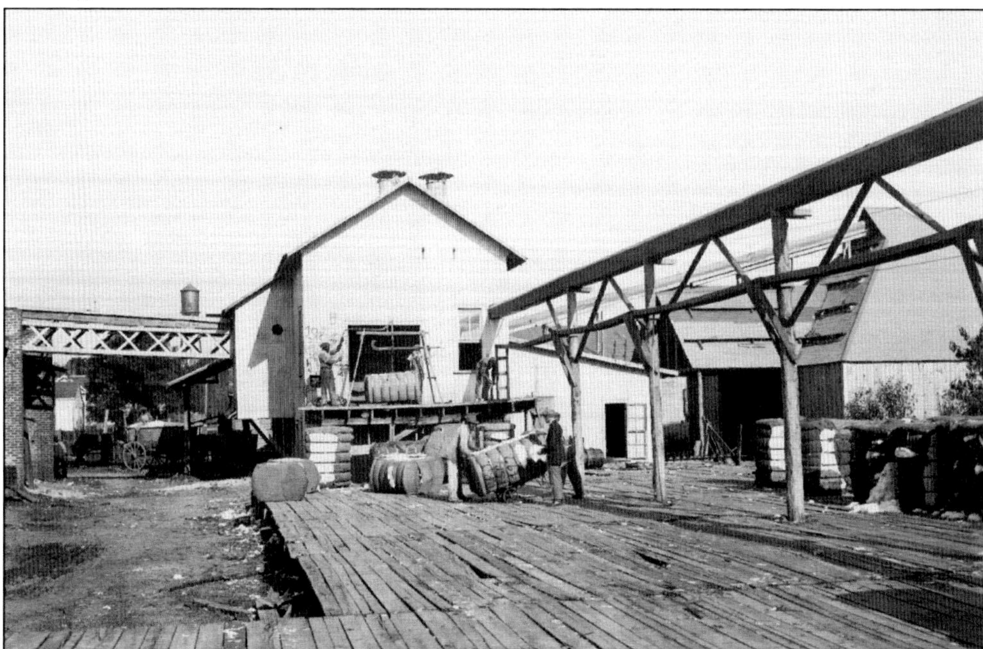

The John G. Barbour and Sons cotton gin, shown here about 1910, featured a large platform for temporarily storing cotton bales. (Courtesy of the North Carolina Division of Archives and History, Raleigh.)

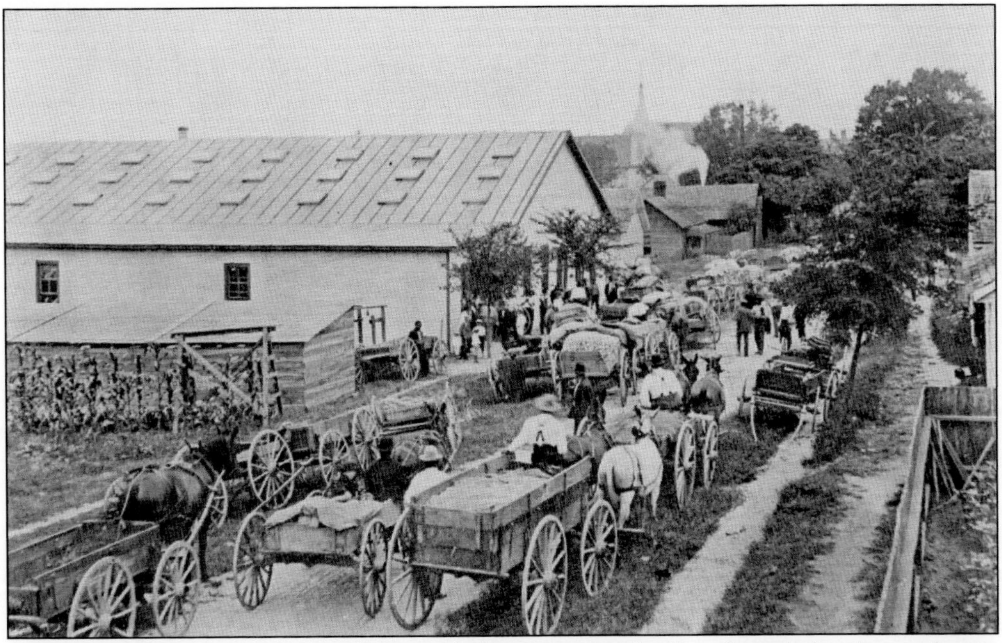

Two tobacco warehouses, the Liberty and the Star, were built and ready for the market in 1909. Wagons were lined up for blocks, waiting for the first tobacco sales, which were held on August 12, 1909. On the first day, 70,883 pounds were sold.

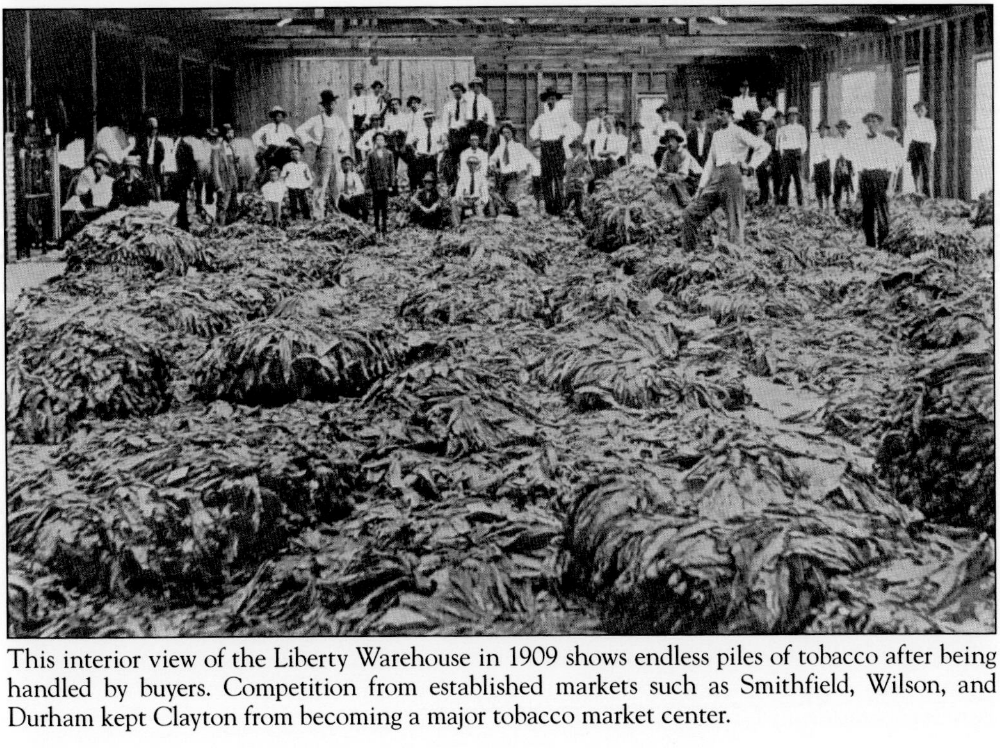

This interior view of the Liberty Warehouse in 1909 shows endless piles of tobacco after being handled by buyers. Competition from established markets such as Smithfield, Wilson, and Durham kept Clayton from becoming a major tobacco market center.

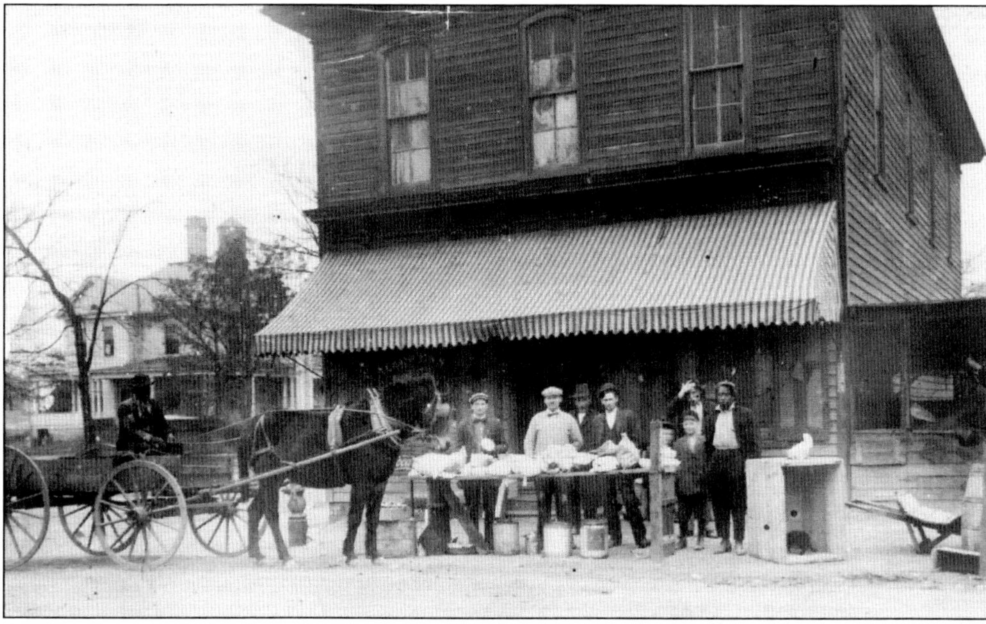

Brothers L. H. and Matthew Champion operated the Champion Brothers Store on the corner of Church and Main Streets about 1915. The stately house in the background was built in 1910 for the John Wesley Massey family. (Courtesy of Sybil T. Champion.)

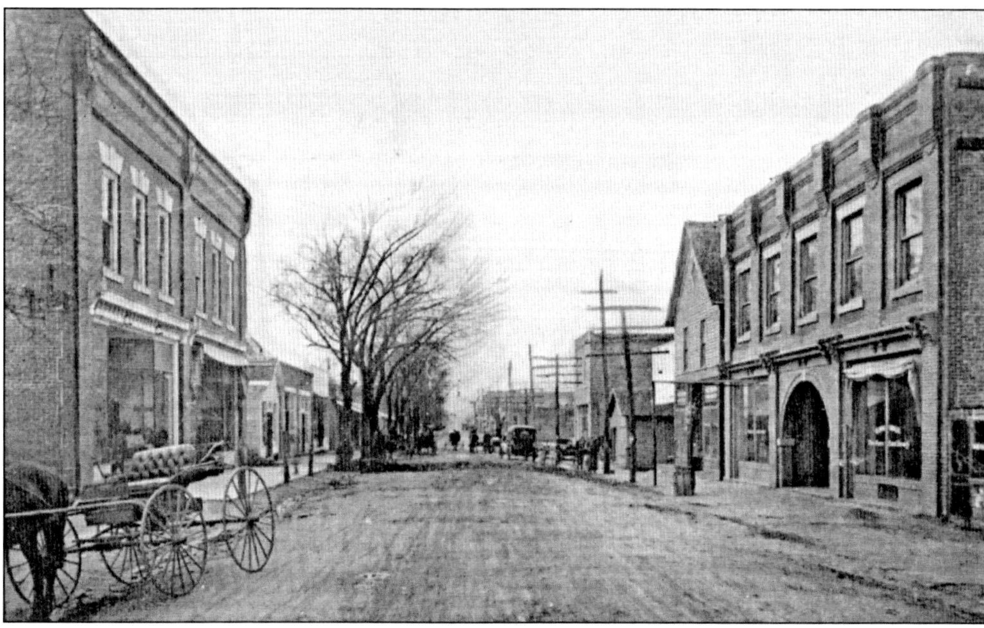

This Main Street view from about 1918 shows, on the left, the Mayo Building, which housed a clothing and furniture store. The Farmers Bank, on the right, opened on July 1, 1918. The officers were John Arch Vinson (president), Dr. J. A. Griffin (first vice president), C. W. Pender (second vice president), and J. M. Turley (cashier). This bank consolidated with the Clayton Banking Company in 1926. (Courtesy of Joyce T. Barbour.)

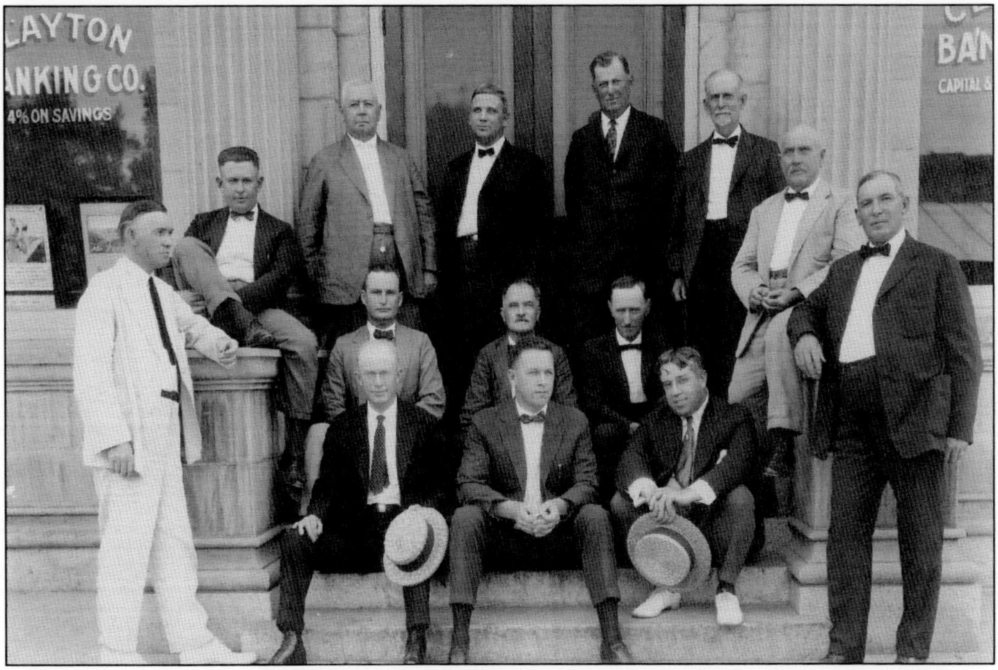

The board of directors of the Clayton Banking Company poses in front of the new Main Street building in the early 1920s. The members are, from left to right, (first row) Dr. J. J. Young, Eliot Poole, Dwight Barbour, Charles W. Horne, and R. Wall; (second row) Swade Barbour, R. W. Sanders, L. F. Austin, Battle M. Robertson, and W. A. Barnes; (third row) D. H. McCullers, John T. Talton, Dr. E. H. McCullers, and C. P. Ellis.

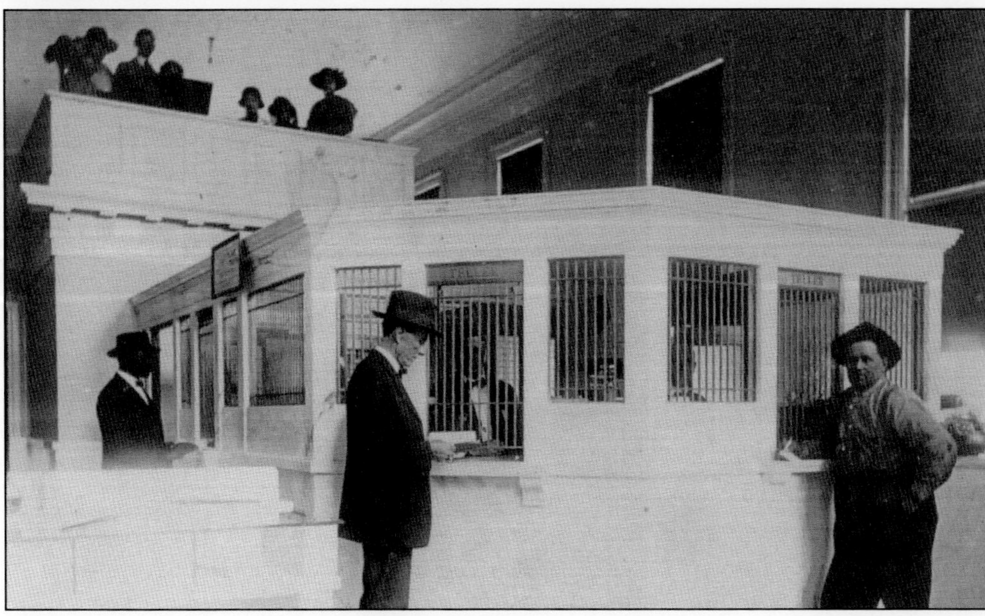

The interior of the new Clayton Banking Company on Main Street is shown in this 1920 photograph. From left to right are unidentified, B.M. Robertson (customer), John T. Talton (cashier), and Larkin Wilder (customer). Shown in the balcony are bookkeeper Blanche Ellis (seated, left) and several visitors. (Courtesy of Sam Robertson.)

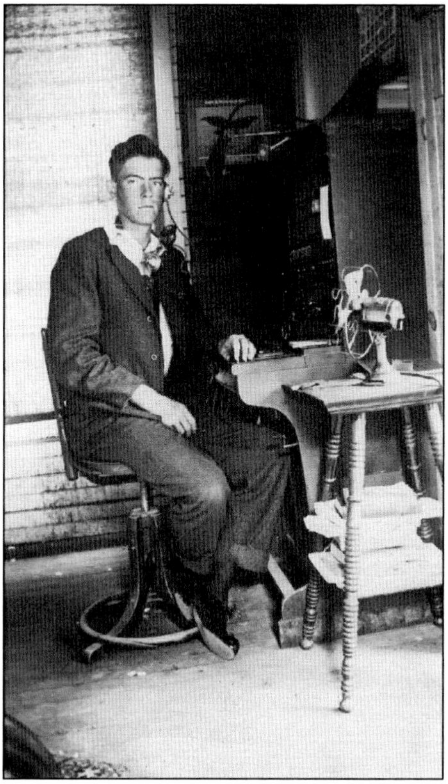

An unidentified operator, shown around 1915, works the switchboard for the Clayton Telephone Company, chartered in January 1907. The first telephone boys were paid a dollar or two per week. Clayton had 30 telephones by September 1906. A new dial telephone instrument was in use by December 1928.

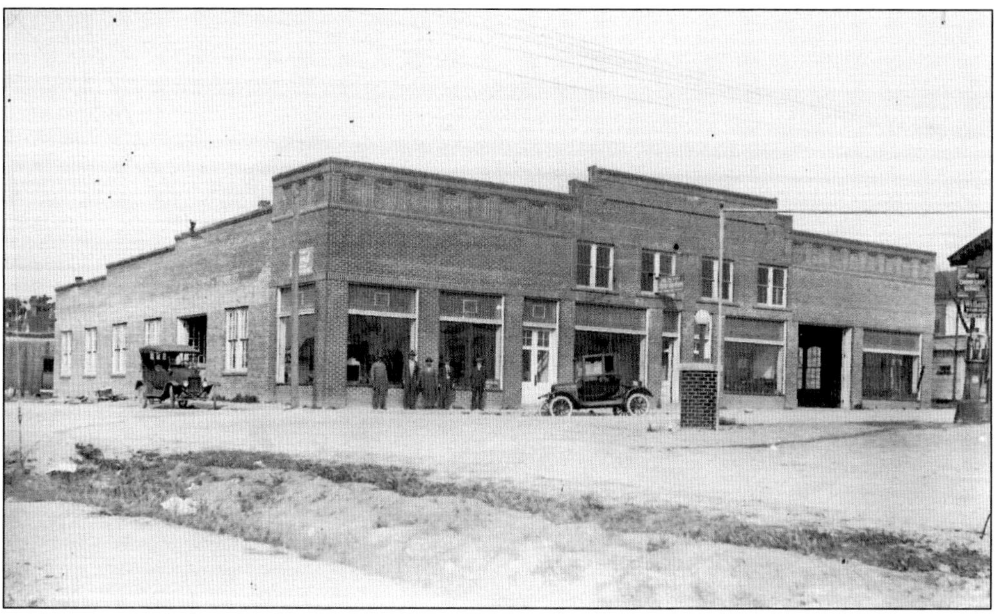

Construction of Clayton's first Ford agency and garage was completed by 1921. John Arch Vinson was the owner, and George Ellis was the building supervisor. The building, located on the corner of O'Neil and Main Streets, is seen here in 1923. An advertisement dated February 23, 1922, listed a Ford touring car for $348, a sedan for $645, and a tractor for $395. (Courtesy of Turner Vinson Jr.)

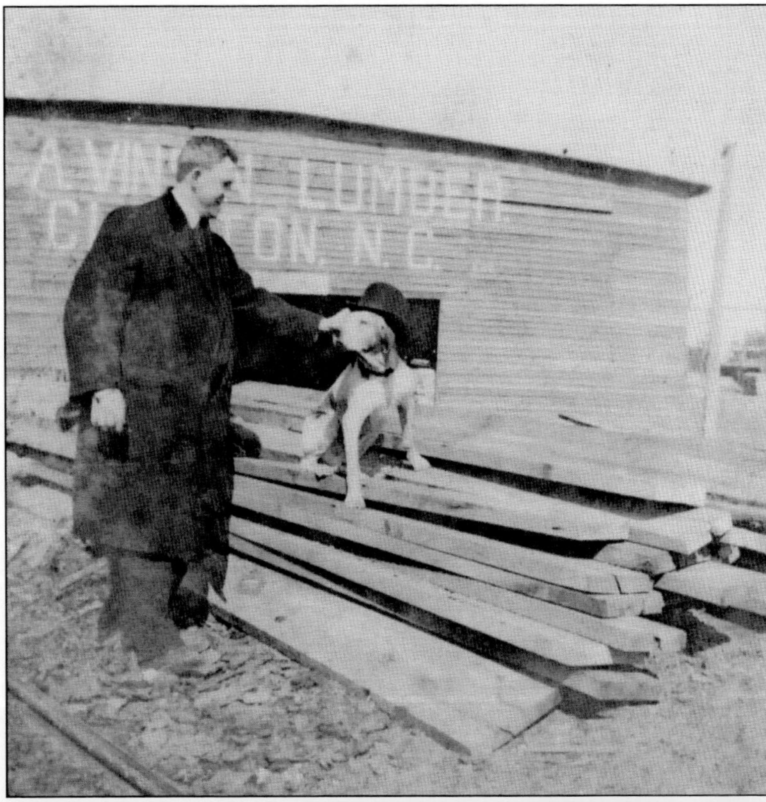

J. A. Vinson Lumber, pictured in the early 1920s with an unidentified businessman, was located on Main Street by the railroad. Vinson was the owner and operator of the lumber mill and had sawmills in several counties. Residents recall caravans of lumber wagons going out at dawn and returning at dusk, hauling logs to the mill. (Courtesy of Turner Vinson Jr.)

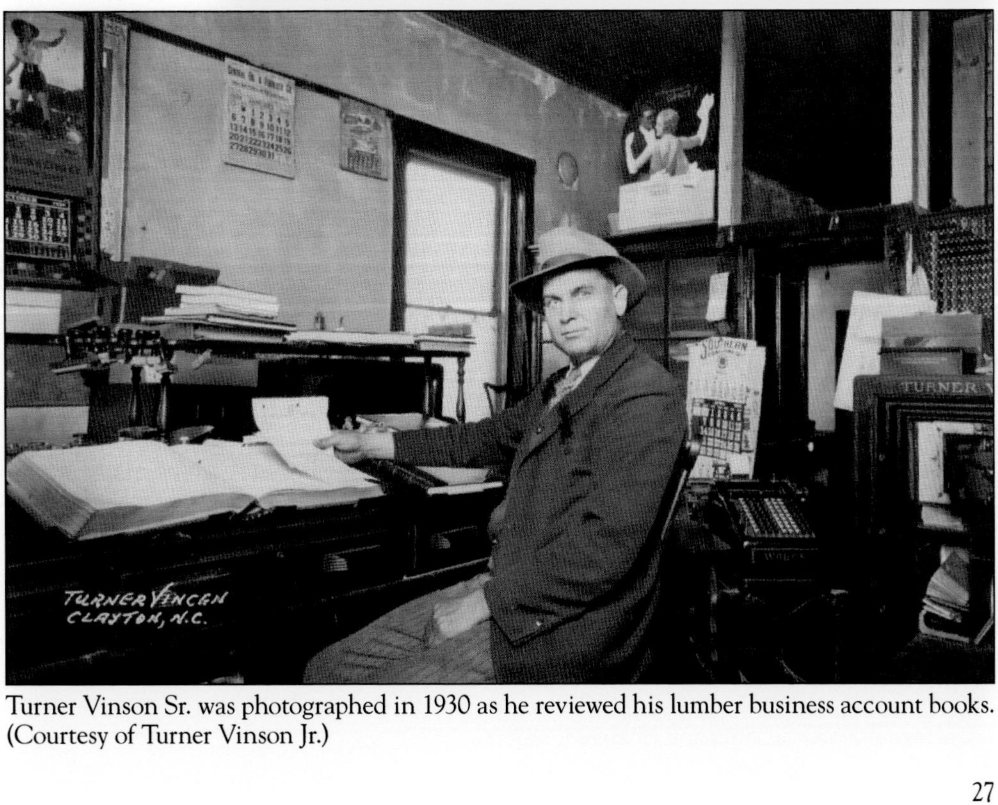

Turner Vinson Sr. was photographed in 1930 as he reviewed his lumber business account books. (Courtesy of Turner Vinson Jr.)

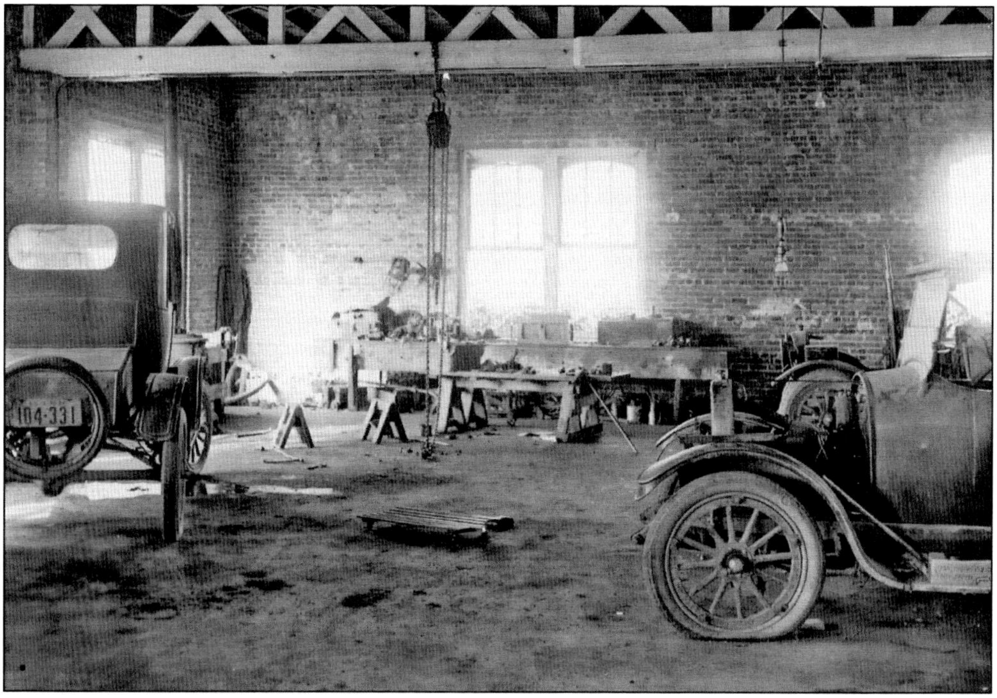

This 1923 photograph shows mechanics' tools and Model T vehicles inside the J. A. Vinson Ford dealership. The license number was 104-331, and the tag showed the plate expired in 1924. (Courtesy of Turner Vinson Jr.)

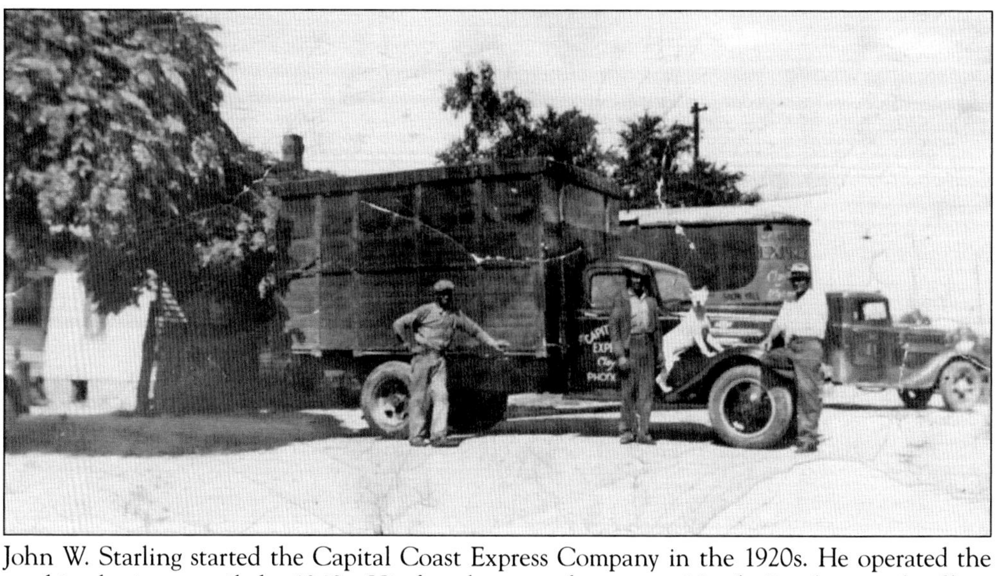

John W. Starling started the Capital Coast Express Company in the 1920s. He operated the trucking business until the 1940s. His franchise was for eastern North Carolina, with offices in Raleigh, Kinston, New Bern, and Clayton. He had a fleet of trucks that hauled to the coast. Shown in this late 1930s photograph are two unidentified drivers (left) with Starling (right). (Courtesy of Hazel Starling and Mildred Gordon.)

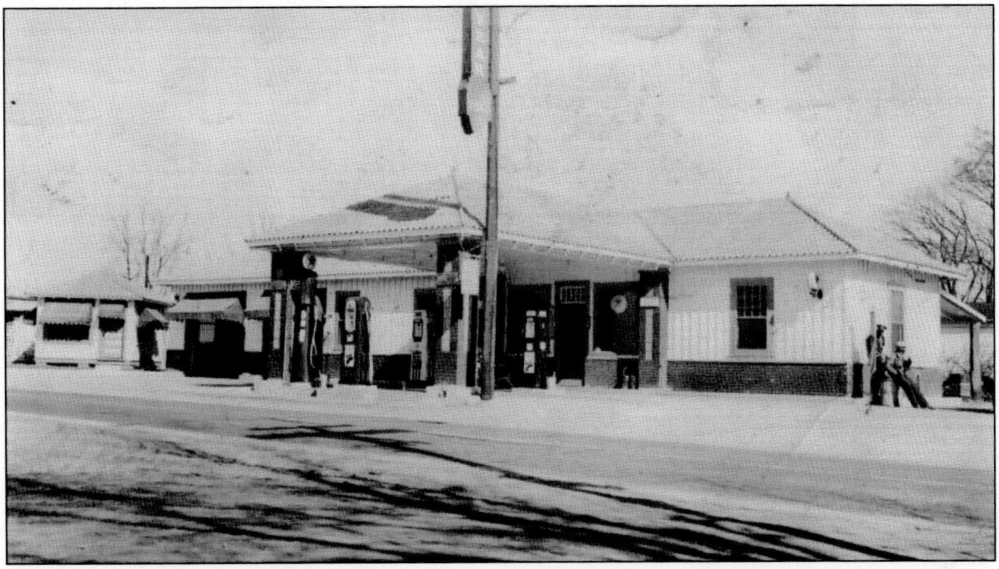

J. L. Hinton owned and operated Luke's Service Station, seen in 1936. This Texaco station was located on the corner of Main and Robertson Streets. (Courtesy of Marcia Amaon.)

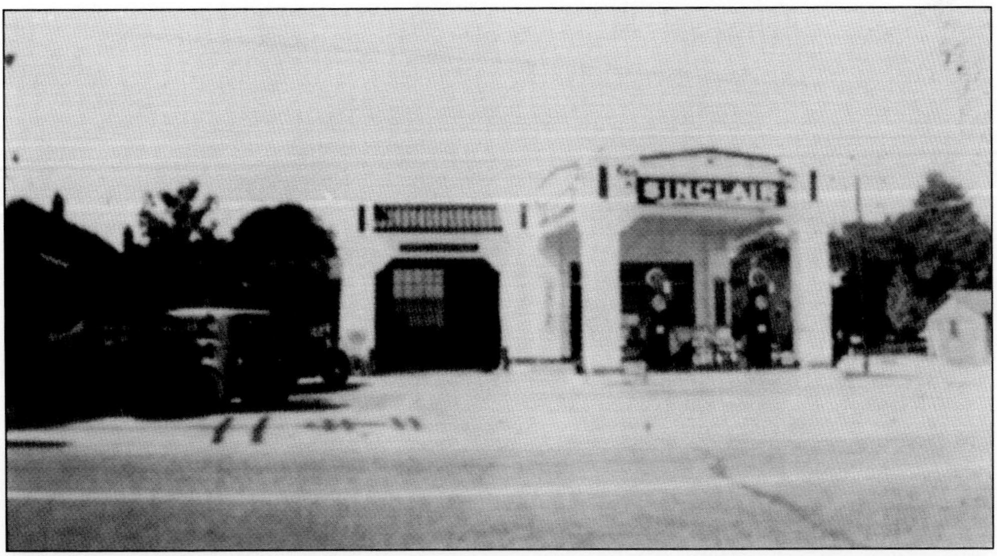

The Sinclair Oil Company built a filling station on the corner of Main and Church Streets in 1935. The station, shown in 1936, was built in the Spanish stucco style, and construction cost was approximately $3,000.

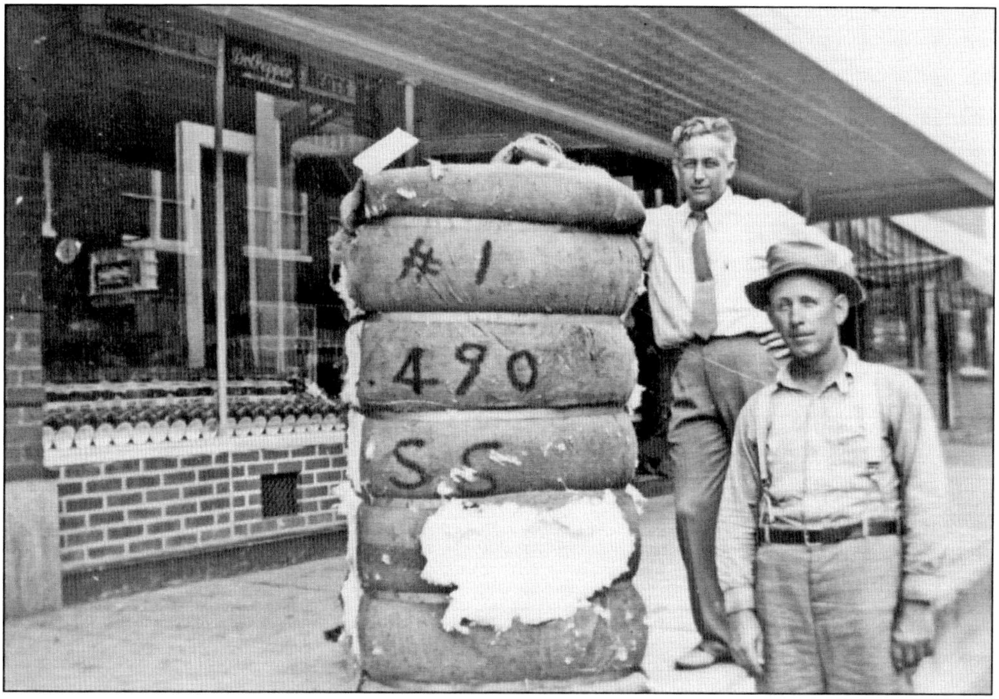

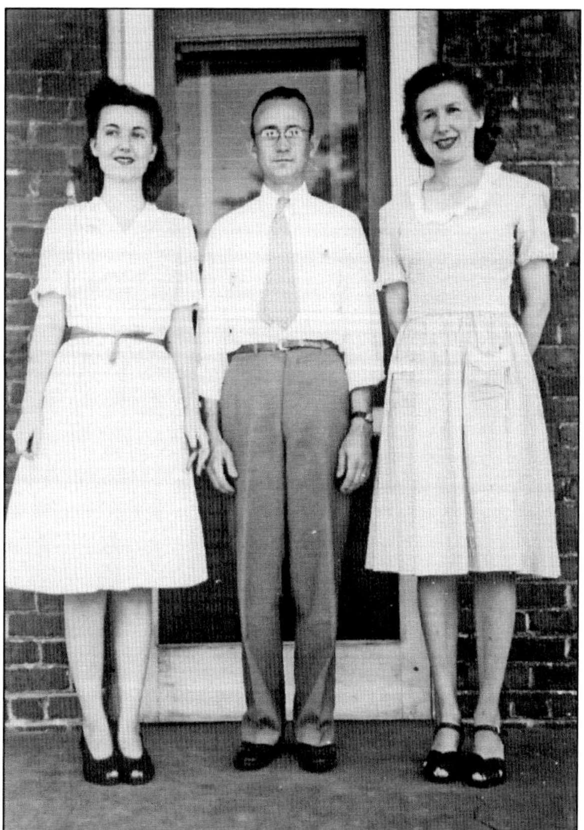

Sam Spence (front), a farmer in the early 1940s, brought in the first bale of cotton for the season at the Cooper–Peele Company. Lawrence Cooper, also pictured, was a cotton buyer for the company. The bale weighed 490 pounds. (Courtesy of Margaret Canady.)

The office employees of Clayton Spinning Company (formerly the Clayton Cotton Mill) in 1940 were, from left to right, Aldine Lancaster, Vernon Corbett, and Mary Ellen Ellis. (Courtesy of the Leon Smith family.)

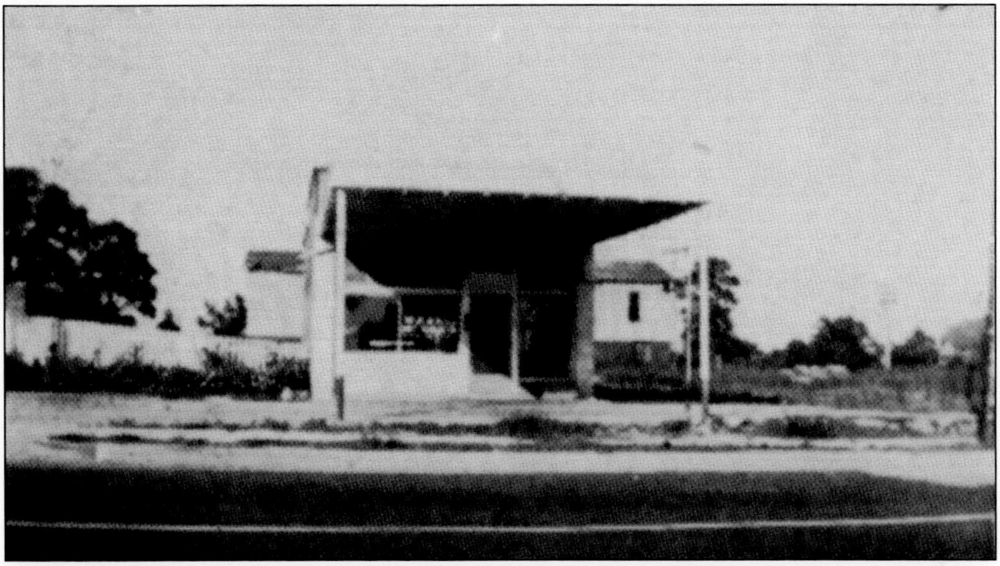

W. J. Akins Dry Cleaning Service on Main Street, pictured in 1936, was one of Clayton's earliest African American businesses. Akins had his "pressing club" in operation as early as 1920. His business offered a delivery service.

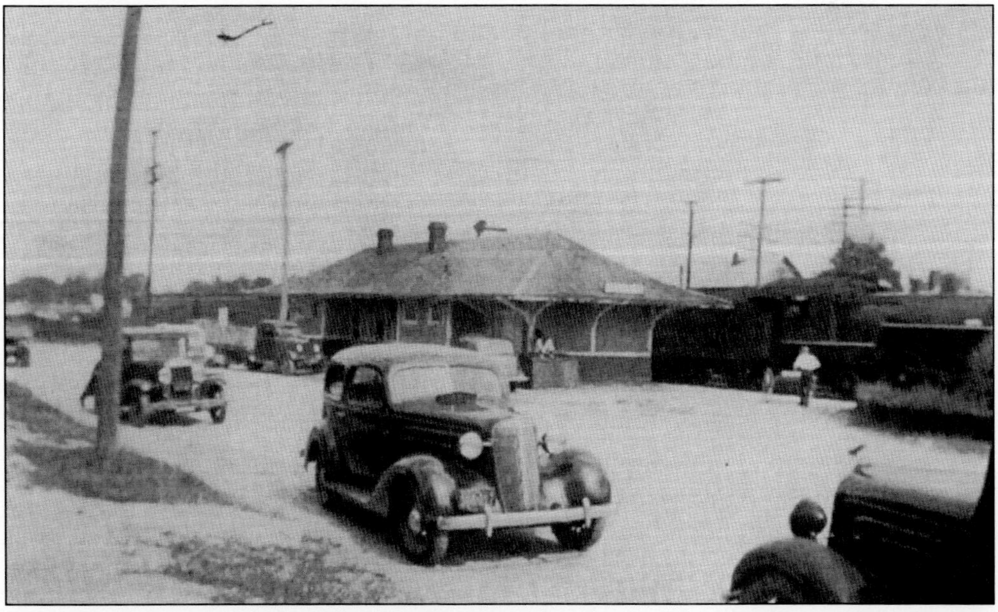

The railroad depot was still a hub of activity when this photograph was taken in 1936. Trucking companies were transporting an increasing number of goods, but businessmen still relied on the railroad for large shipments and for items from distant places.

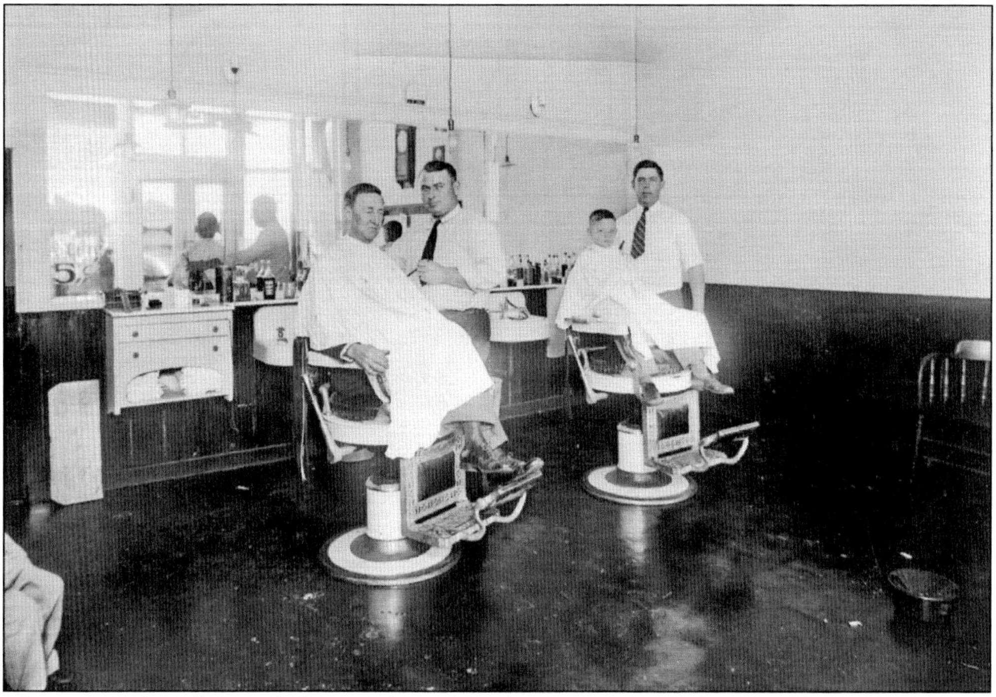

Elbert Jones (standing, right) opened Jones' Barber Shop in March 1934, about the time this photograph was made. His shop on Main Street advertised haircuts for 25¢ that year. Mal Gower, another experienced barber, also worked in the shop. (Courtesy of Bernice Jones.)

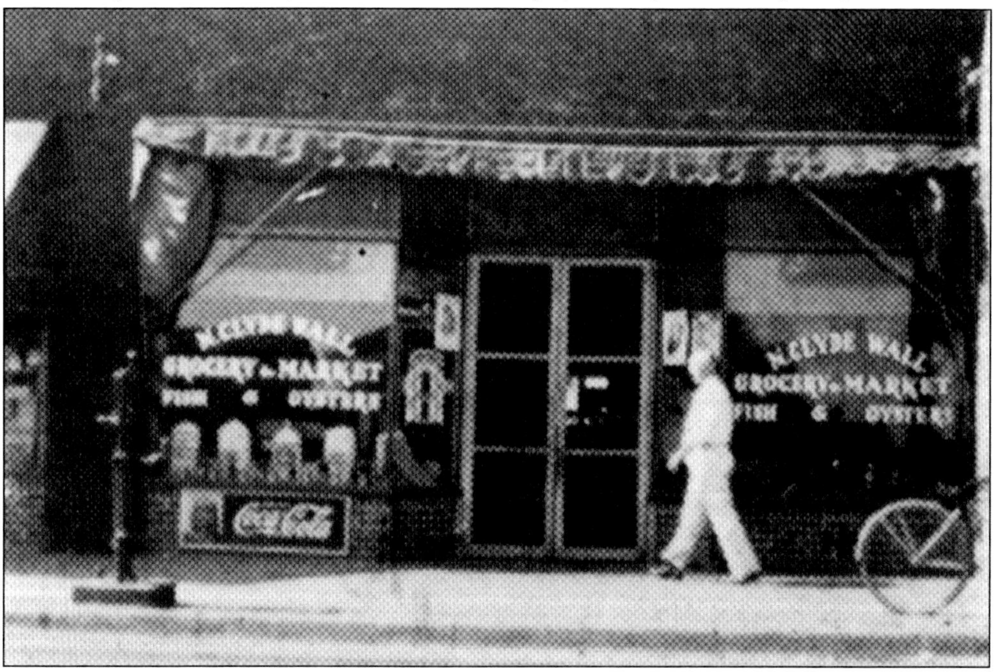

Clayton had one grocery chain, Piggly Wiggly, as early as 1928, but locally owned and operated grocery stores were still the rule when this photograph of Clyde Wall's business was taken in 1936.

Susie Jane Watson, a 1938 graduate of Cooper High School, attended Stark's Beauty College in Raleigh and had opened her own Acme Beauty Shoppe in Clayton by 1945. (From *The Zenith*, Cooper High School yearbook, 1946.)

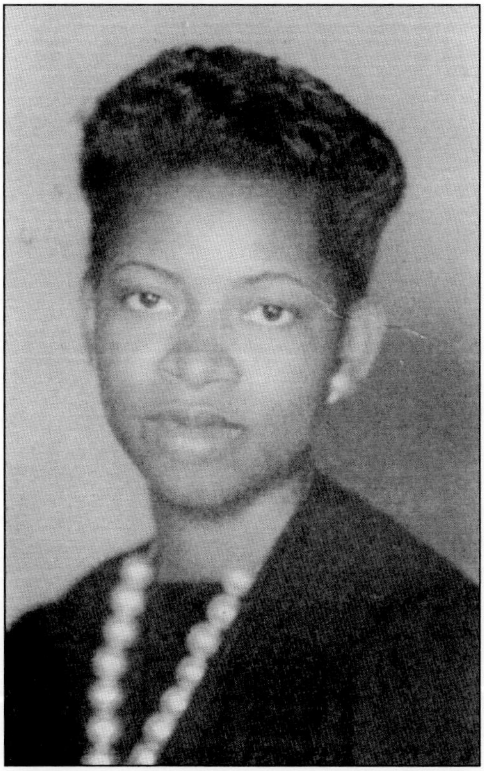

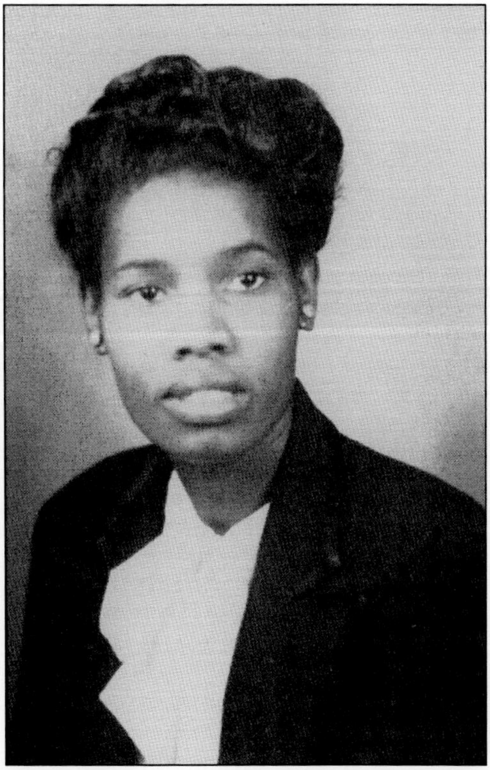

Ora Clarke Rodgers, a member of the Cooper High class of 1936, was one of several Cooper alumni who attended Stark's Beauty College. She joined Susie Watson as a cosmetologist at the Acme Beauty Shoppe by 1945. (From *The Zenith*, Cooper High School yearbook, 1946.)

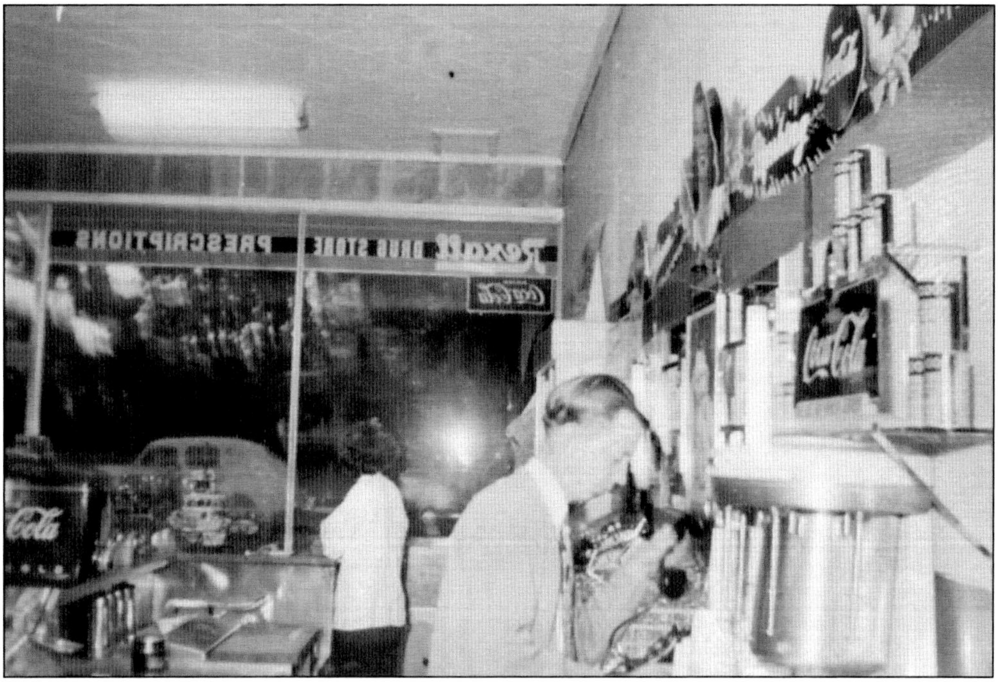

Charles (Colonel) and Edgar Beddingfield took over the former Pope and Stallings drugstore and opened Beddingfield Brothers in 1919. Their popular drugstore, pictured in the 1940s, is now Clayton's oldest business establishment. (Courtesy of Charles H. Beddingfield Jr.)

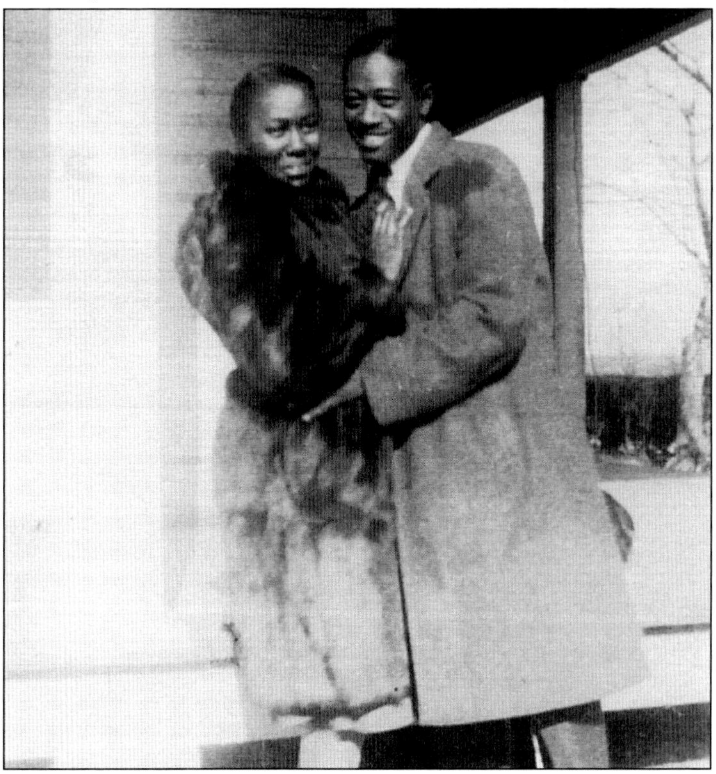

Harold Toole, shown here with his wife, Lucy Hicks Toole (DeLaine), about 1940, was a porter for the Beddingfield Brothers drugstore in the 1930s and also had the first radio and television repair service in Clayton. Lucy Toole became Johnston County's first Negro Home Demonstration Agent with the North Carolina Cooperative Extension Service in 1936, serving 31 years. (Courtesy of Lucy T. DeLaine.)

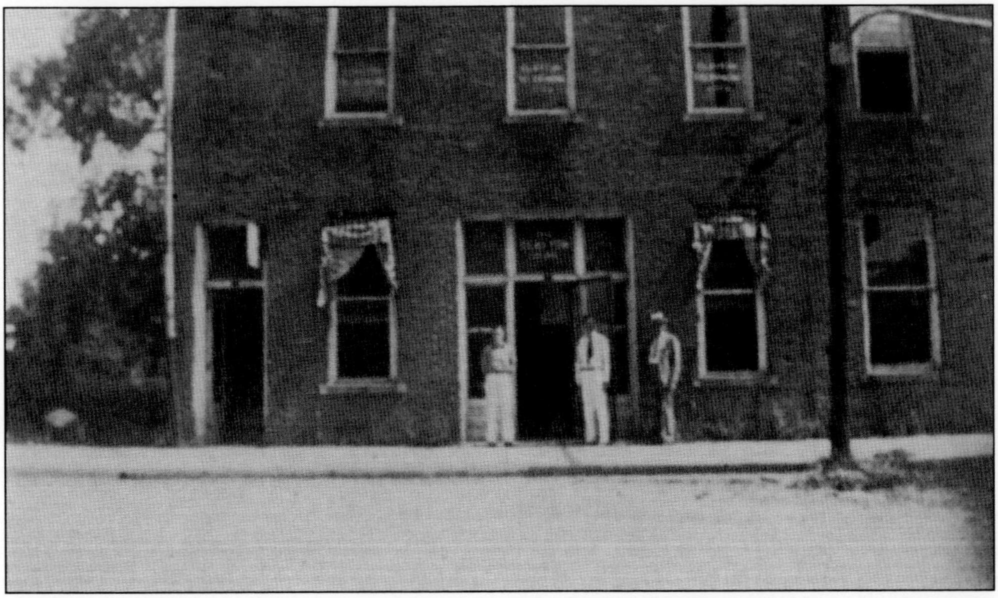

The *Clayton News* was organized in 1911 as a weekly newspaper. W. S. Penn was the editor and publisher. A print shop was also operated on the site. The first newspaper was a six-column, four-page paper. Penn published the paper until a few months before his death in 1934. The newspaper resumed publication in September 1943, with Weisner Farmer, a Clayton attorney, as the news editor.

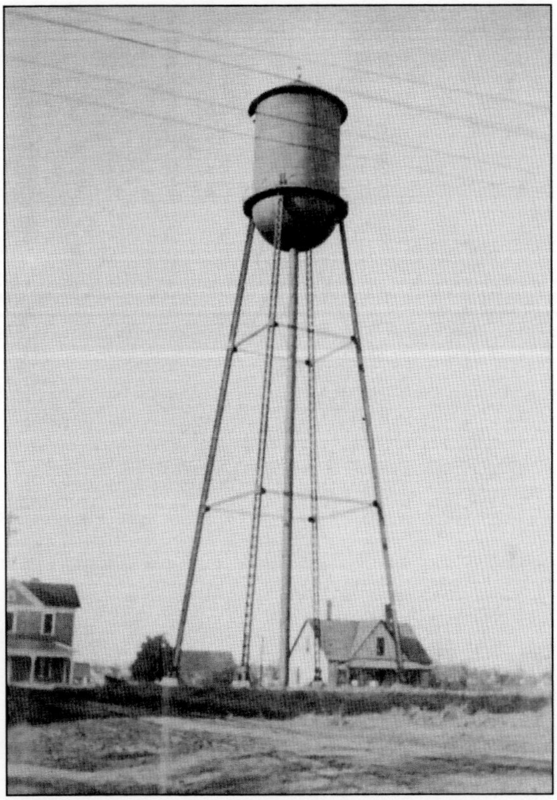

The *Clayton News* of October 14, 1915, reported that a 750-watt electric light shone from the top of the water tank, 150 feet above the ground. It would serve as an advertisement for the town, the newspaper added, since it could be seen for miles in every direction at night. (Courtesy of Joyce T. Barbour.)

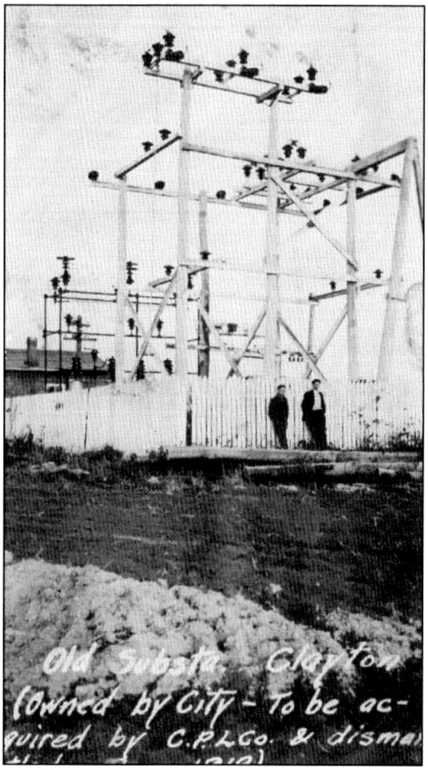

Clayton's power station and all of its electrical and waterworks equipment were destroyed by fire on September 20, 1918. The town was without power for more than a year until Carolina Power and Light started furnishing power to the station in early December 1919. Many businesses used gasoline engines for power during the interim period.

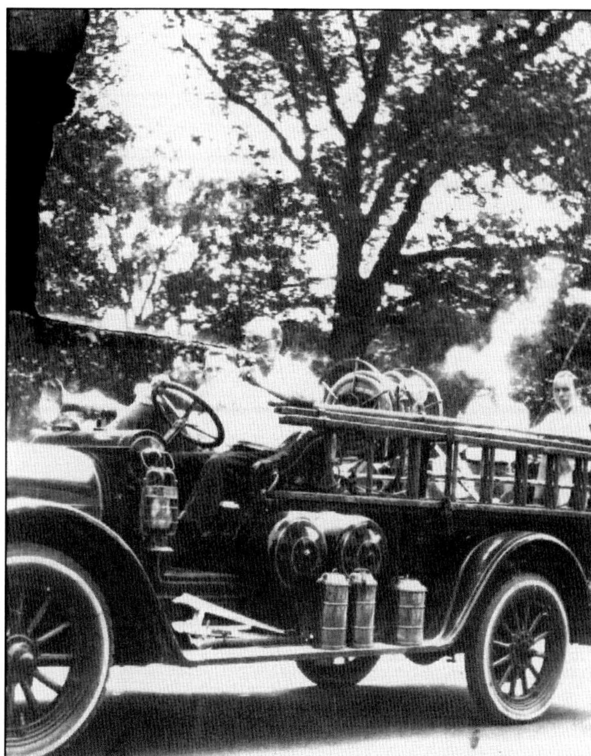

This 1930s photograph shows O. B. Garris driving an early fire truck. A new fire engine was bought in 1906, and a storage house was built for the engine and other equipment in 1907. E. L. O'Neil was chief of the fire department from the early 1900s until 1914. The *Clayton News* reported the purchase of a hook-and-ladder wagon in May 1917. Beginning in December 1919, every Monday at noon the fire alarm was tested by one blow of the siren. (Courtesy of the Garris family.)

Sam Ellis, pictured here, was a night policeman and assistant to the police chief during the 1930s. Max E. Barbour was the chief of police during this time. In 1917, Hal O. Ellis succeeded J. L. Ellis, who had held the office for a number of years. (Courtesy of Jackie Smith.)

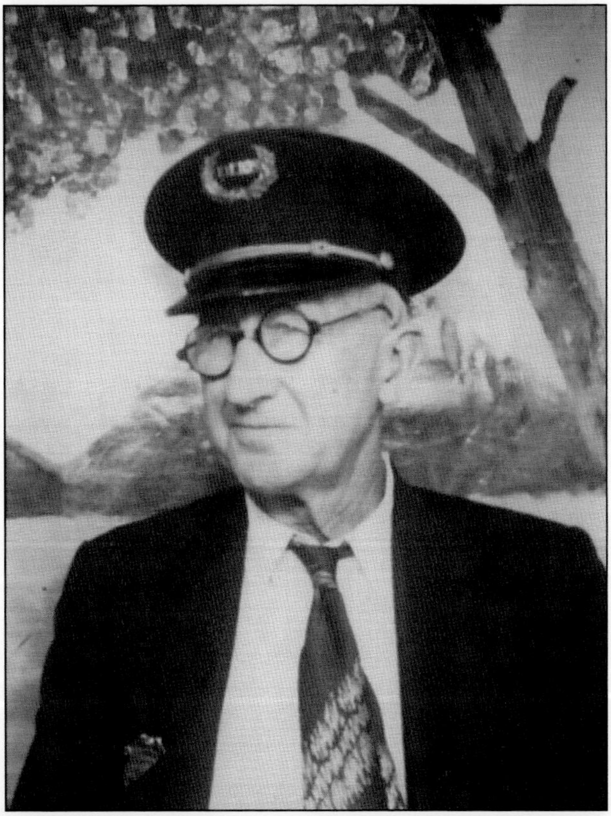

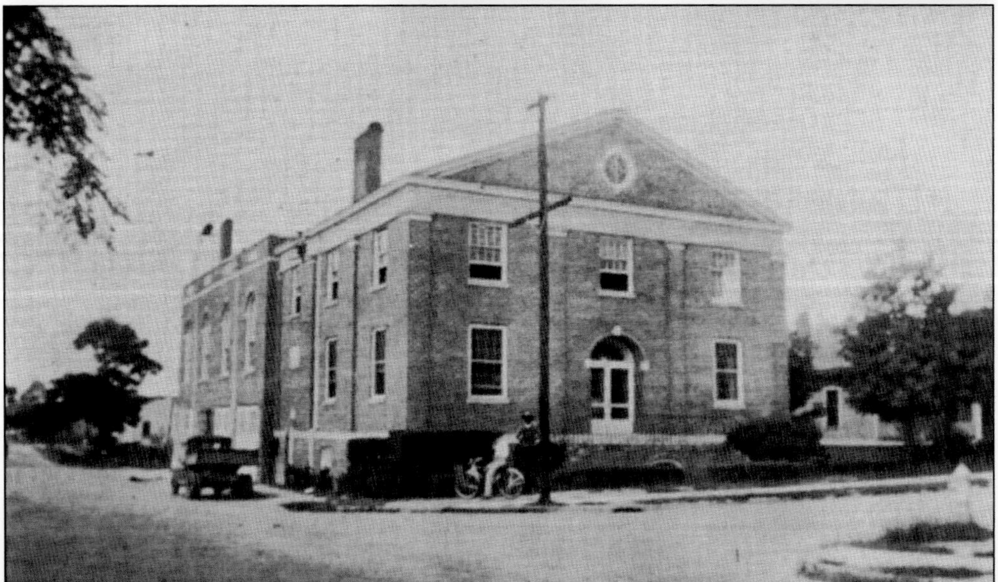

Clayton's town hall was completed in 1927. The building housed the municipal offices, police and volunteer fire departments, a courtroom, and a jail. The Woman's Club of Clayton was instrumental in obtaining a space for a library in the town hall and collected more than 500 books. The library opened in May 1931 for two afternoons a week.

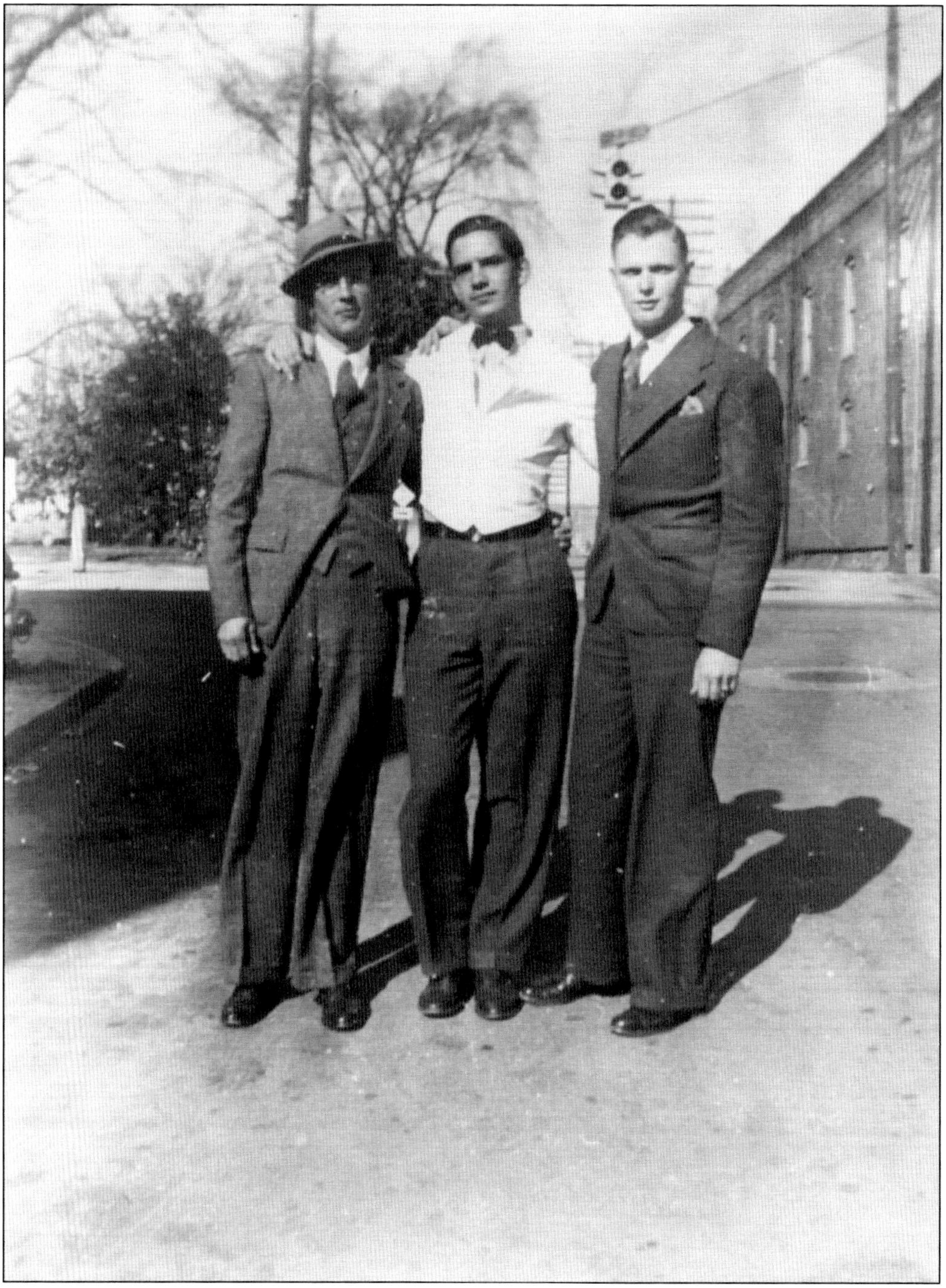

Two stop lights were installed at the busiest intersections during 1935. This photograph shows the intersection of Lombard and Main Streets in 1939. The two-story building on the right was the Horne Building. The friends are, from left to right, unidentified, Colin Hamilton, and James Thomas Vinson. Hamilton worked at the drugstore nearby.

Two

HOMES AND FAMILIES

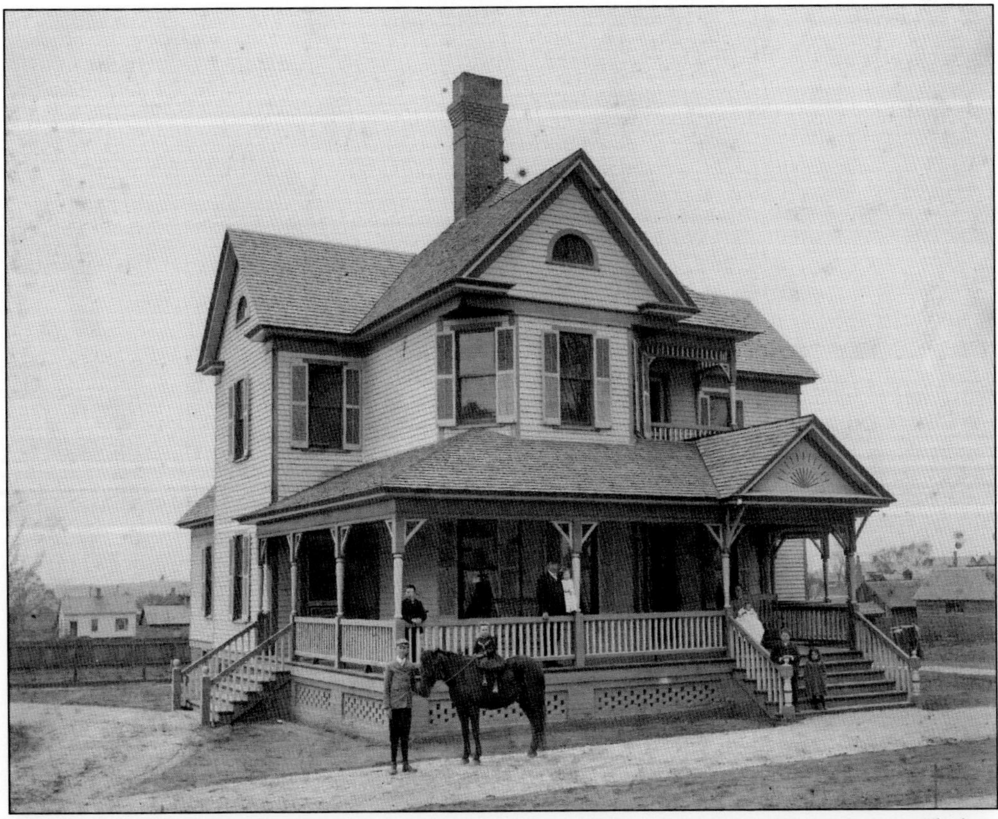

The A. Julian Barbour family poses for this picture in 1904 at their Main Street home. Thelma is sitting on the pony, while Dwight keeps the animal steady. Swade and Winnie are on the first step. From left to right on the porch are Roger, A. J., Grace, and Annie, who is holding Helen. This home was located on Main Street. Julian Barbour was the son of John G. Barbour and helped operate the family business until his death in 1911. (Courtesy of Carey Barbour.)

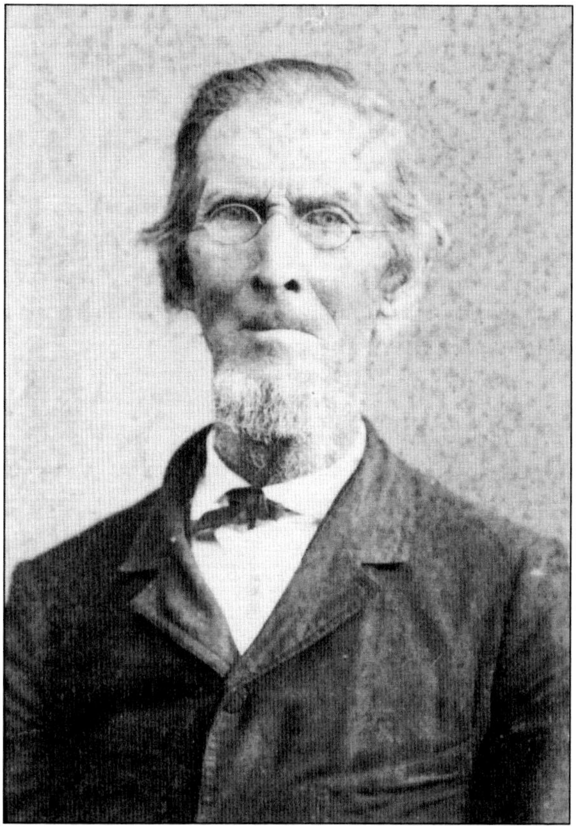

Needham G. Gulley (1820–1899), pictured about 1889, was the first postmaster at Gulley's Store in 1845 and was succeeded in 1846 by his father, John G. Gulley. After the Civil War, N. G. Gulley was a farmer-merchant, justice of the peace, active Democrat, and a founder of the Granite Lodge. His son Needham Yancey Gulley was the founder and longtime dean of the School of Law at Wake Forest College.

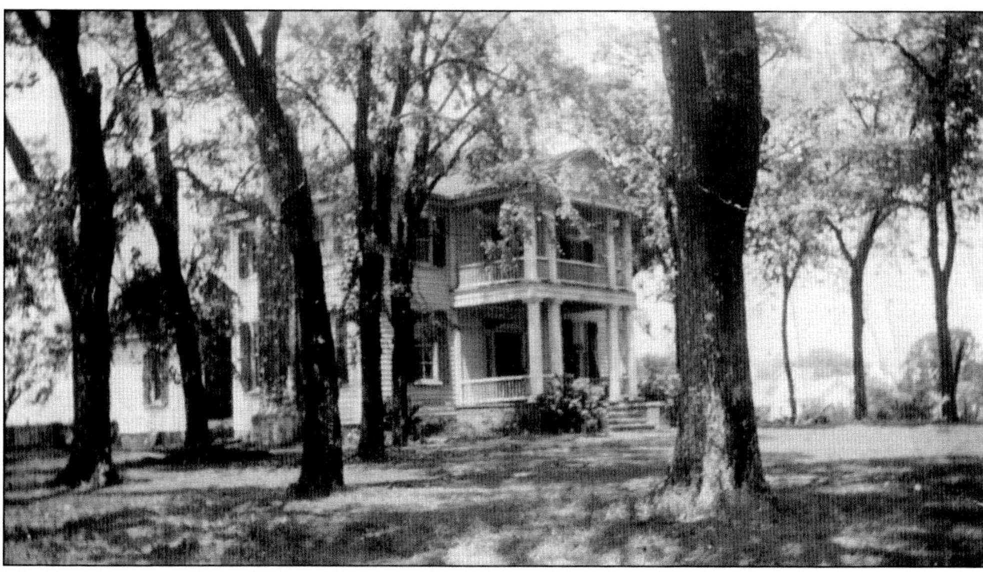

This Greek Revival–style home, now known as the Compton House, was built around 1840 by Joseph M. Smith, a planter and merchant. Henry L. Winton, a teacher, lived with the Smith family as early as 1850, according to the U.S. census. Smith traded the home to Harry Durham for land in Greene County in the 1870s. Harry's daughter Emma married Sheriff J. T. Ellington and inherited the house. (Courtesy of Sam Robertson.)

Jesse T. Ellington (1842–1910) was considered a man of extraordinary ability by his peers. A Confederate veteran, he became active in the Democratic Party after the war and was elected to the state legislature in 1885. He was the sheriff of Johnston County from about 1885 to 1904. He also farmed, taught school, and wrote poetry, much of it on sheriff's stationery.

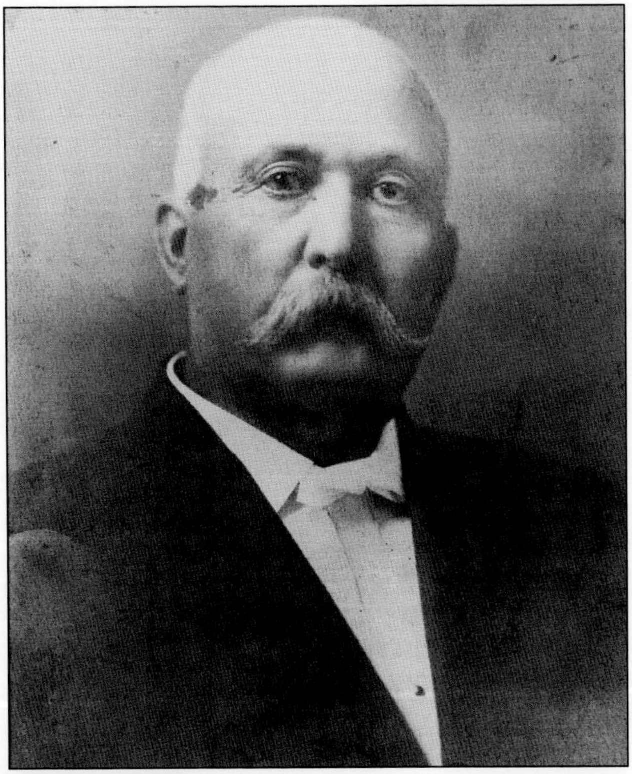

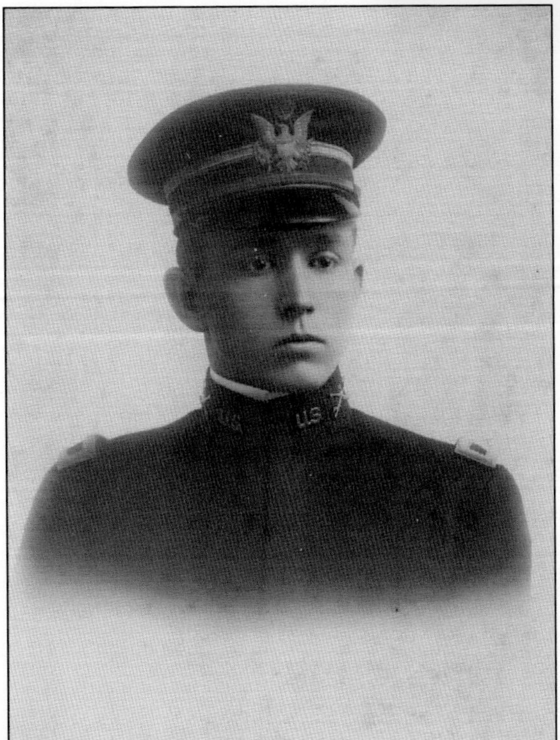

Eric Lamar Ellington (1884–1913), son of Sheriff Jesse T. Ellington by his second wife, Sallie Williamson, entered the U.S. Naval Academy at the age of 16 but requested a transfer to the army upon graduation. He joined the fledgling aviation corps in 1912 and was killed in an airplane crash near San Diego, California, in June 1913. Ellington Air Force Base in Houston, Texas, was named in his memory when it opened at the beginning of World War I in 1917.

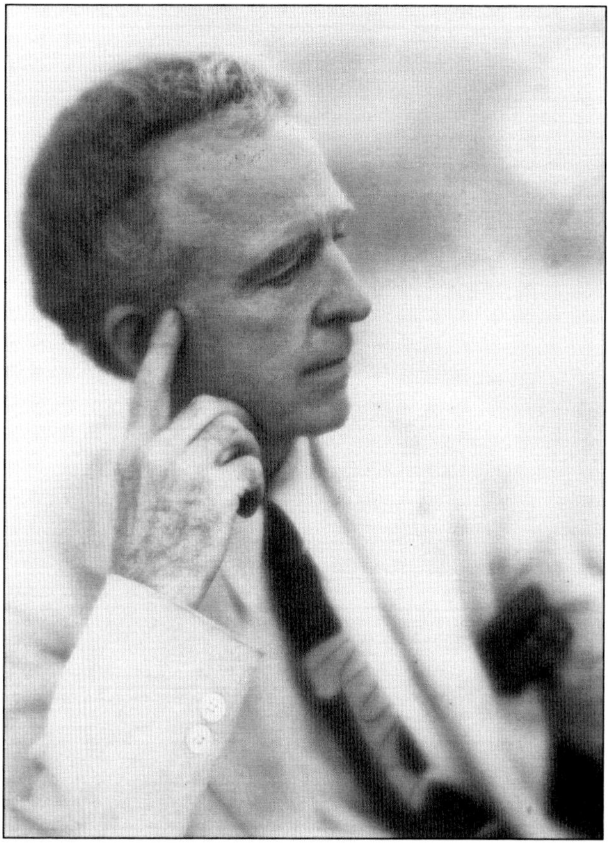

Douglas D. Ellington (1886–1960), son of Jesse T. and Sallie Williamson Ellington, was an internationally known architect in Asheville. After attending the Clayton Utopian Institute and Randolph-Macon College, he studied at Drexel Institute and the University of Pennsylvania in Philadelphia. In 1913, he was accepted into the Ecole des Beaux Arts in Paris, where he became the first American to win the coveted Prix Rougevin for architecture and the first Southerner to win the Prix de Paris.

Ashley Horne built this mansion, shown below about 1904, at the urging of Col. J. S. Carr of Durham, who believed a man of such great means should have a home to reflect his economic stature. Constructed between 1894 and 1897, the house passed out of the family in the late 1920s. It was demolished in 1970.

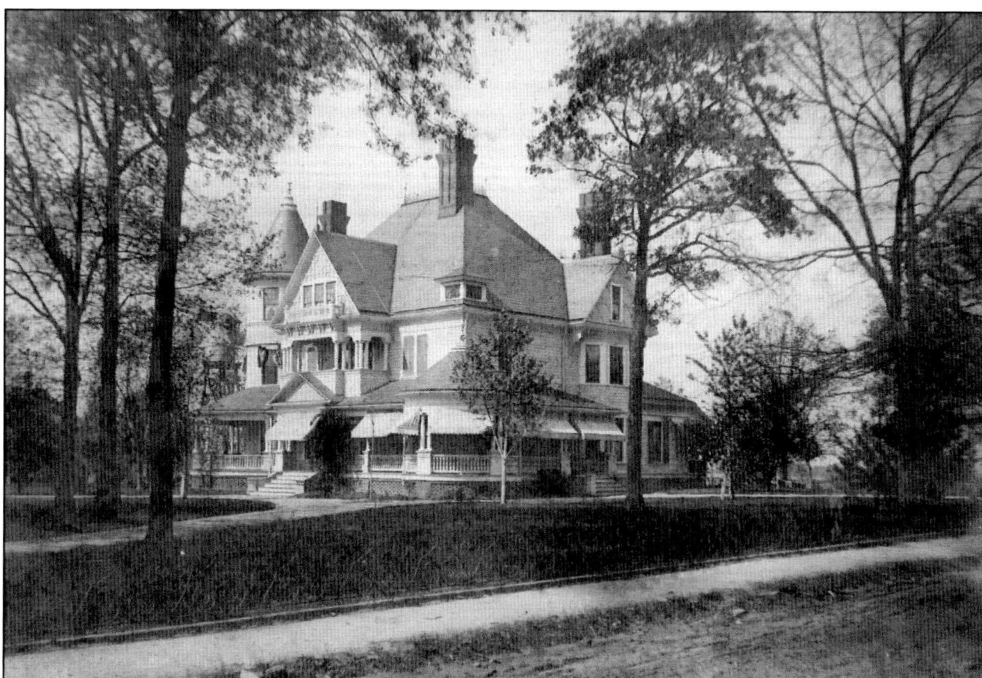

Ashley Horne (1841–1913) was Clayton's wealthiest citizen in the early 20th century. Returning from Confederate army service in 1865, he discovered his family's livestock had been taken by Union forces. He began building his fortune by planting a crop of corn and melons using two horses he stole back from a Union encampment near Raleigh. By 1900, he had large business interests in Clayton, Raleigh, and elsewhere. He was a state senator (1884–1885) and ran unsuccessfully for governor in 1908.

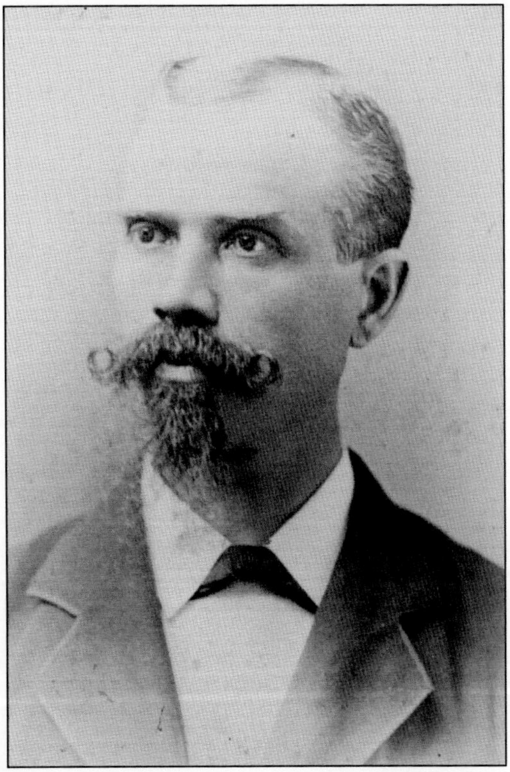

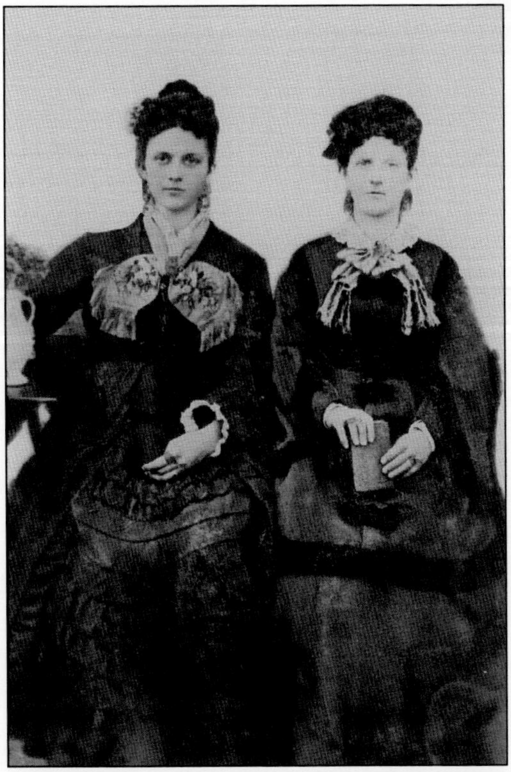

Cornelia Lee Horne (1849–1885), at right, was Ashley Horne's first wife. She posed for this photograph about 1880 with a sister, probably Laura Elizabeth "Bettie" Lee Battle. In Battle's book, *Forget-Me-Nots of the Civil War* (1909), she recalled "Nealy" as the belle of Clayton in the years immediately following the Civil War. She was crowned the "Queen of Love and Beauty" at a state horseracing tournament held in Clayton in 1869.

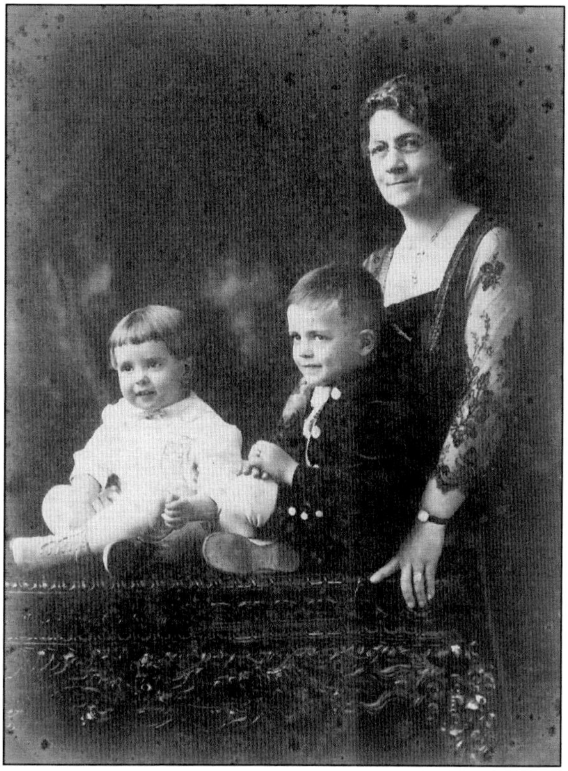

Rena Beckwith Horne Hunter, the second wife of Ashley Horne, is shown with grandsons Robert and Charles Priddy after moving to Wichita Falls, Texas, to live with her daughter Swannanoa in the late 1920s. A native of the Holly Springs vicinity in Wake County, she attended the Boston Conservatory of Music before coming to Clayton in 1886 to join her brother Exum G. Beckwith as assistant principal and music teacher at the Clayton Academy. A local reporter aptly characterized her as "a lady of high culture."

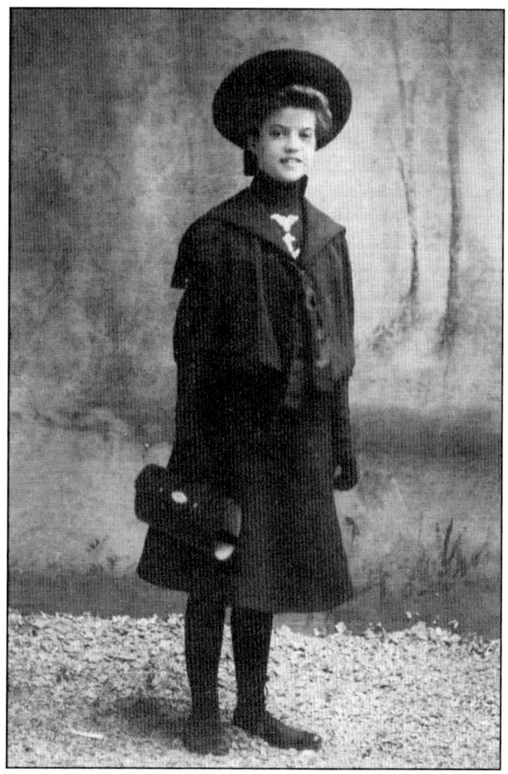

Swannanoa Horne (1889–1981), the daughter of Ashley and Rena Beckwith Horne, is shown in the early 1900s. Like her mother, she was remembered as an accomplished musician. After attending the Clayton High School, she attended Raleigh's Meredith College, founded by her uncle O. L. Stringfield, and later transferred to Hollins College in Roanoke, Virginia, where she graduated in 1911. Her wedding to Walter Priddy in 1914 was the social event of the season, after which the newlyweds settled in Wichita Falls, Texas.

Ida Harrell Horne, the wife of Ashley Horne's brother Hardee, was active in Clayton's civic and religious life for most of her adulthood. She was particularly well known for her intellect and poetry writing. A number of newspapers across North Carolina published her poems under the nom de plume Carmine, and her son Herman compiled her works into two books, *Southern Lyrics* (1916) and *Simple Southern Songs* (1916).

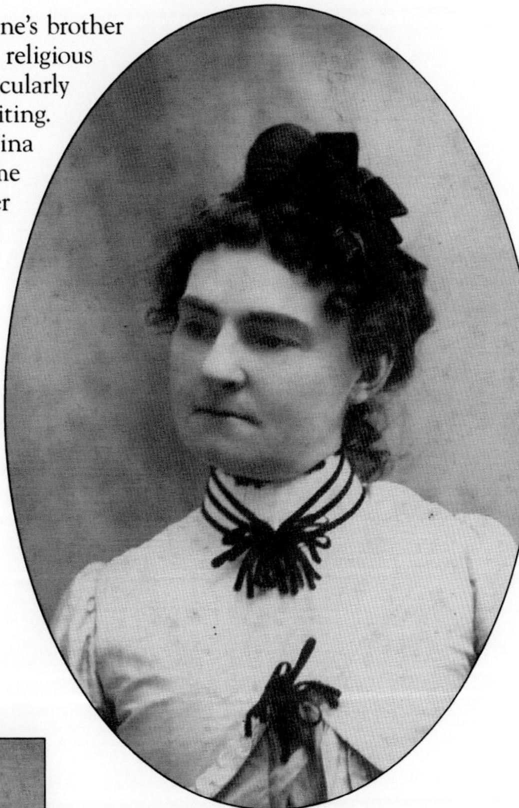

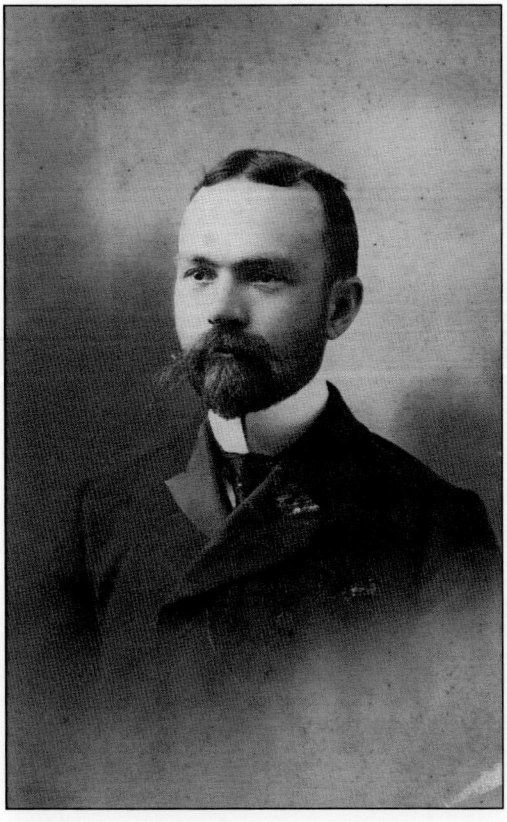

Herman Harrell Horne (1874–1946), son of Hardee and Ida Harrell Horne, was a leader in his class at the Clayton Utopian Institute in the early 1890s. After earning a Ph.D. at Harvard in 1899, he taught for 10 years at Dartmouth College and for more than 30 years at New York University. A prolific writer, he published some 20 books during his career. At the time of his death, he was planning to return to Clayton to spend his last days at the old Horne family home.

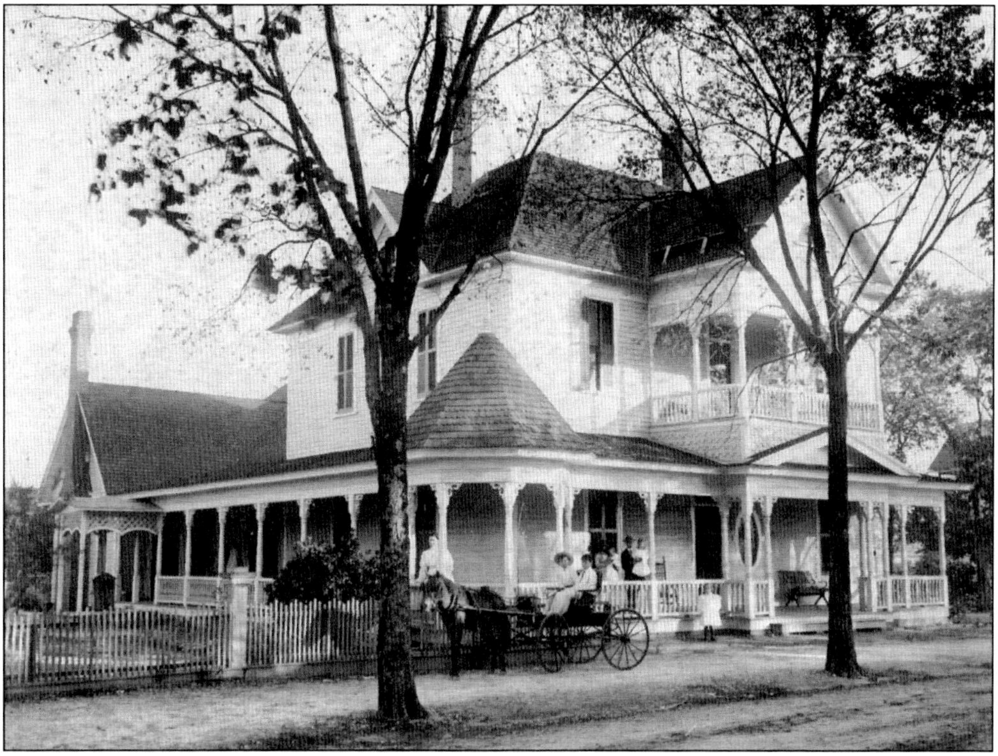

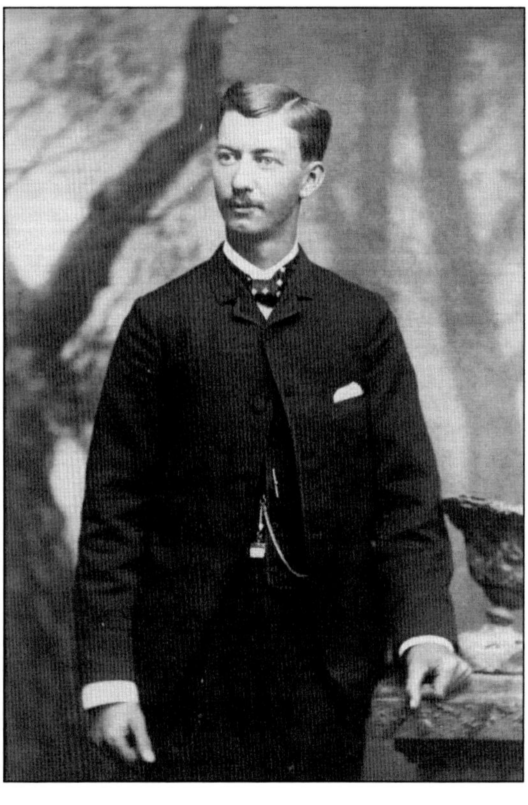

Pictured around 1909, the home of Delano Houston McCullers (1853–1935), a dry-goods merchant, was located on the corner of Fayetteville and Main Streets. Delano and three of his brothers operated the family business, W. H. McCullers and Sons, after the death of their father in 1890. Delano's brother William H. (1858–1921) is pictured at left about 1885.

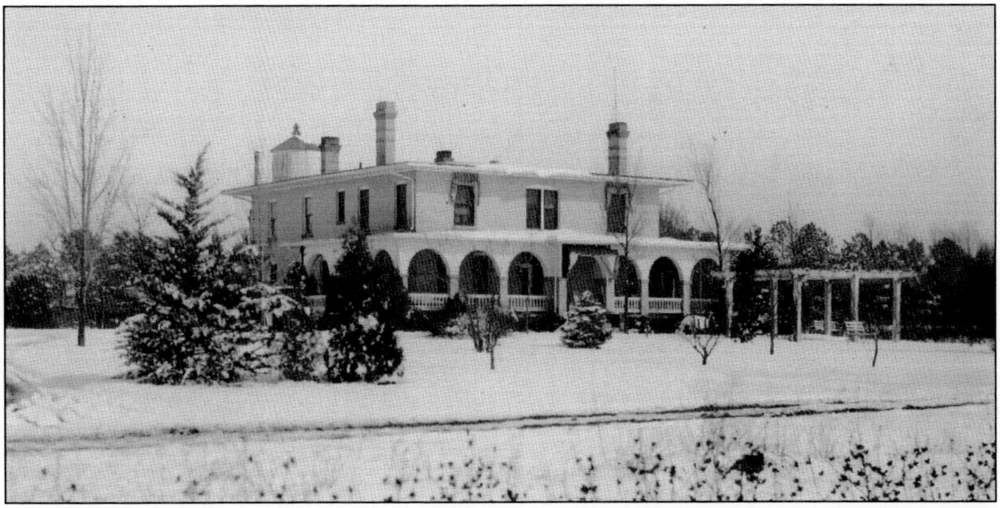

Jesse Mercer Battle, a wealthy St. Louis pharmaceutical executive, built this impressive Spanish Revival house (above), called Roxborough Hall, in 1910 for his wife, Clayton-native Laura Elizabeth "Bettie" Lee. Battle commented in his memoirs in 1911 that Bettie and her mother would have thought him the wildest dreamer during their courtship in the 1870s if he had said he would build the most expensive house in town, complete with every convenience and comfort imaginable. "And this is exactly what I have done," he added. While in Clayton from about 1909 to 1914, the Battles built a Catholic church (St. Joseph's) and opened Johnston County's first movie theater, the Palace. The Battles are pictured below about 1912 with daughter Helen and son-in-law Eugene Smith and the grandchildren in St. Louis. Laura Battle's nephew Charlie Horne purchased the home, and it was sold to Ollin S. Benson in 1935.

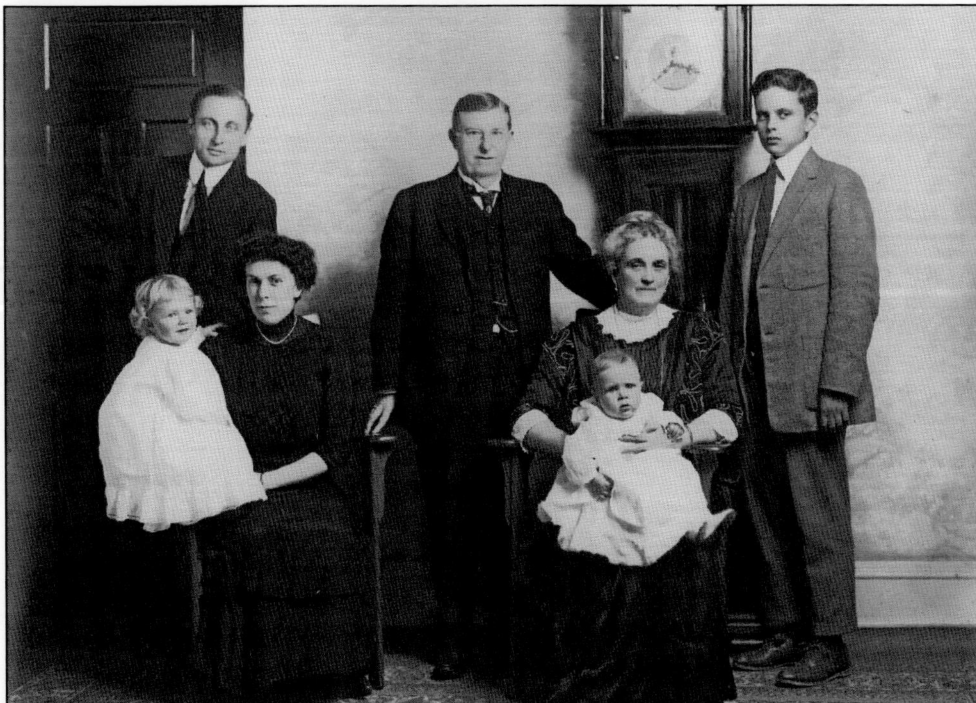

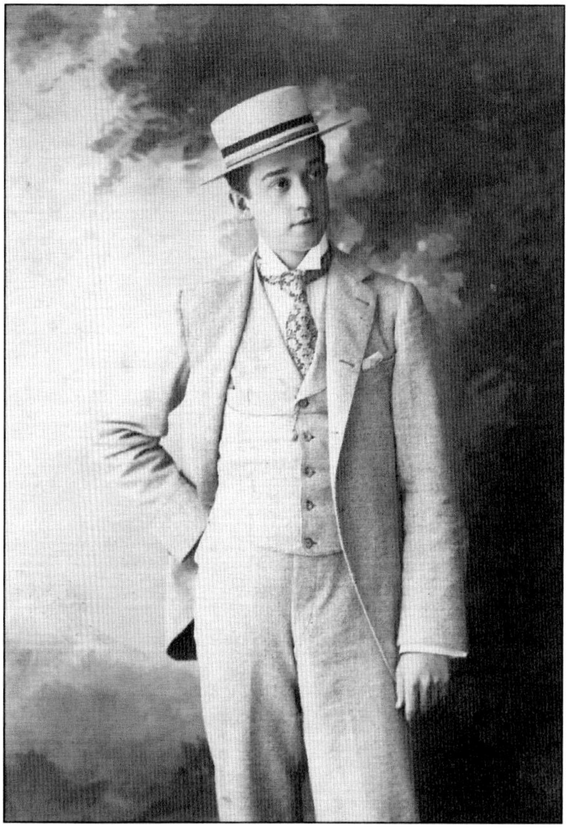

A debonair Charles Whitehurst "Charlie" Horne, son of Ashley and Cornelia Lee Horne, was photographed about 1900 in a Newark, New Jersey, studio, probably while on a buying trip for Ashley Horne and Son's mercantile business. While his father was getting a cotton mill started, Charlie joined J. Arch Vinson in the lumber business. According to the *Smithfield Herald* of January 26, 1900, Vinson and Horne had bought up enough timberlands to keep two lumber mills operating for five years.

The Quinton F. Pool family members are shown below around 1900. From left to right are (first row) Mattie Ruth, Alice, Quinton, and Elsie; (second row) Robert and Nellie. Quinton operated a general merchandise store. Elsie married Ashley Horne Jr.

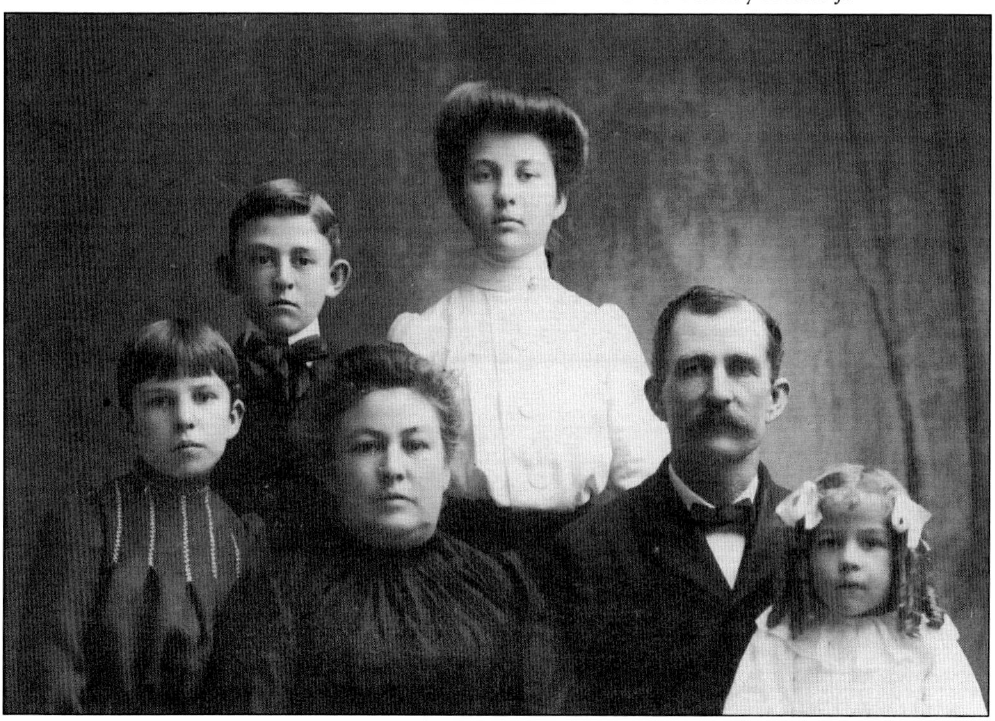

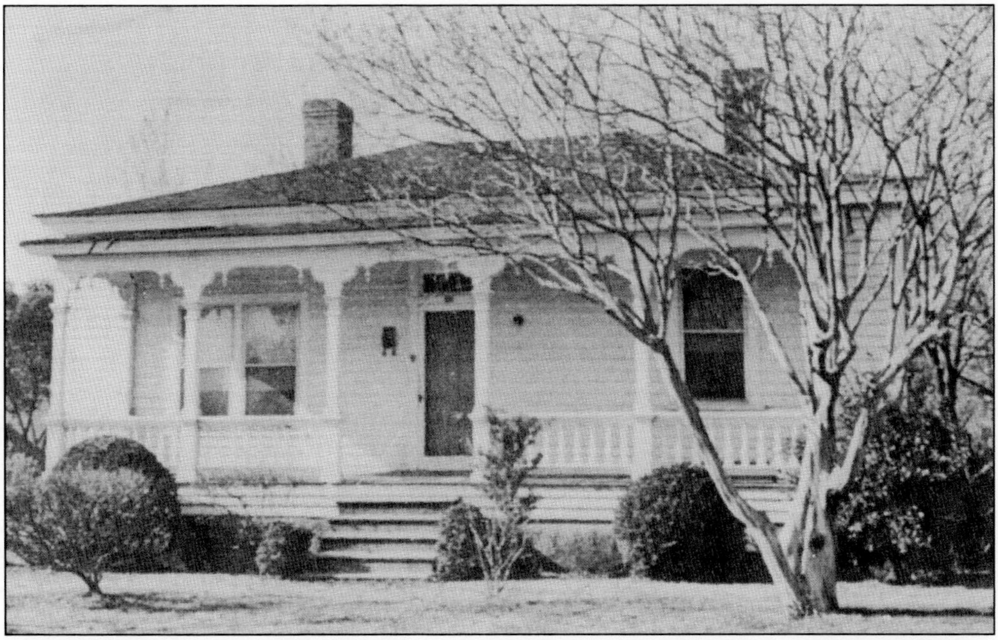

The Wiley Wooten Cox (1830–1908) home, located on the corner of First and Church Streets, is one of the oldest in Clayton. Cox, one of Clayton's first merchants, built a store on one of the lots sold by Sarah Stallings in the mid-1850s. He operated the store until the 1870s, when he sold the business to John M. Cox. Wiley married Mary Anne Eliza Poole, the daughter of Lewis and Elizabeth Talton Poole. He was a Mason and a charter member of the Granite Lodge.

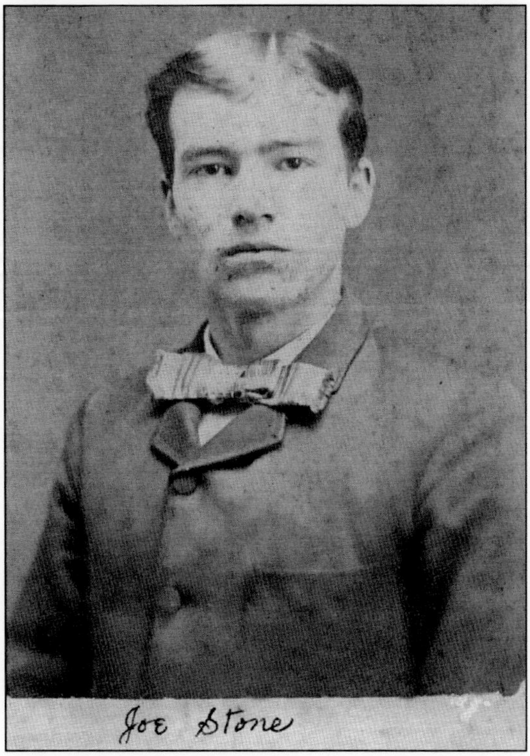

Joseph J. Stone, shown here in about 1890, purchased N. R. Richardson's interest in the town's newspaper, the *Clayton Bud*, in January 1886. He and business partner John R. Wedding continued the paper with Stone as the editor. The *Clayton Bud* was first issued on February 27, 1883. Stone and Henry A. McCullers were cocaptains of the Clayton Red Stockings baseball team of 1883.

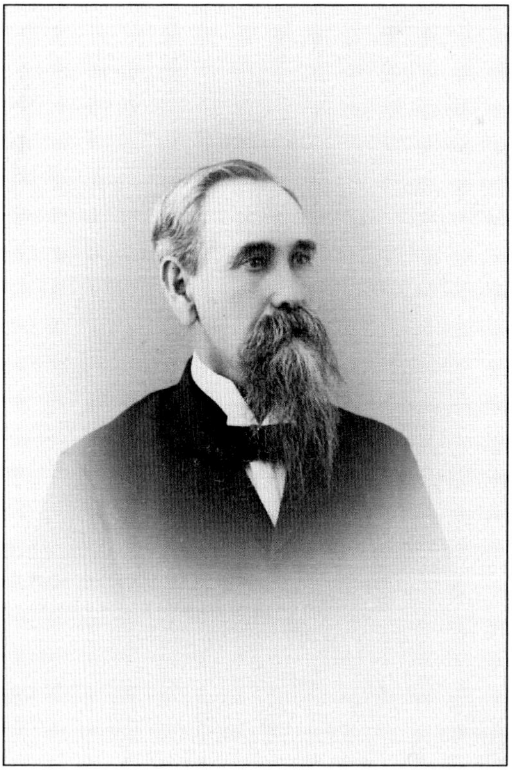

Dr. James Battle Robertson (*c.* 1835–1910) graduated from the University of Pennsylvania and served as an army surgeon during the Civil War. After the war, he began a medical practice and drugstore in Clayton. He served the community as a doctor for 50 years. He and his wife, Julia, owned and operated the Robertson Hotel until 1906. (Courtesy of Sam Robertson.)

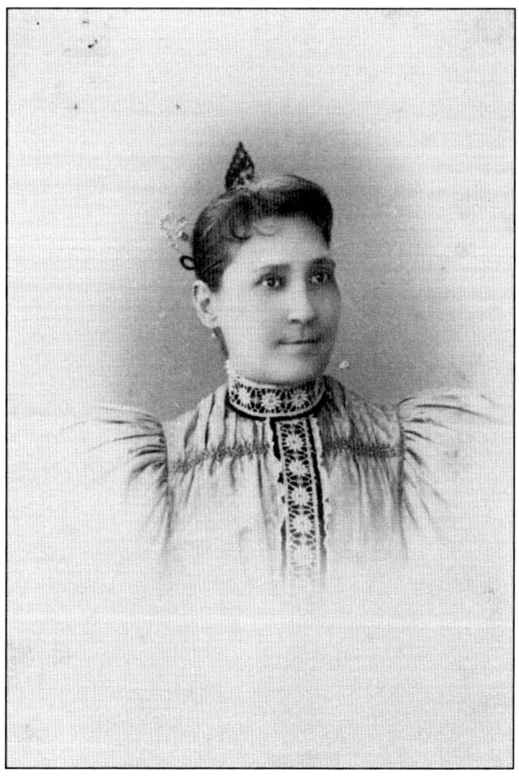

Julia Avera Ellington Robertson (1845–1912) was the daughter of Rev. John F. and Christiana Avera Ellington and the wife of Dr. James B. Robertson. Julia taught piano and organ during the 1880s at the Clayton Institute. She was the mother of Mrs. J. J. (Margaret) Young, Mrs. J. B. (Pearl) Blades, Will, John, and Roy Robertson. (Courtesy of Sam Robertson.)

Charles Manly Creech of O'Neals Township came to Clayton by the early 1890s, when this photograph was taken, and became heavily involved in public life. He was elected a town commissioner in 1894 and won a seat in the state legislature in 1896. He also made captain of the Clayton baseball club that same year. In 1897, he left town briefly to accept a position with the Caraleigh Phosphate Works, a Raleigh fertilizer plant, but he died in his prime the following year.

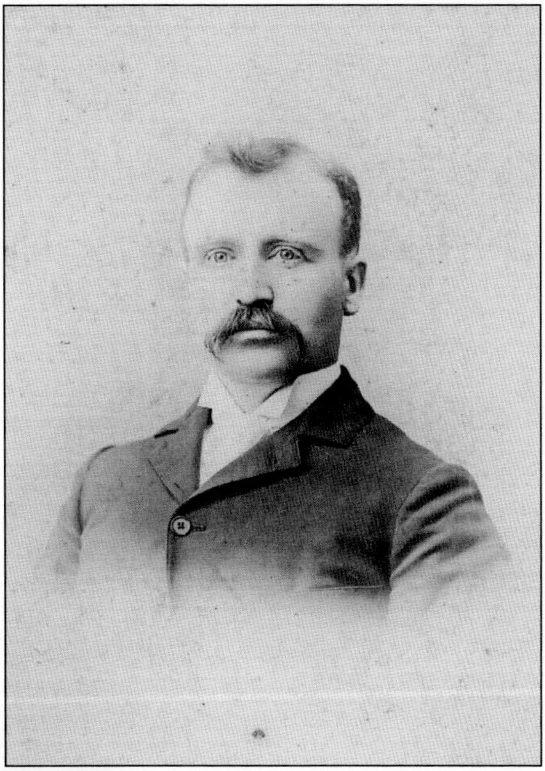

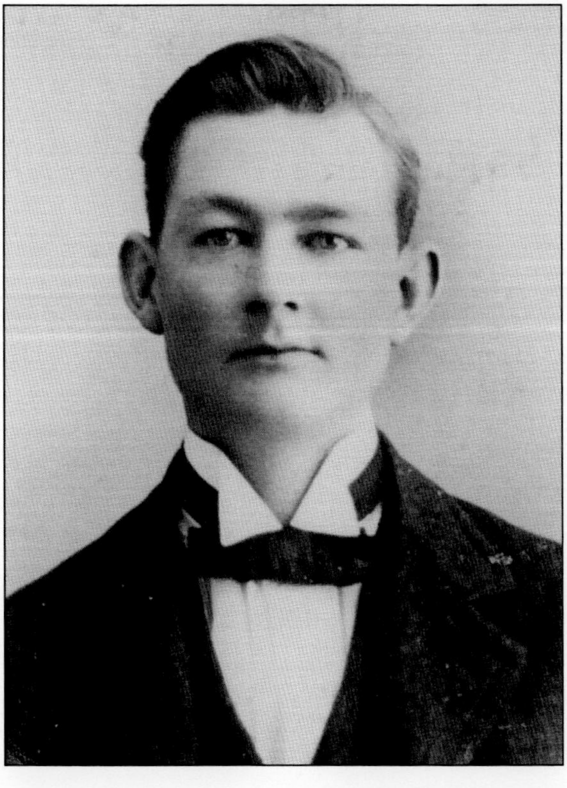

Wilfred Ivan Whitley (1876–1949), shown here in 1898, was a Clayton merchant, town mayor and commissioner, a registrar, and a member of the Knights of Pythias. Ivan married Nina Duncan in 1901. Nina was the daughter of A. R. and Betty Turner Duncan. (Courtesy of the Rasor family.)

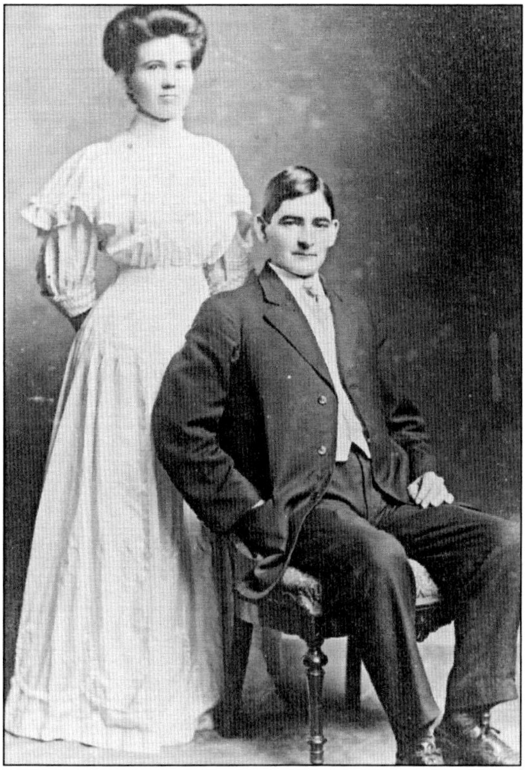

L. H. Champion (1878–1968) married Ada Hinton in 1908. He taught school, worked with Ashley Horne and Son, and then opened a store with his brother Matthew. He worked with the North Carolina Prison Department, served as the first judge of Clayton's recorders court for almost 10 years, and was a town road commissioner, registrar, and justice of the peace. (Courtesy of Sybil T. Champion.)

The Ernest L. Hinton home (shown below) was built in 1899 on First Street. Hinton was the son of Malachi and Elizabeth Hood Hinton. He married Lela Ellington in 1893. He was mayor of Clayton from 1899 to 1915, a county commissioner, and an employee of J. G. Barbour and Sons from 1888 to 1920.

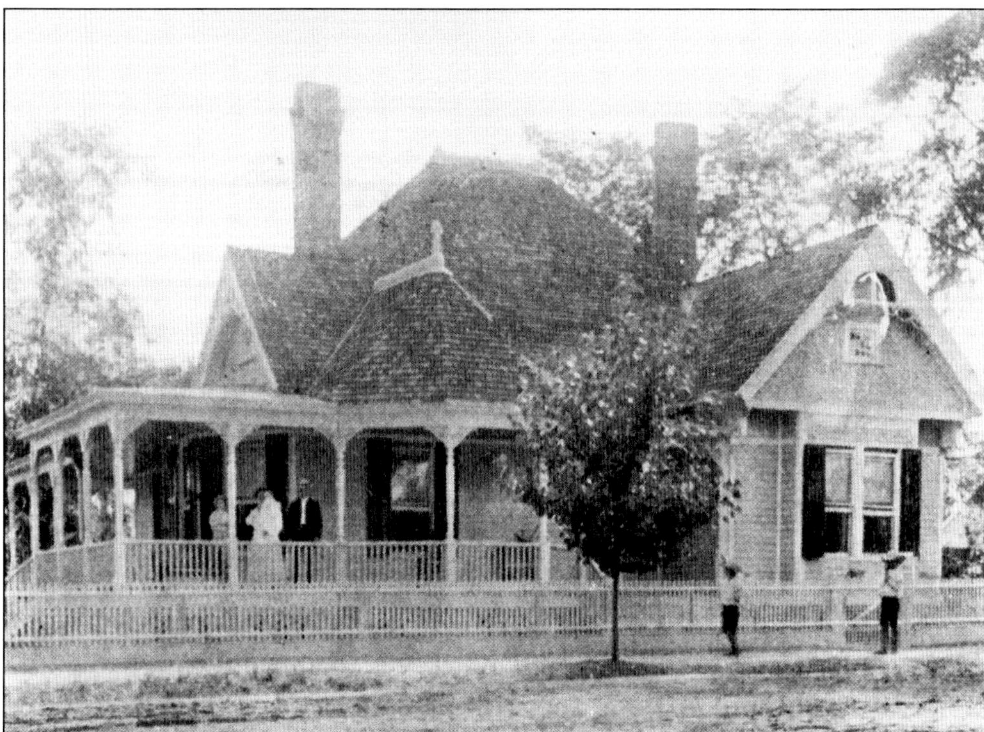

Henry Rufus Goodson (1854–1932), pictured at right, was born during slavery but was from a free African American family living near Eagle Rock, Wake County. He attended Shaw University and as a young man began accumulating farmland. By the early 20th century, he was a sizeable landowner in Wake and Johnston Counties and a leader in Clayton's First Missionary Baptist Church, as well as in the National Baptist Convention's Johnston County Baptist Association. In the second decade of the 20th century, he worked with fellow Baptists to raise money to build Johnston County's first high school for blacks in Smithfield. He was married first to Sarah Hall and later to Sadie Lewis, and was the father of 19 children. His home in Clayton, shown below, is still standing.

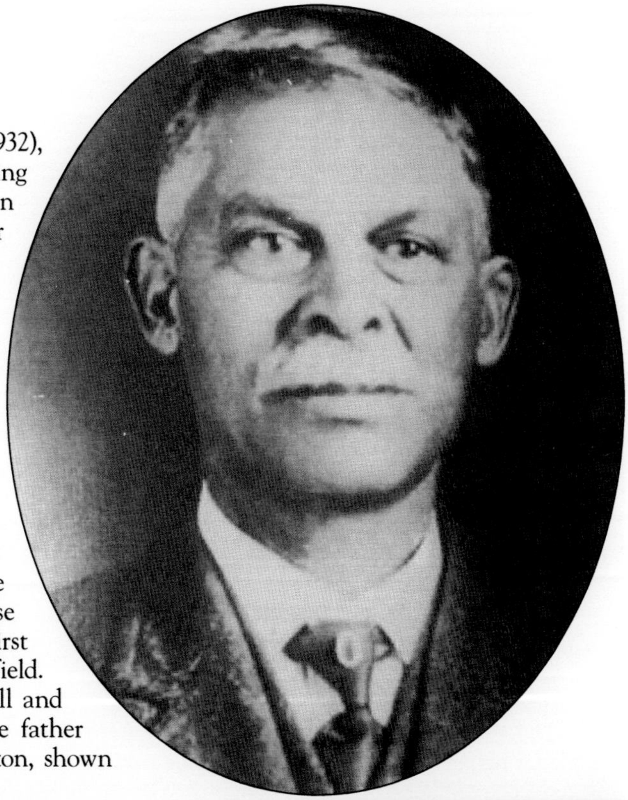

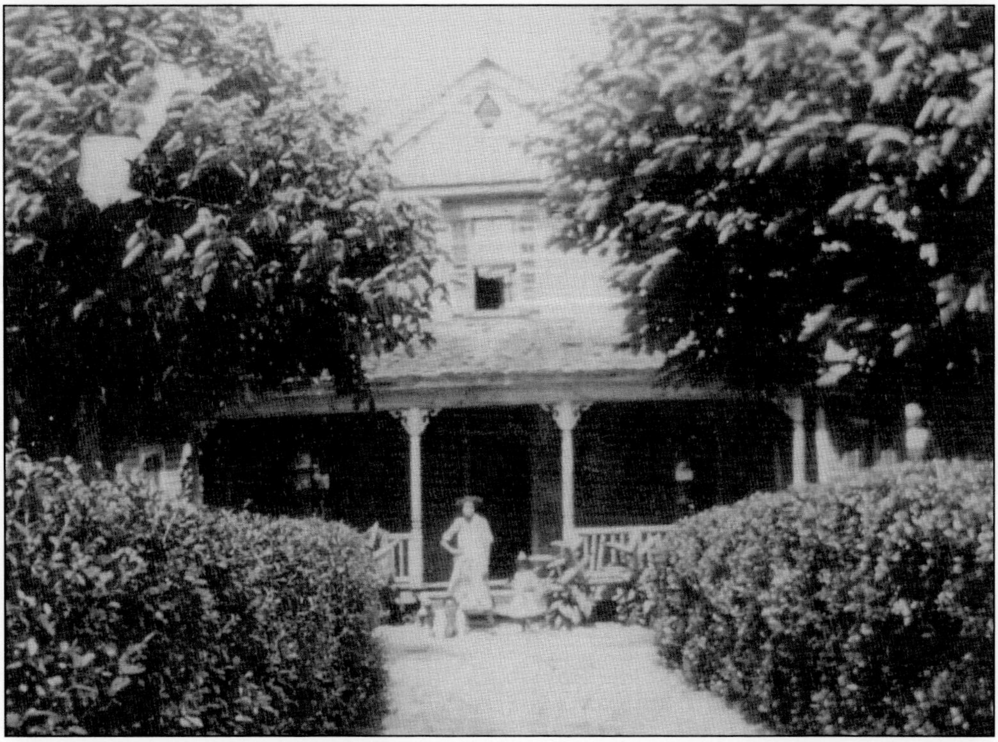

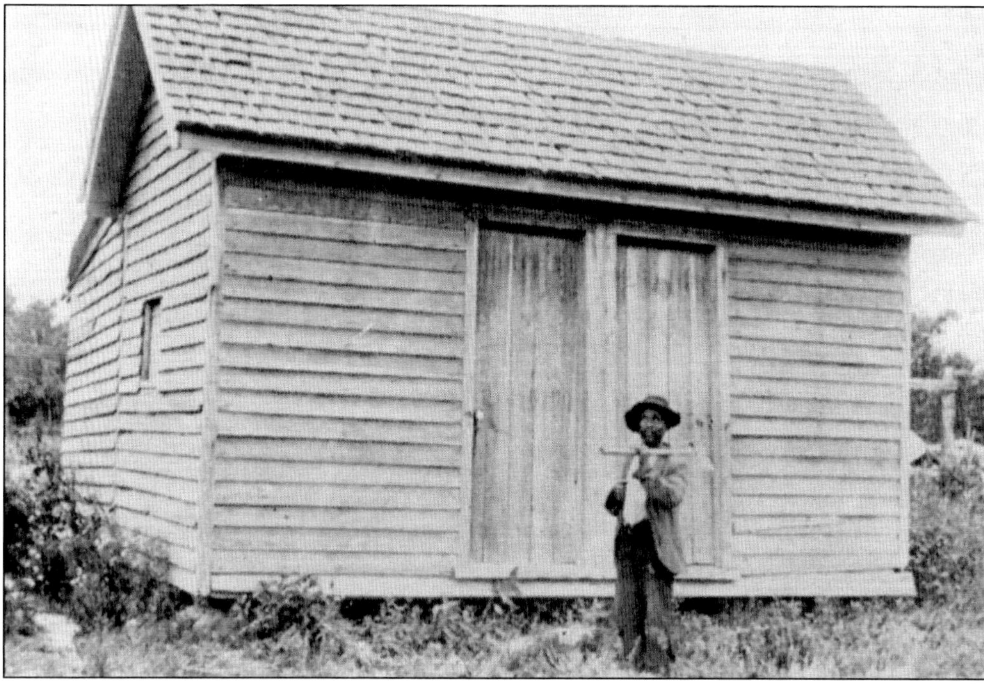

Woodcutter Alsey Horton was characterized as a "noble specimen of Clayton energy" in 1909. He had been totally blind for about 15 years, John T. Talton wrote, but was never known to beg anyone for help. "He can go to any woodpile in town unaided," Talton added, "and it is nothing unusual to be awakened before it is light by the stroke of his axe chopping wood."

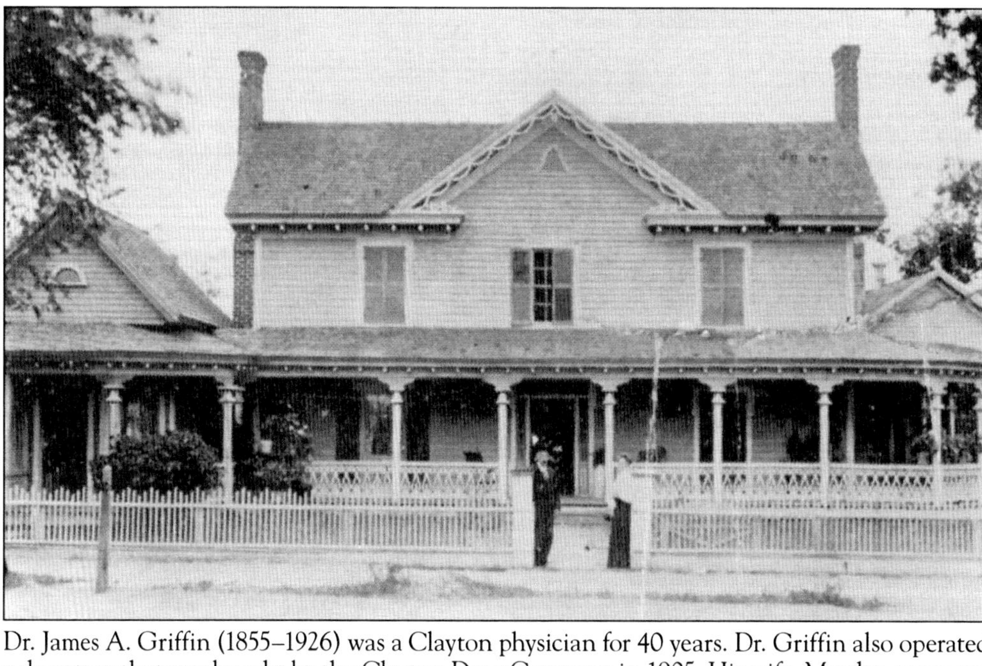

Dr. James A. Griffin (1855–1926) was a Clayton physician for 40 years. Dr. Griffin also operated a drugstore that was bought by the Clayton Drug Company in 1905. His wife, Martha, managed a millinery shop. This 1909 picture shows the Griffins' Main Street home, built around 1880, with the wraparound porch and the doctor's office on the back right.

Dr. B. A. Hocutt (1879-1946) is shown in 1906, when he graduated from the University of North Carolina Medical School in Raleigh. He served the community as a general practitioner for 42 years. Dr. Hocutt was a leader in town, church, and county organizations.

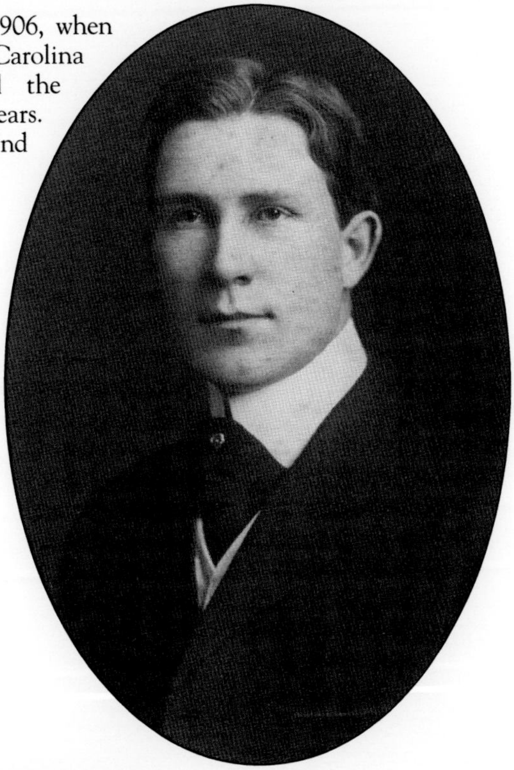

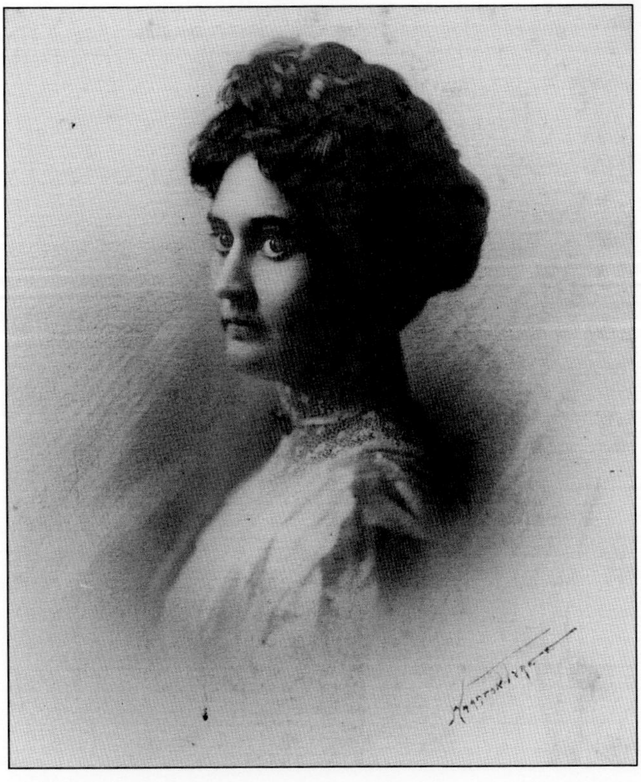

Lucile Ellington Hocutt (1882–1974), pictured in about 1910, was the wife of Dr. B. A. Hocutt and the daughter of Jesse T. and Delia Ellington. Known as "Miss Lucile," she was a leader in the First Baptist Church, working with the Woman's Missionary Union and teaching various classes. She was a vital part of the Woman's Club of Clayton and helped to establish the town library. She deeded her home on Second Street to the town for the location of the Hocutt-Ellington Memorial Library.

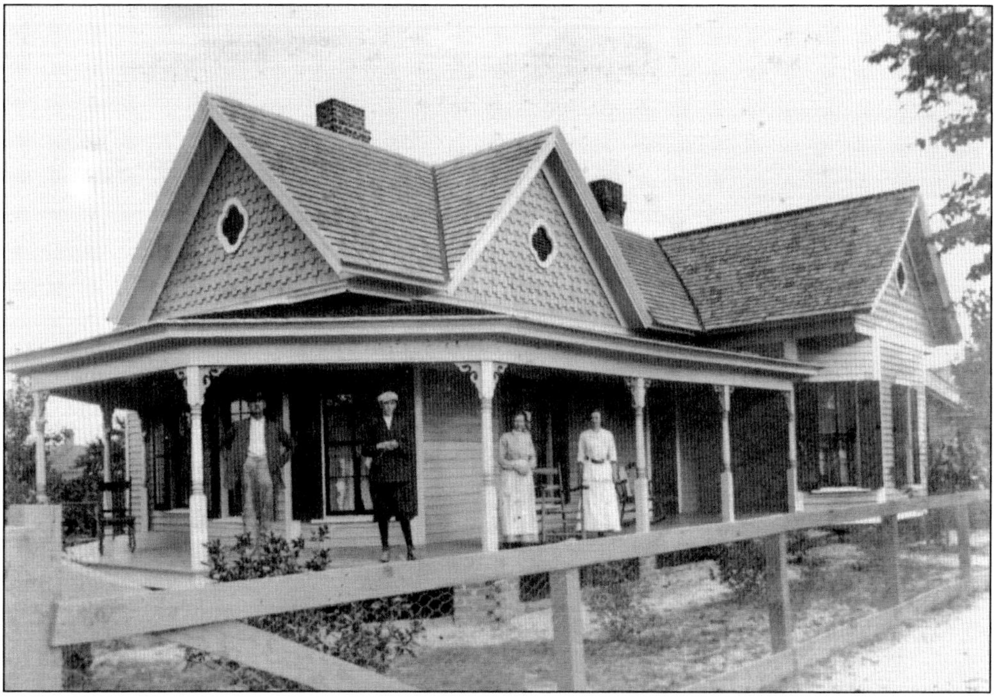

D. Q. Lowry built this Page Street residence around 1910, shortly before this photograph was taken. Pictured on the porch from left to right are D. Q. Lowry, Charles (son), Laura (wife), and Pearl (daughter).

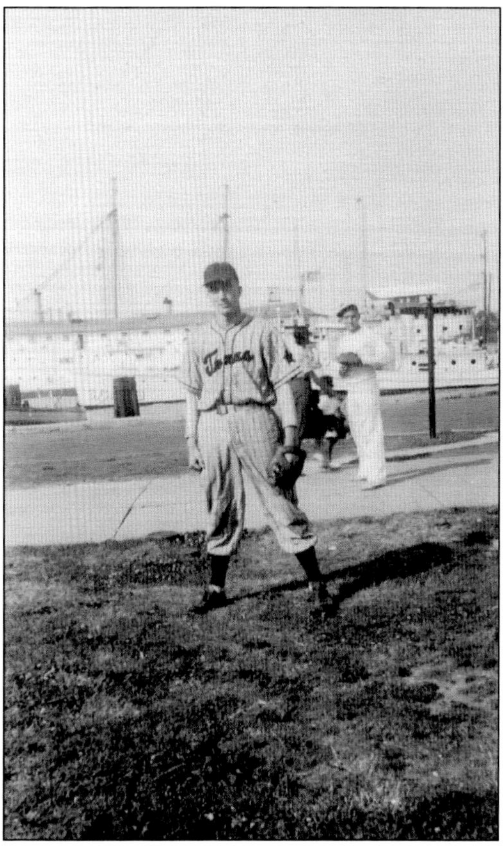

Belvin Womble Maynard Jr. was photographed in a Texas baseball uniform about 1940, a short time before enlisting to serve in World War II. He was grandson of Dr. A. A. Maynard, a physician who practiced in Clayton in the 1880s, and son of Belvin W. Maynard, a famous minister-aviator known as the "Flying Parson." After his father died in a stunt plane crash in 1922, his mother married Hunter Hamilton and brought the family to Clayton.

Nixon Louis Cannady (1905–1991), at right, was a native of Smithfield and came to Clayton in 1931 as the principal and a teacher at the Clayton Negro School. He worked his way through Shaw University by shining shoes at Raleigh's Yarborough House and later earned a master's degree from Columbia University. Under his leadership, the Clayton school grew, by 1946, from a three-teacher elementary institution to a high school with a faculty of more than 20. His wife, Flossie Davidson Cannady (1908–1975), shown below, came to teach with him in 1933. A native of Statesville, she was educated at the Winston-Salem Teachers College and New York University. She and her husband were both active in Clayton's civic and church life. He retired in 1970 and she in 1973 after a combined 80 years of service to the public school system.

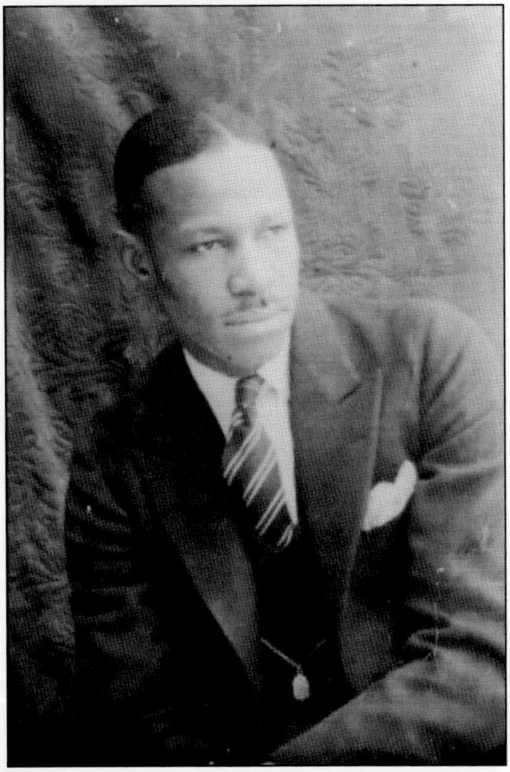

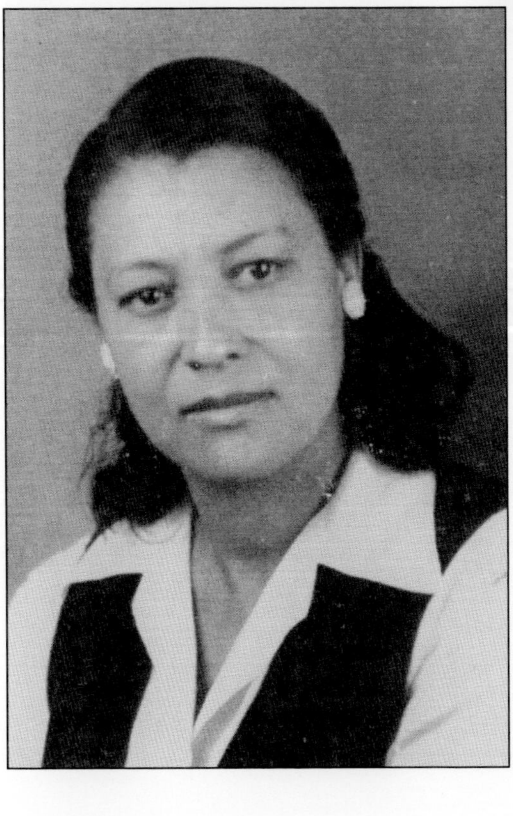

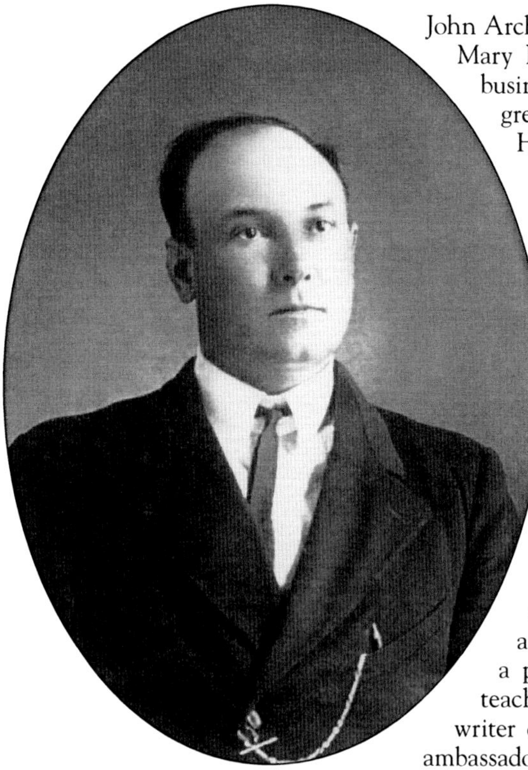

John Arch Vinson (1871–1923), son of Ahasuerus and Mary Elizabeth Turner Vinson, started a lumber business in Clayton in the 1890s. The business grew and became one of the largest in the area. He built Clayton's first Ford dealership on the corner of O'Neal and Main Streets. Arch was the first president of the Farmers Bank. He was a Mason and a member of the Knights of Pythias. (Courtesy of Turner Vinson Jr.)

William E. Dodd (1869–1940), shown with his wife, Mattie Johns Dodd, in the 1930s, was one of Clayton's most well-known native sons. With financing from his great-uncle Ashley Horne, Dodd graduated from Virginia Polytechnic Institute and earned a doctorate from the University of Leipzig in Germany in 1900. He returned home and launched his teaching career at Clayton's Liberty School, a one-room public school. He soon accepted a position at Randolph-Macon College, later teaching at the University of Chicago. A prolific writer of history, he was best known as the U.S. ambassador to Germany, from 1933 to 1937.

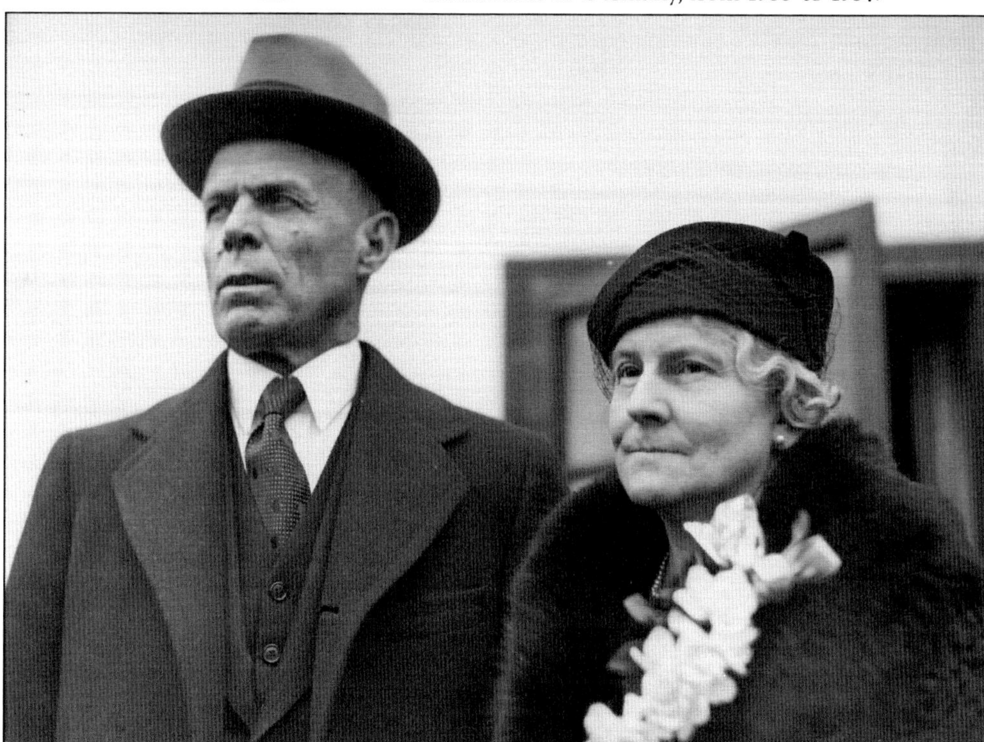

Three

CHURCHES

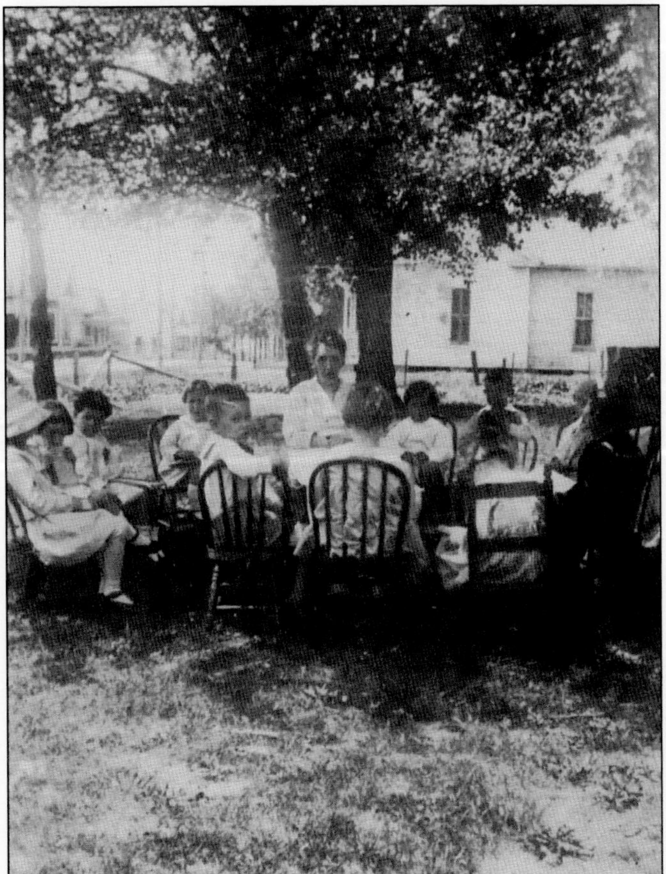

This photograph from about 1920 shows a local lady, thought to be a Sunday school teacher, taking advantage of the nice weather and treating a group of youngsters to an outdoor learning session. (Courtesy of Joyce T. Barbour.)

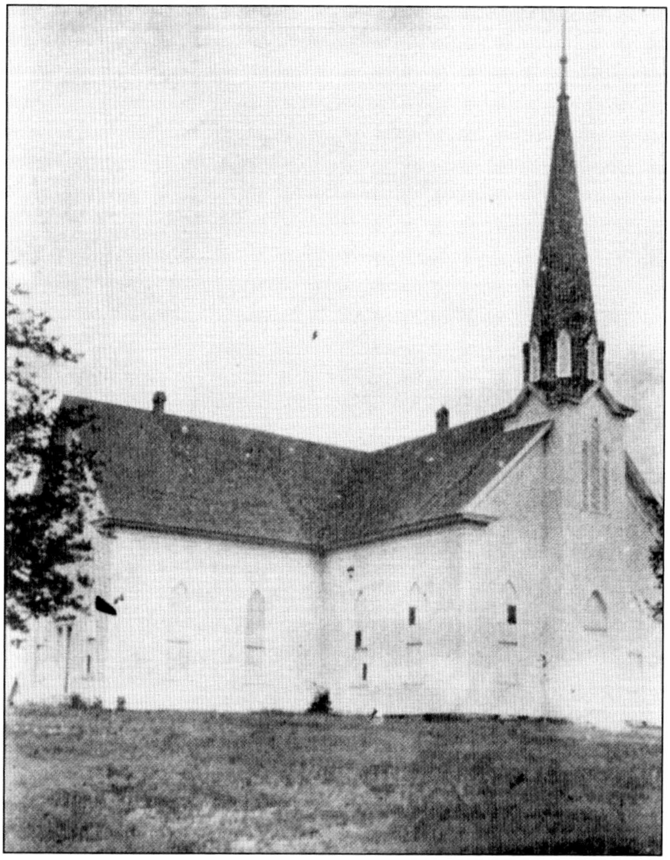

The First Baptist Church was organized as the Baptist Church of Christ at the Johnston Liberty Meeting House in 1811. A decision was made to move the church to a lot on the corner of Whitaker and Fayetteville Streets in 1882, and the name was changed to the Clayton Baptist Church. This building was occupied in 1883 but was not completed until 1885. (Courtesy of First Baptist Church.)

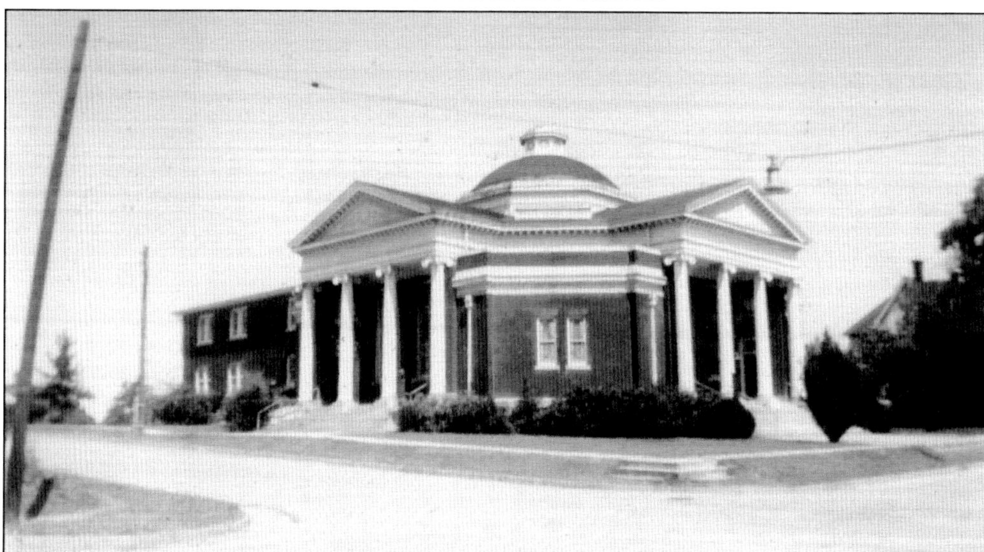

The First Baptist Church began construction of this brick building (still standing) in 1913 and held a dedication service in January 1923. The church, shown here in 1939, was built at a cost of $65,000 and featured 53 stained-glass windows. A new pipe organ was installed in 1920. (Courtesy of Joyce T. Barbour.)

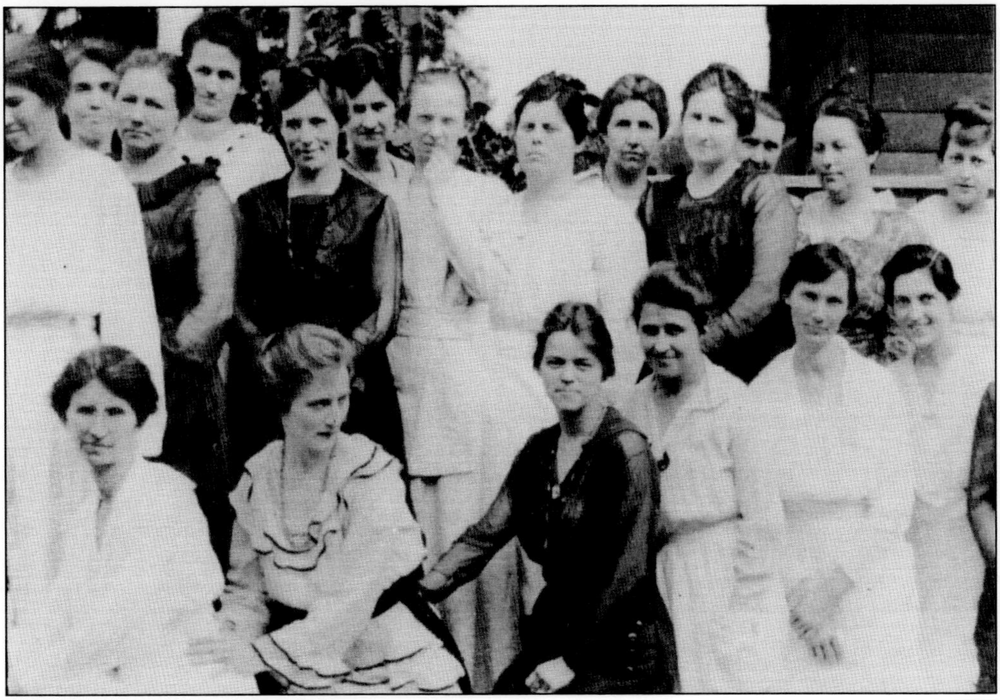

The 1919 Philathia Class of the First Baptist Church met at the home of Janie Gulley. The members are, from left to right, (first row) Elizabeth Hinton, Duba Turley, Larue Jeffreys, Lovie Ellis, Hallie Austin, and Gladys Barbour; (second row) Ione Creech, Mrs. Beck Parrish, Roberta Hilliard, Mrs. Jesse (Viola) Ellis, Ola Coats, Annie Hoyle, Lillie Coats, and Melba McCullers; (third row) unidentified, Myrtie Smith, Lucile Morris, Janie Gulley, and Kiva Allen. (Courtesy of First Baptist Church.)

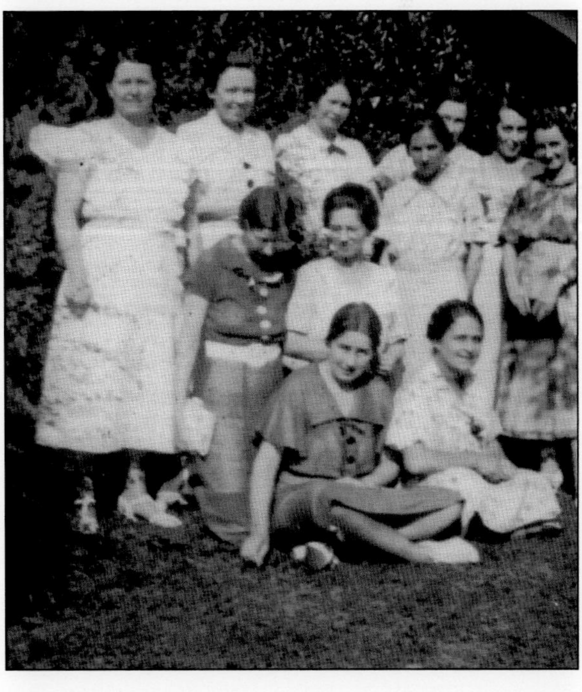

This 1936 First Baptist Church ladies group includes, from left to right, (first row) Maggie Gulley and Lovie Ellis; (second row) Ruth Yelverton and Bernice Smith; (third row) Annie Mae Ferrell, Winnie Barbour, Minnie Page, Clyde Ellis, unidentified, Louise Duncan, and Barbara Montague. (Courtesy of First Baptist Church.)

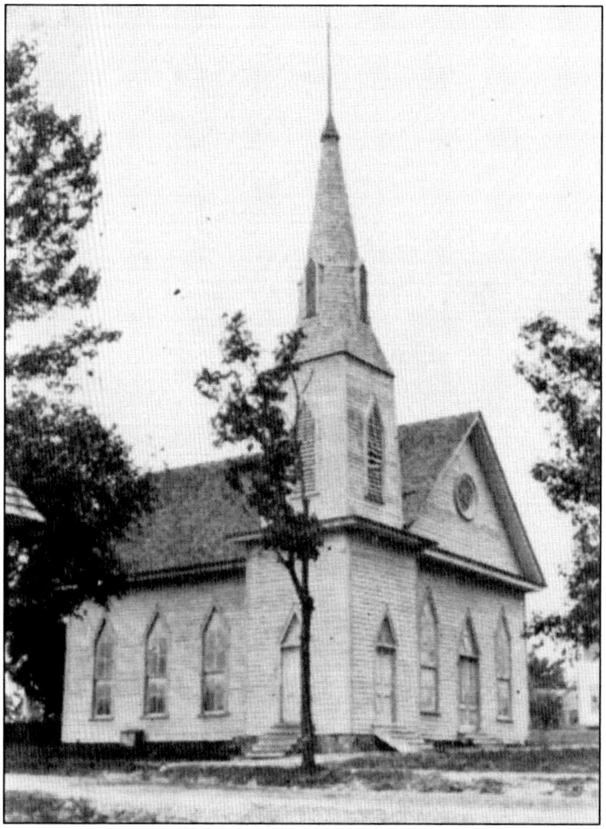

The Horne Memorial Methodist Church was formed in 1859 and was first named the Clayton Methodist Episcopal Church. Joseph M. Smith deeded a half-acre of land to the church in April 1859. This frame building was replaced in 1912 when the present brick church was built.

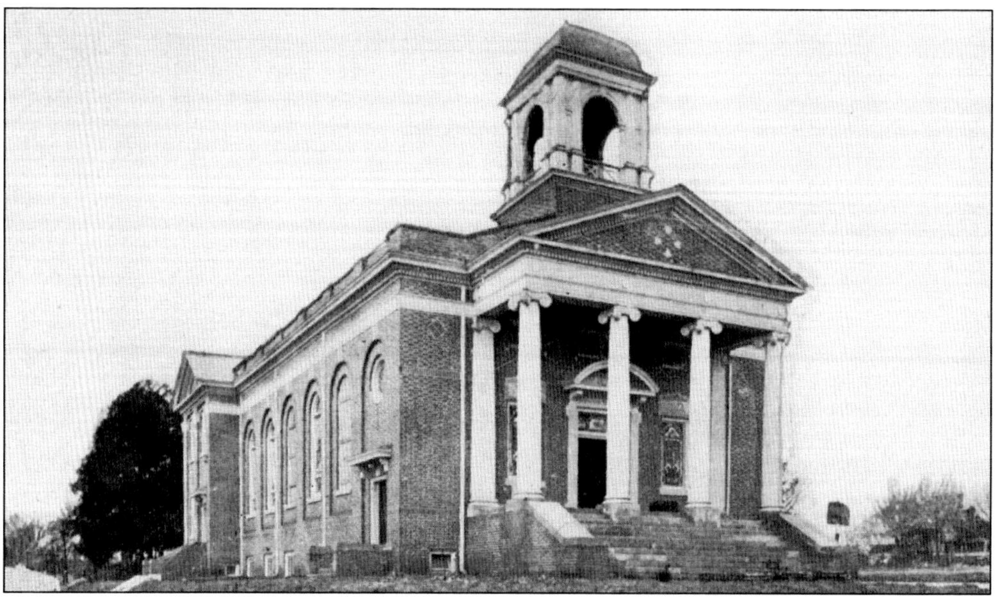

This *c.* 1916 postcard showcases the new brick Horne Memorial Methodist Church (still standing), constructed between 1912 and 1916. The church's stained-glass windows depicting biblical scenes are believed to have been made by Tiffany Studios in New York. (Courtesy of Carey Barbour.)

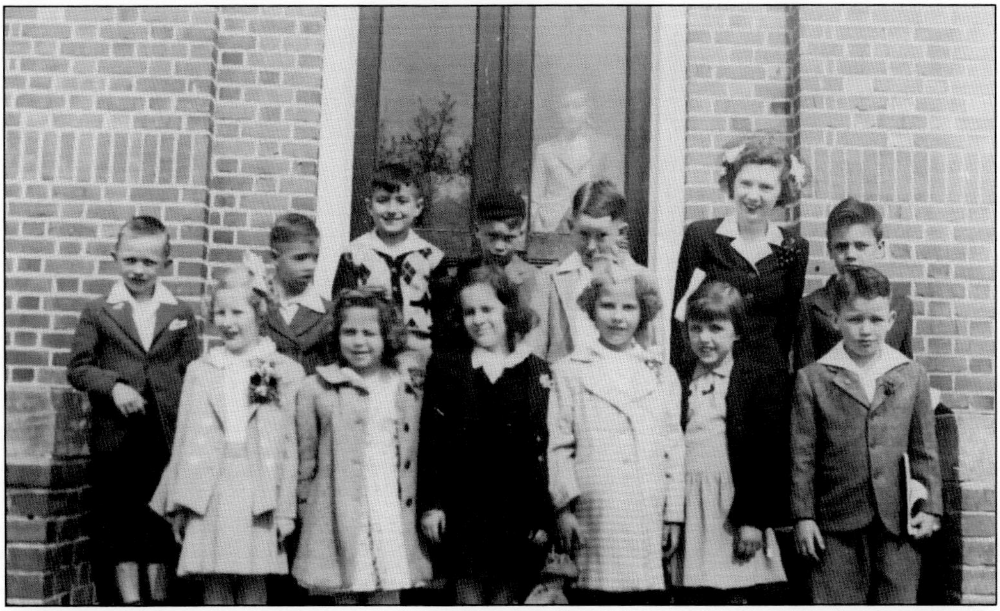

This early 1940s photograph was taken on Easter Sunday at Horne Memorial Methodist Church. From left to right are (first row) Caroline Nelson, Sue Mitchell, Jeannie Welch, Sue Cavanaugh, unidentified, and Bobby Dodd; (second row) Bat Robertson, Ellsworth Barbour, Jimmy Moore, Johnny Welch, Bill Peele, Virginia Lee Satterfield, and William Sherron. (Courtesy of the Horne Memorial Methodist Church.)

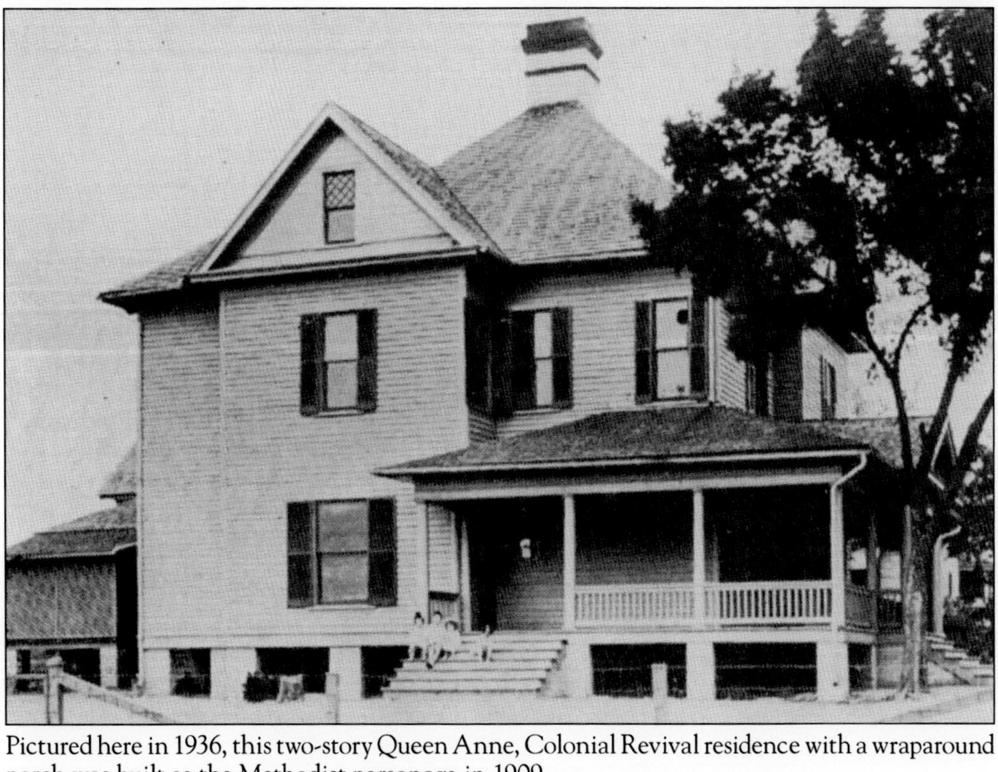

Pictured here in 1936, this two-story Queen Anne, Colonial Revival residence with a wraparound porch was built as the Methodist parsonage in 1909.

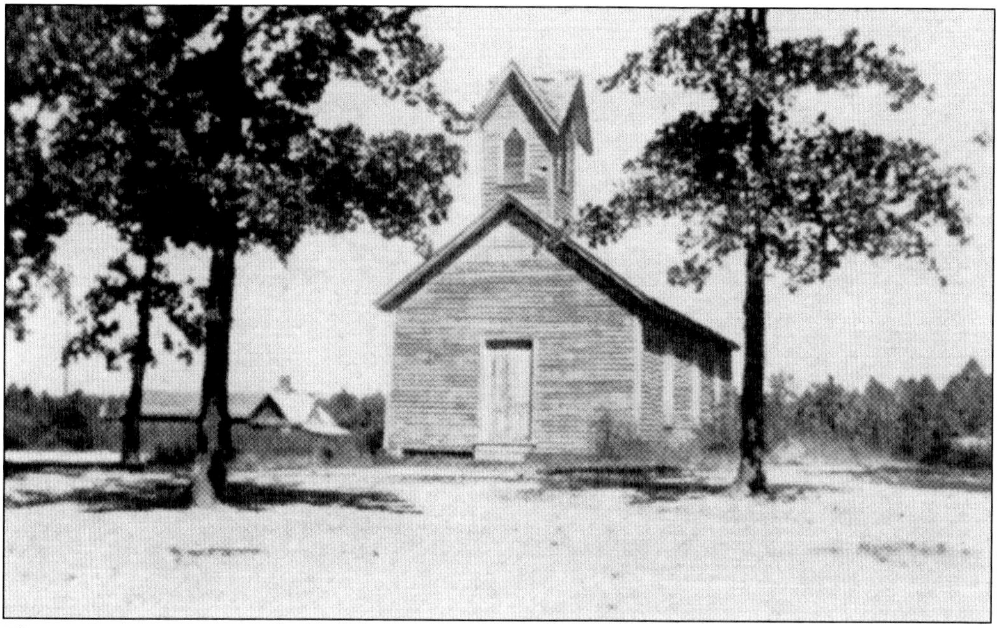

The Primitive Baptists used this building, shown in 1909, for their services in the early 1900s. The building was built as the Liberty Free School and was used as a church on Sundays. Jesse Ellington taught Latin here, and his daughter Lucile attended this school. Dr. William E. Dodd taught one summer term there to help pay for his college expenses. Located on Stallings Street, the building was taken down in 1968.

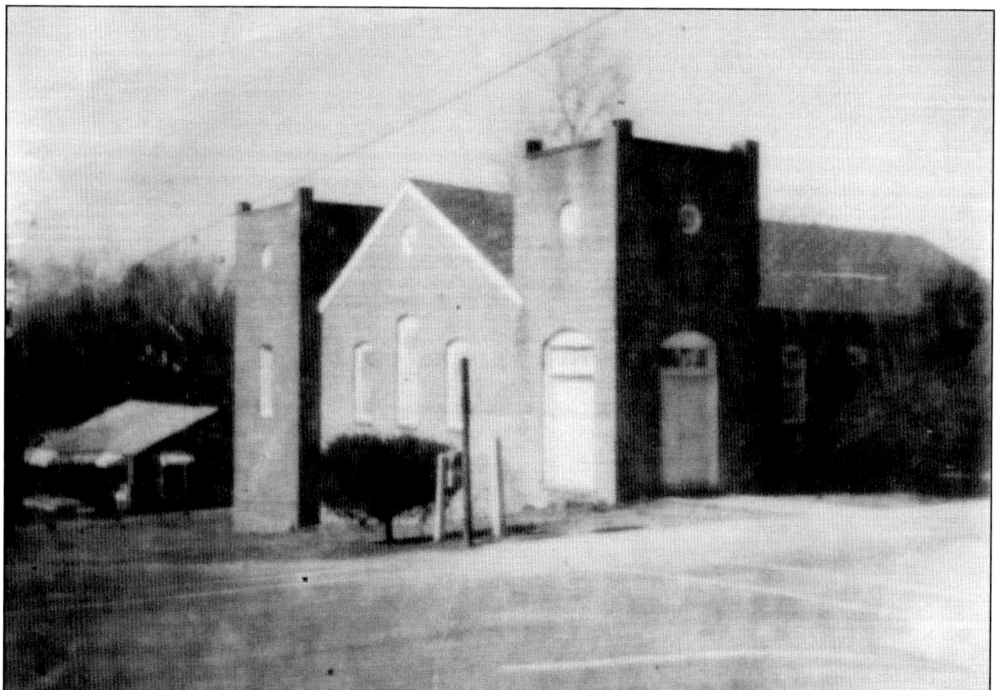

The First Missionary Baptist Church, located on the corner of Lombard and East Stallings Streets, was organized in 1870 by former slaves. This brick structure (still standing) dates to 1926.

W. B. Everett founded the Free Will Baptist Church around 1903. The original building, shown in this 1936 photograph, was located on Front Street. The congregation included 74 people in 1917.

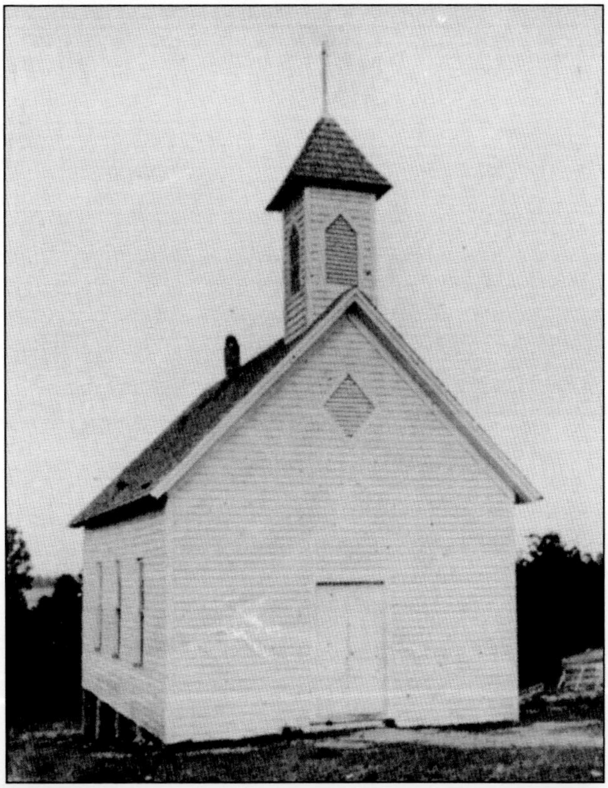

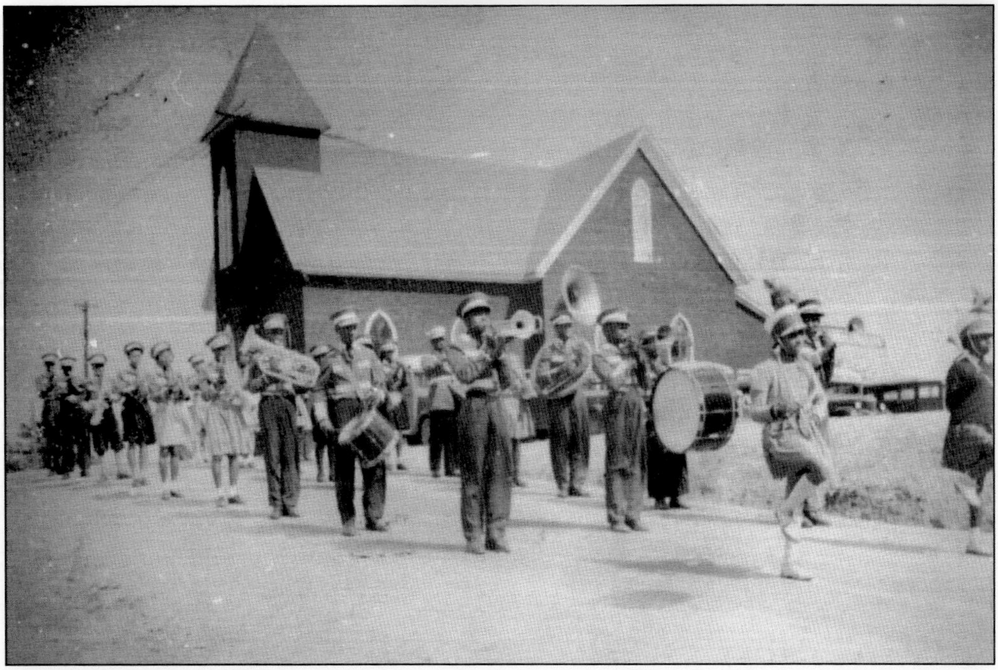

The Mount Vernon Christian Church, located on the corner of Lombard and Hinton Streets, was established in 1910. This 1940s photograph shows the Cooper High School band during a marching exercise.

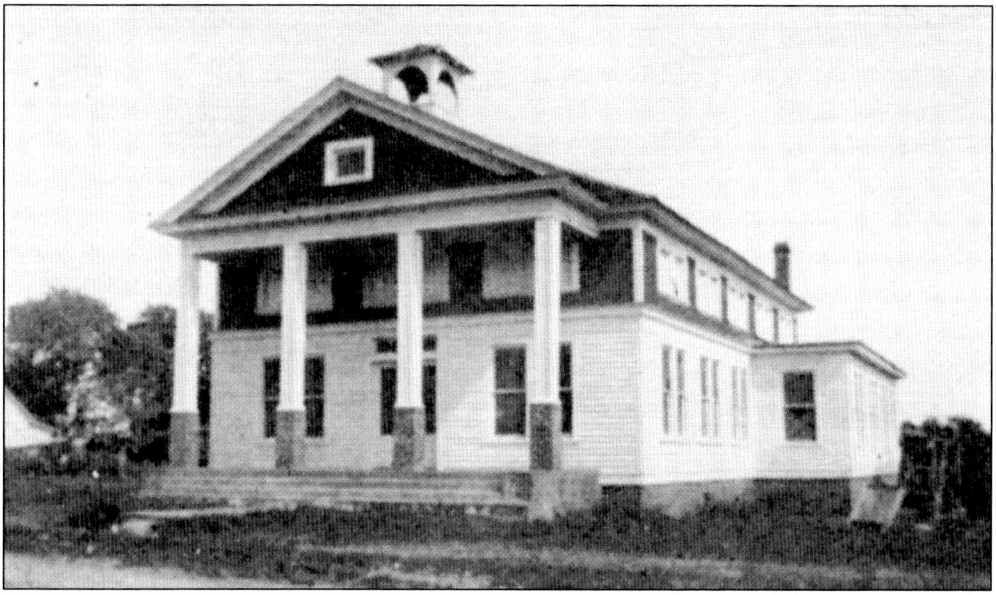

The Clayton Christian Church was organized in July 1920 as a branch of Amelia Christian Church. The church, shown in 1936, was located on the corner of Second and Robertson Streets.

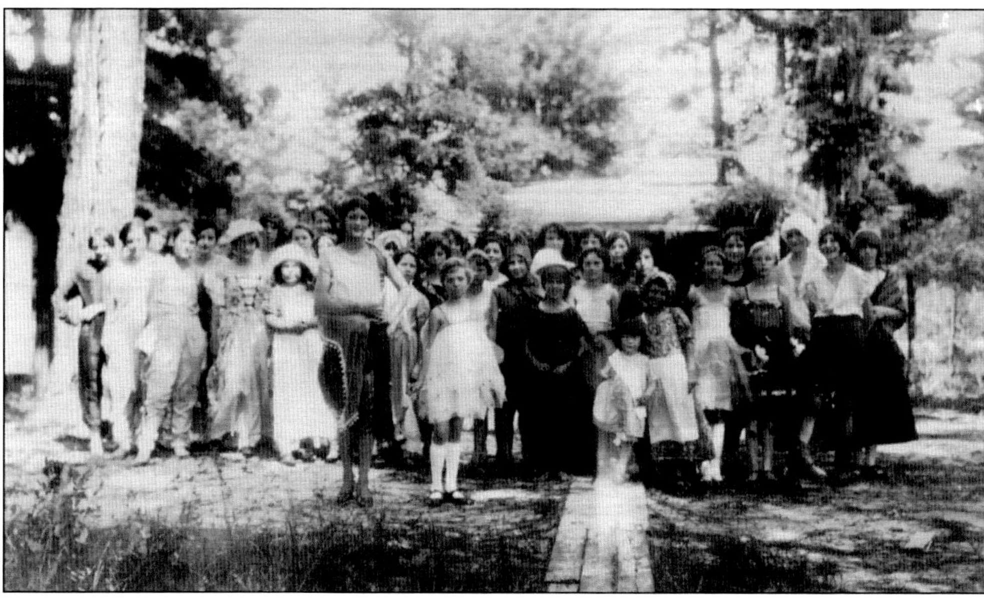

The Girls' Auxiliary of First Baptist Church is shown in the 1930s on a summer visit to White Lake. Lucile Ellington Hocutt was a leader of the group for many years.

Four

Schools

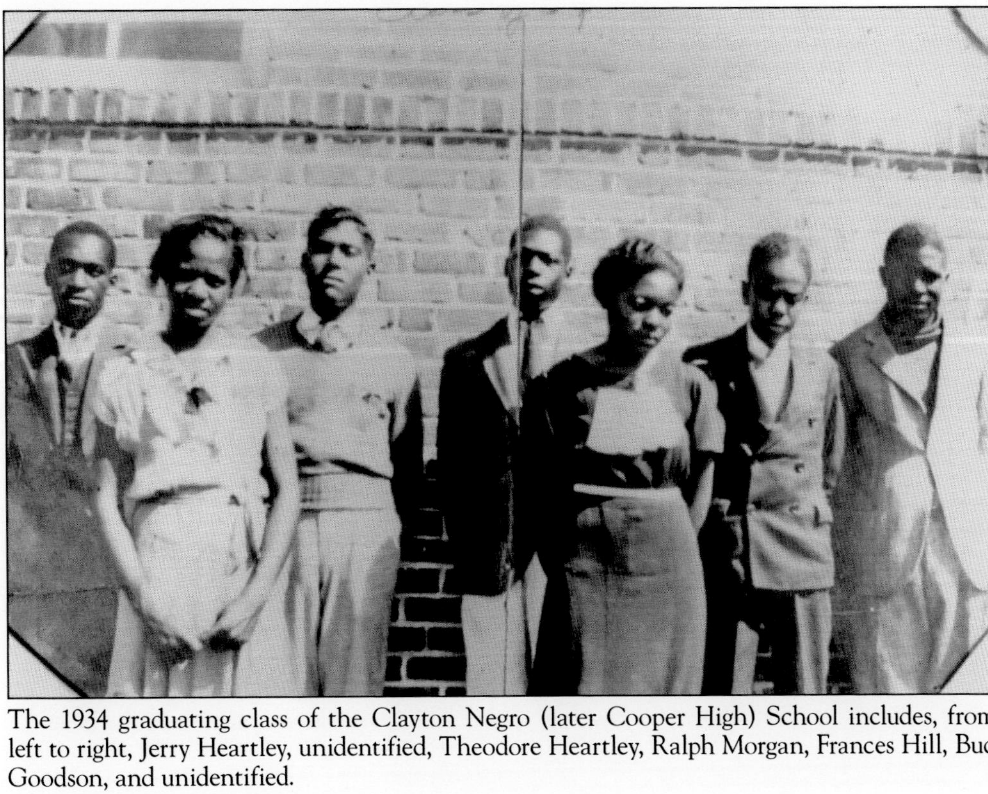

The 1934 graduating class of the Clayton Negro (later Cooper High) School includes, from left to right, Jerry Heartley, unidentified, Theodore Heartley, Ralph Morgan, Frances Hill, Bud Goodson, and unidentified.

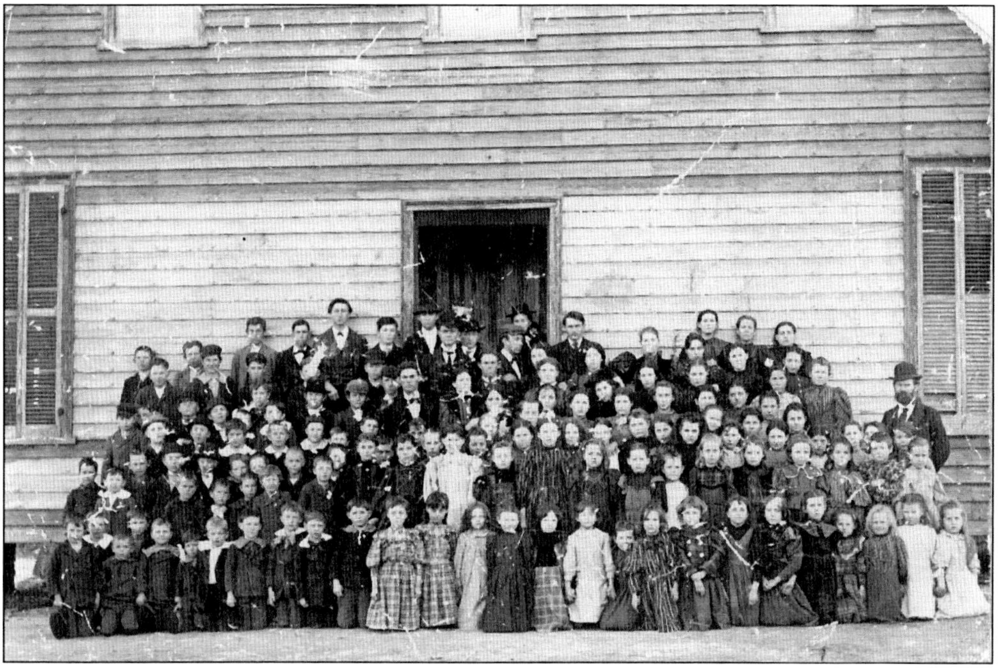

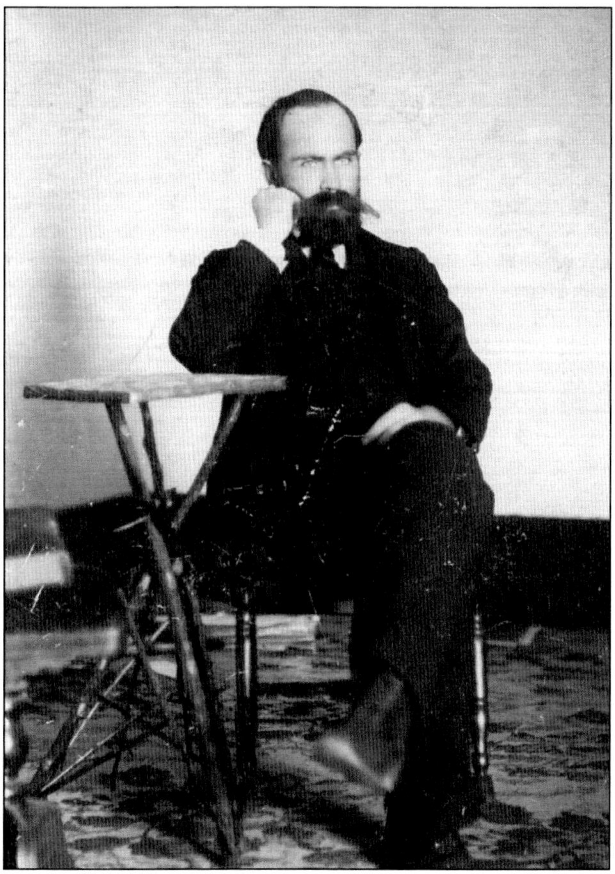

This photograph (above) of Utopian Institute students was taken in 1895. The school had 125 students in 1896. John Robert Williams, the principal and a teacher, is the bearded man on the right. Two other teachers were Jessie Ellington and Essie Watson. The Utopian hosted bazaars, benefits, and concerts on Friday nights. (Courtesy of First Baptist Church.)

John Robert Williams (1862–1938), at left, was the principal and a professor of the Clayton Academy and the Utopian Institute during the 1890s and early 1900s. He began a law practice in 1909 in Clayton. Williams was a member of the board of trustees for the University of Chapel Hill, a member of the general assembly in 1919, and an active member of the First Baptist Church. (Courtesy of First Baptist Church.)

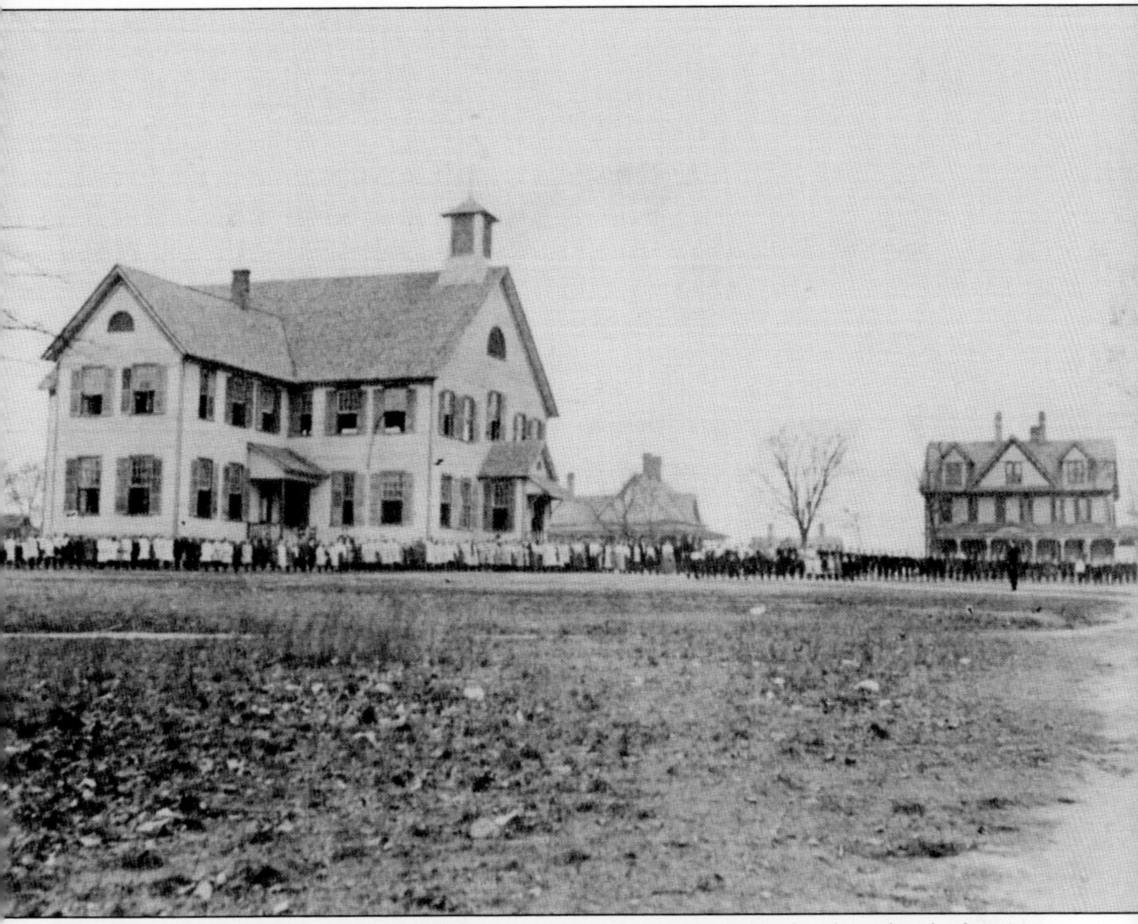

This Clayton High School building (left), featured in the 1904–1905 school catalog, had 10,000 square feet and contained 10 classrooms, all with patent desks. An auditorium was on the second floor. The school dormitory, shown on the right, was an important feature allowing rural students to attend in the pre-automobile days.

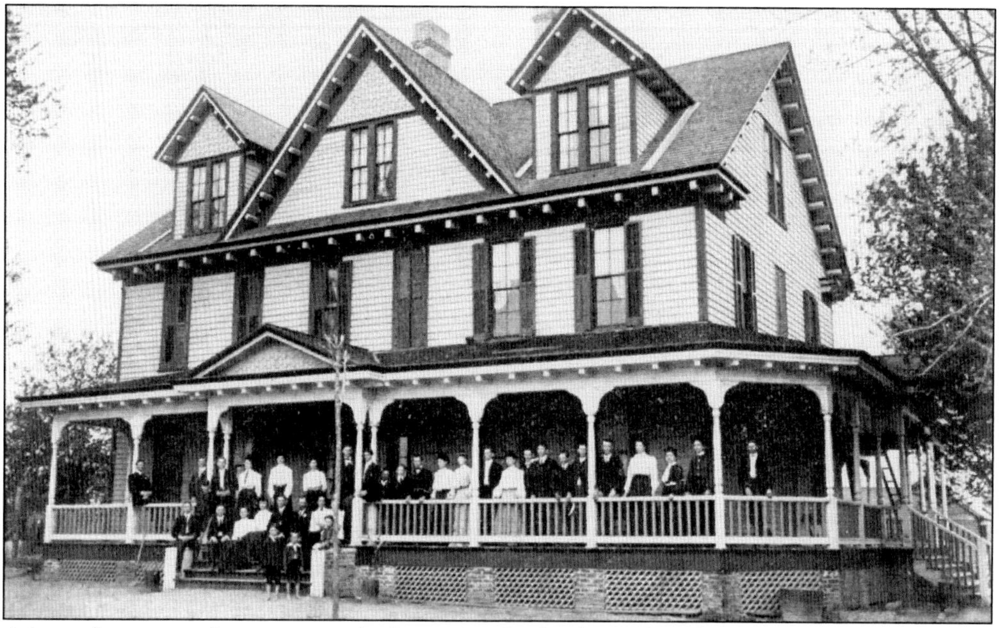

A large three-story dormitory was built in 1901 for faculty and students. Located on the corner of Fayetteville and Second Streets, the dormitory accommodated 40 students. Students and faculty in this 1904–1905 photograph were supervised by dormitory director James Ellis. The boarding fee was $8 a month.

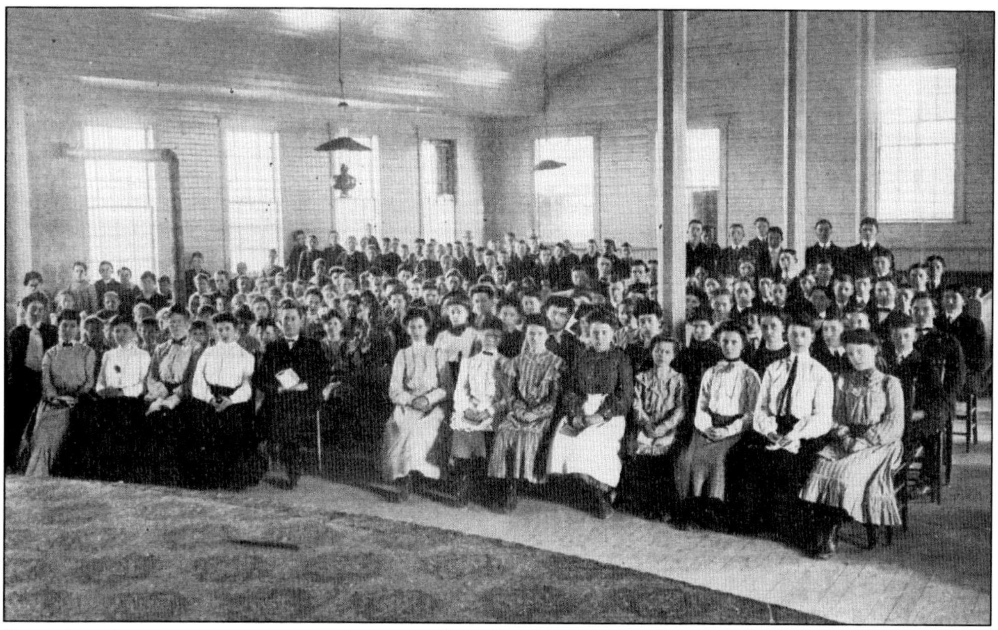

Devotional exercises were a morning ritual at the Clayton High School when this photograph was taken about 1904. The upstairs auditorium, shown here, was well lit by windows during the day and had kerosene lamps hanging from the ceiling for evening gatherings.

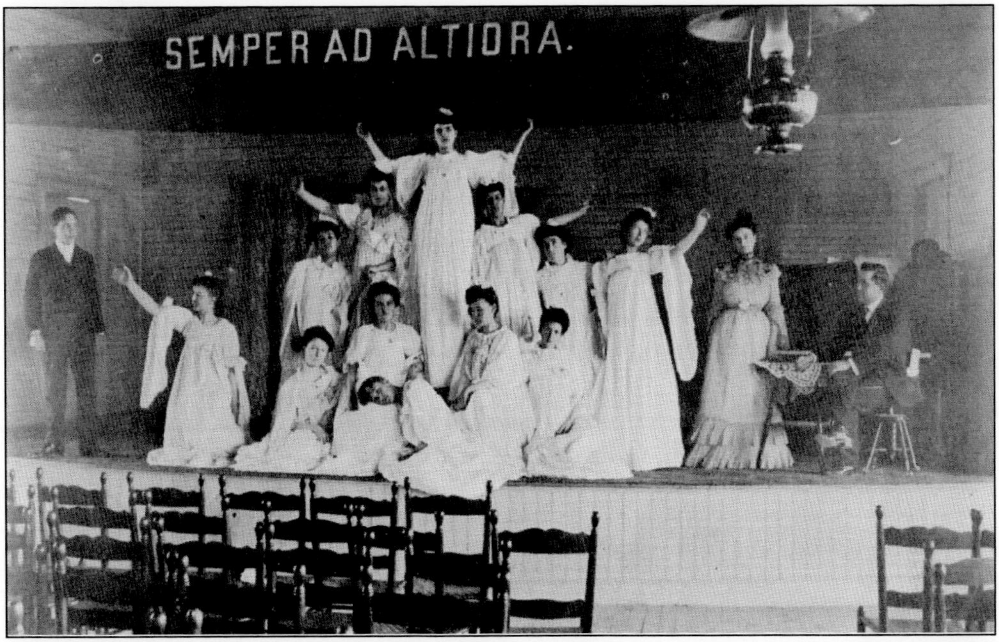

The Clayton High School placed great emphasis on effective communication skills. A school catalog pointed to the fact that people in every profession and vocation were often unable to express what they had in their minds. However, only a handful of students, pictured above about 1904, took advantage of this "training of the body and voice."

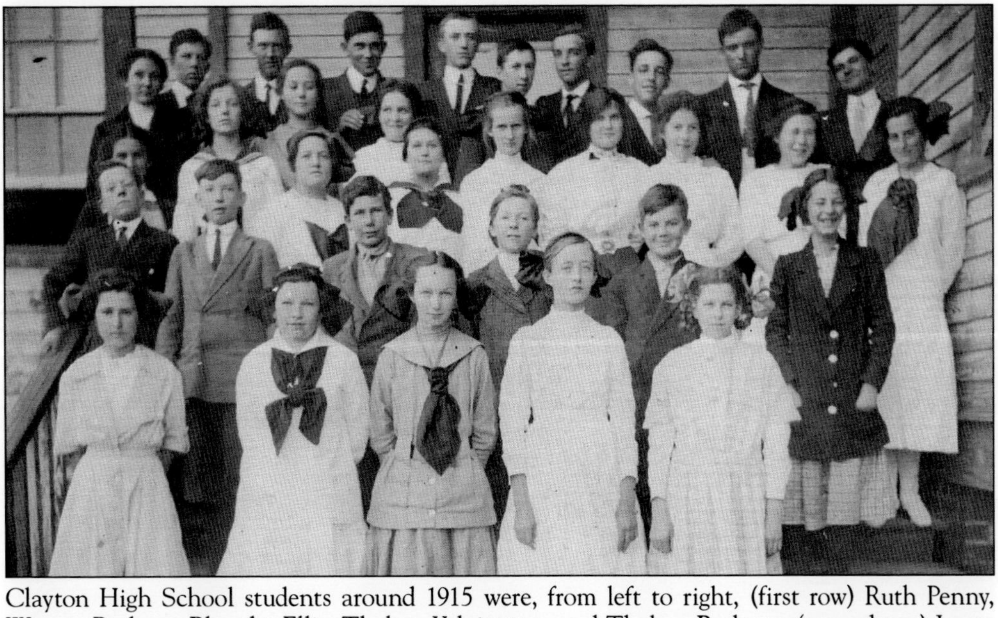

Clayton High School students around 1915 were, from left to right, (first row) Ruth Penny, Winnie Barbour, Blanche Ellis, Thelma Yelvington, and Thelma Barbour; (second row) James Hall, Willard McCullers, unidentified, Carlton Stephenson, Worth Blackwood, and unidentified; (third row) unidentified, Mattie Jones, unidentified, Jessie Gulley, Rosa Hinton, Elsie Poole, Telza Barnes, and Clee Ellis; (fourth row) Pearl Harris, Eugenia Thomas, and Ethel O'Neil; (fifth row) Bennett Poole, Ralph Allen, Herman Duncan, Charles Lowry, Carl Smith, Elsie Gattis, Aubrey Gattis, unidentified, and Ralph Austin.

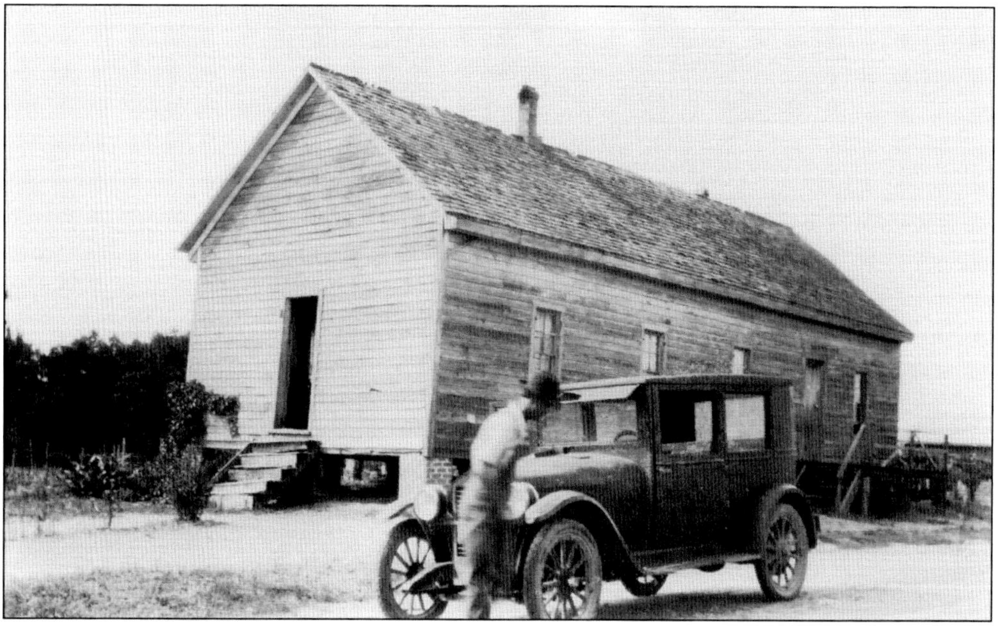

This school building served Clayton's African American community from around the late 1880s until 1924, when a modern brick structure was completed. Quinton C. and Lillie Mials were the teachers during most of this time. Ashley Horne II noted on the back of this photograph, taken in 1932, that he attended the Mials' school for three years from about 1905 to 1907, no doubt with his best friend, Lee Powell. Despite legalized racial segregation, newspaper accounts and photographs indicate these two boys were inseparable, even at school, in their childhood years.

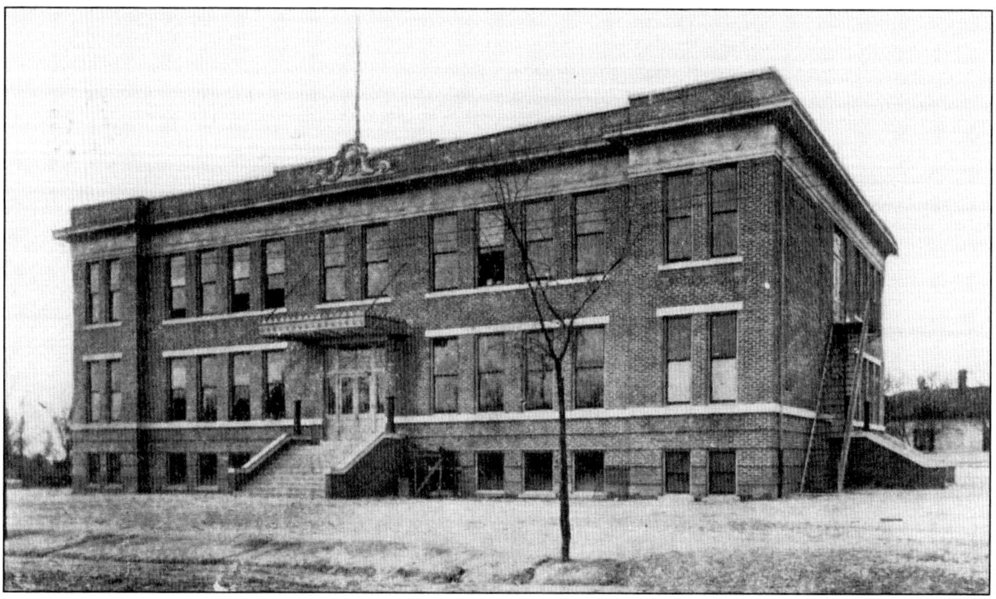

Clayton High School's new building, located on Fayetteville Street, was completed in 1915. A $25,000 bond was passed in May 1913 for construction of the school. (Courtesy of Carey Barbour.)

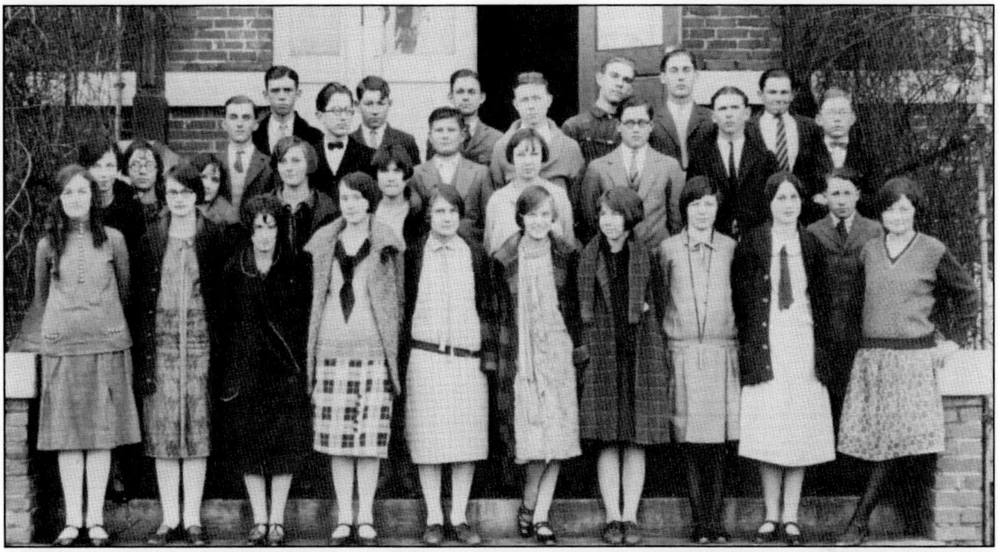

Clayton High School freshmen in 1926 include, from left to right, (first row) Estelle Smith, Ruby Moore, Elva Lloyd, Ruth Stephenson, Maggie Phelps, Ruth Ellis, Guinehl McCullers, Bertie Earp, Annie Coats, and Mona Ellis; (second row) Cornelia Gulley, Kathleen McCullers, Gertrude Lloyd, Emma O'Neil, Pauline Ellis, Ruby Turner, and Glenn Tysinger; (third row) Elton Ellis, Eugene Hinton, Robert Ferrell, Fletcher Wilder, James Clark, and Talmadge Grimes; (fourth row) Nick Jeffreys, Owen Spell, John Mayo, Douglas Boone, Howard Hocutt, Laynelle Johnson, and Alton Talton.

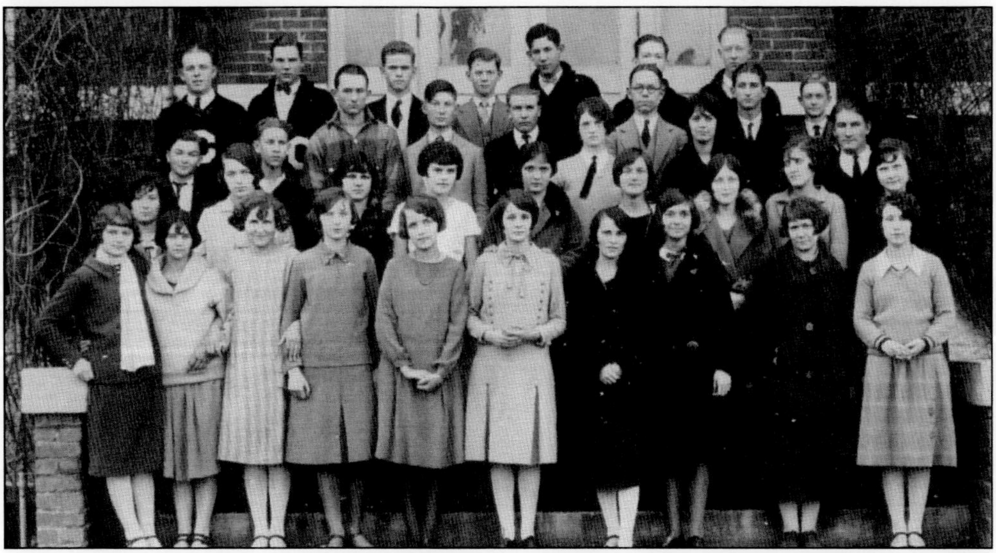

Clayton High School sophomores in 1926 are, from left to right, (first row) Blanche Parrish, Jessie Gale, Nina Little, Grace Robertson, Mary Talton, Gaynelle Hinton, Virginia Gillespie, Frances Gulley, Mae Phelps, and Virginia Fort; (second row) Viola Spell, Melba Dixon, Hocutt Wall, Ethel Ellen, Louise Grimes, Helen Austin, Florence Wilder, Minnie Spinks, and Sarah Kirby; (third row) Harold Self, Herbert Hocutt, Sexton Layton, Everett Austin, Curtis Singletary, Lucille Young, George Coats, Polly Smith, Stephen Wall, Glenn Wall, and Frank Hamrick; (fourth row) Eugene Walters, Tyler Dewar, Eric Whitworth, James White, Wilburn Smith, Millard Boone, and Elmer Jones.

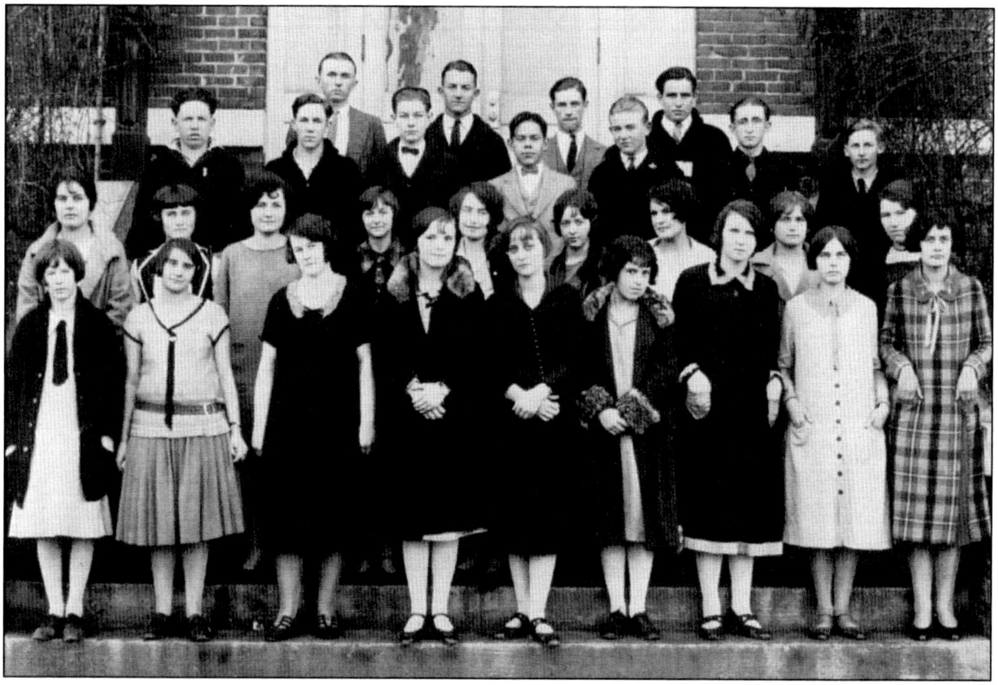

Clayton High School juniors in 1926 include, from left to right, (first row) Elsie Hill, Madelyn Duncan, Madie Hicks, Erdine O'Neil, Janie O'Neil, Thelma Talton, Estelle Clark, Frances White, and Charlotte Thurston; (second row) Mamie Pace, Kiva Coates, Ruby Matthews, Angela Whitley, Elsie Barnes, Vivian Creech, Lenora Hughes, Grace Taylor, and Hazel Woodall; (third row) Charles Duncan, Tom Hassell, Tomlin Farmer, William Penn, George Little, Roy Parrish, and Howard Parrish; (fourth row) William Clark, Clyde Mauney, Burton Wilder, and Joe Barnes.

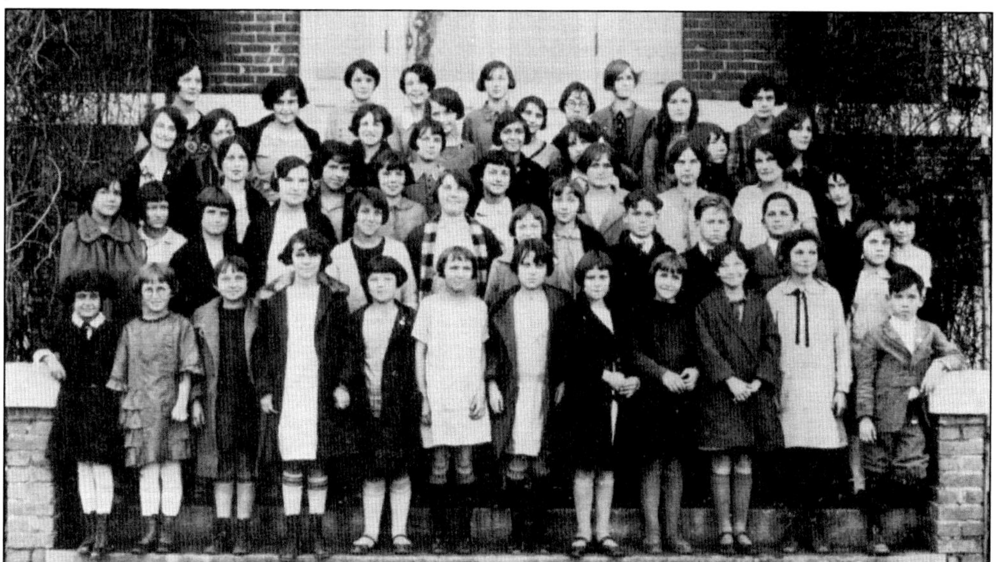

The music classes of Clayton High School, pictured in the 1926 *Wanna Tah Tella* annual, were taught by Norvelle Bryan (piano) and Mrs. Charles G. (Inez) Gulley (piano and voice) in 1926.

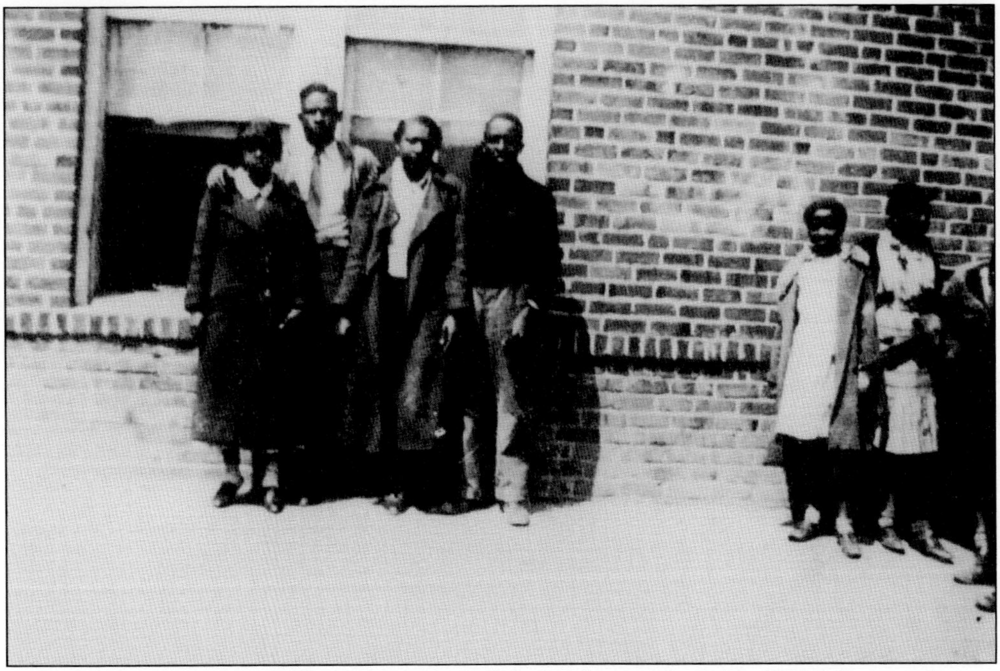

A group of students are caught socializing on the school grounds in this 1930s photograph.

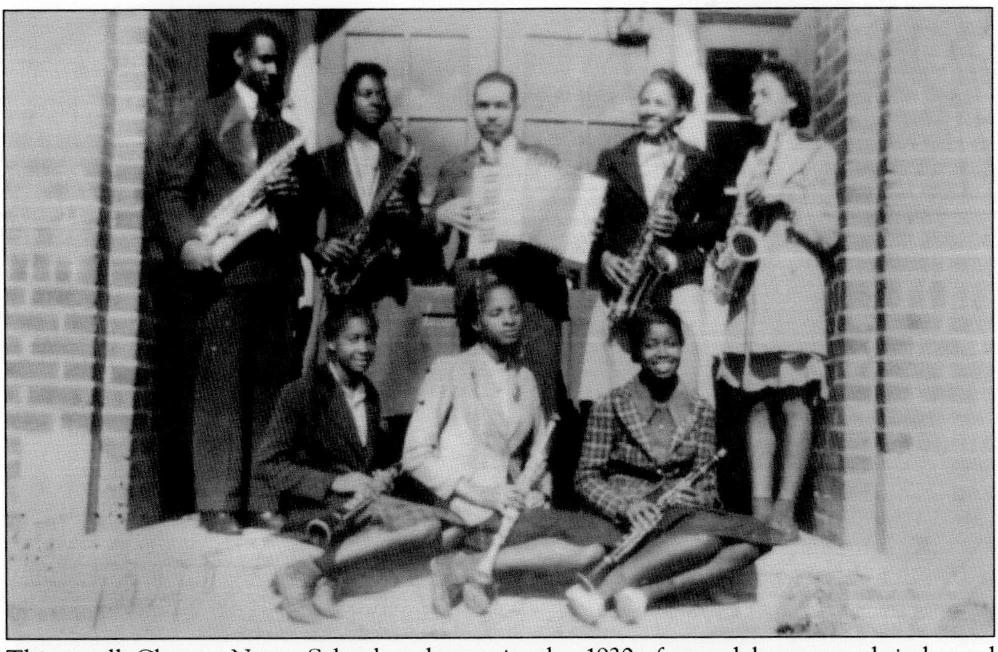

This small Clayton Negro School orchestra in the 1930s featured brass, woodwinds, and an accordion.

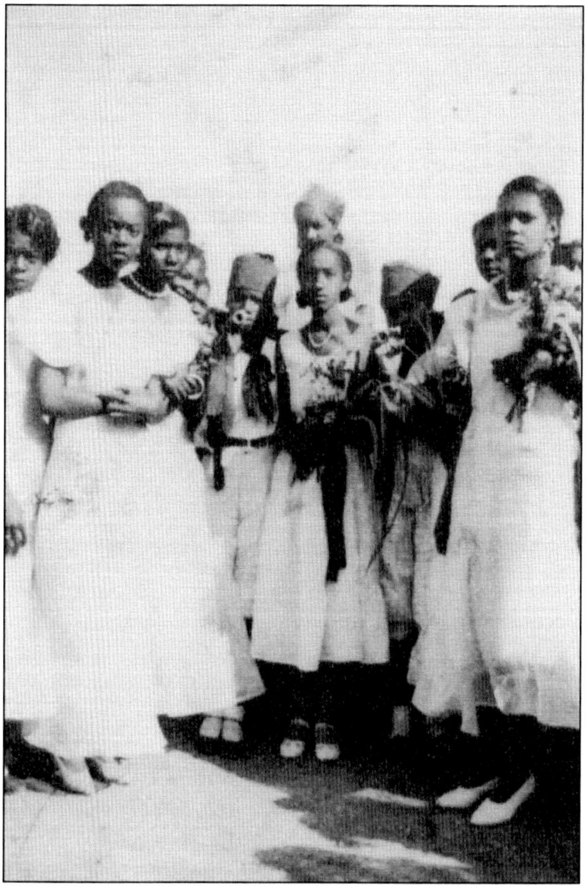

For many years, May Day and homecoming celebrations were the highlights of the year for students and alumni at Cooper High School. This photograph, probably from the 1940s, is thought to include homecoming queens and their court.

Harry E. Payne (first row, far right) is shown with a group thought to be one of Cooper's early graduating classes in the 1930s.

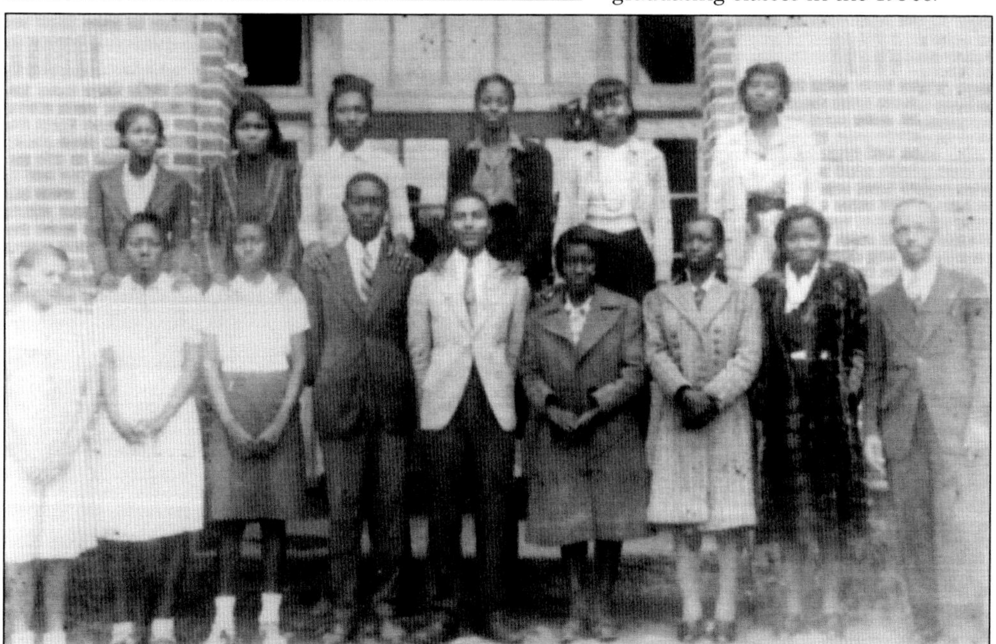

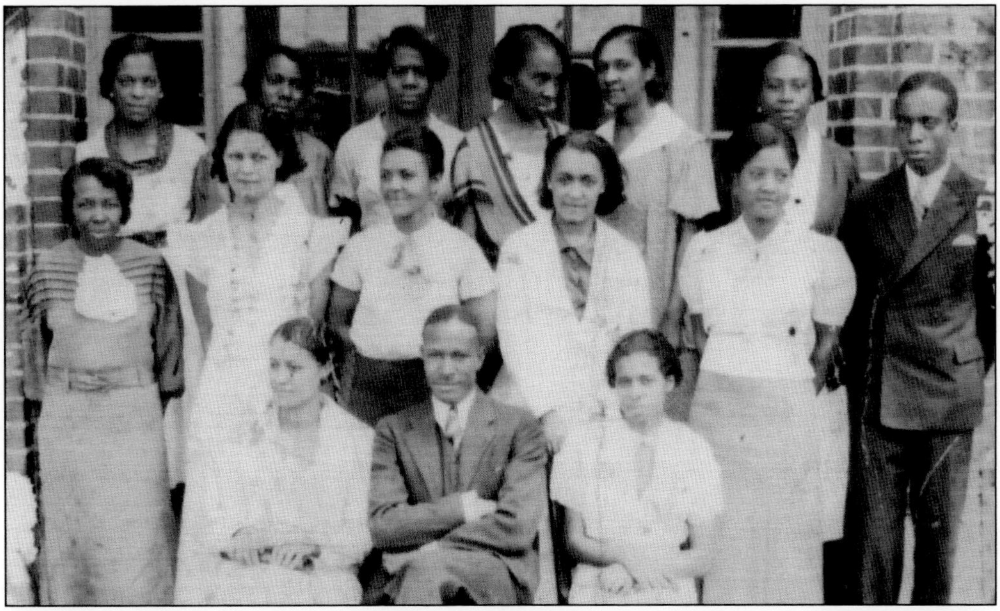

The Clayton Negro School faculty of 1935 includes, from left to right, (first row) Flossie Cannady, Nixon L. Cannady, and Bernice Furlonge; (second row) Matilda Ormond, unidentified, Lola Clark, two unidentified, and Wiley Hammond; (third row) unidentified, Susie McIntosh Hinton, unidentified, Alice Holt, Grace Whitley Kennedy, and Pauline Woodard.

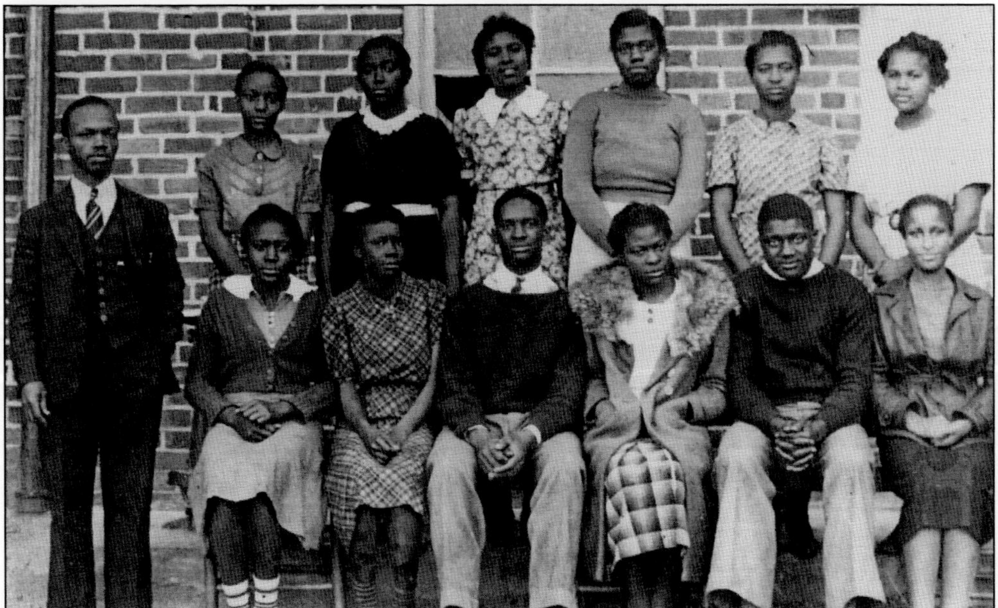

This photograph from 1939 shows the last Clayton Negro School graduating class before the school was renamed the William Mason Cooper High School. Pictured from left to right are (first row) homeroom teacher Harry Edgar Payne Sr., Pearl Agnes Burt, Essie Belle Mitchell, Booker Taliaferra McNeil, Bernice Marie Hill, William Burt Jr., and Emily Louise Cannady; (second row) Doris Jean McNeil, Pernell Bell, Doris Marie Lewis, Eunice Rae Campbell, Bessie Beatrice Mitchell, and Lois Mae Watson.

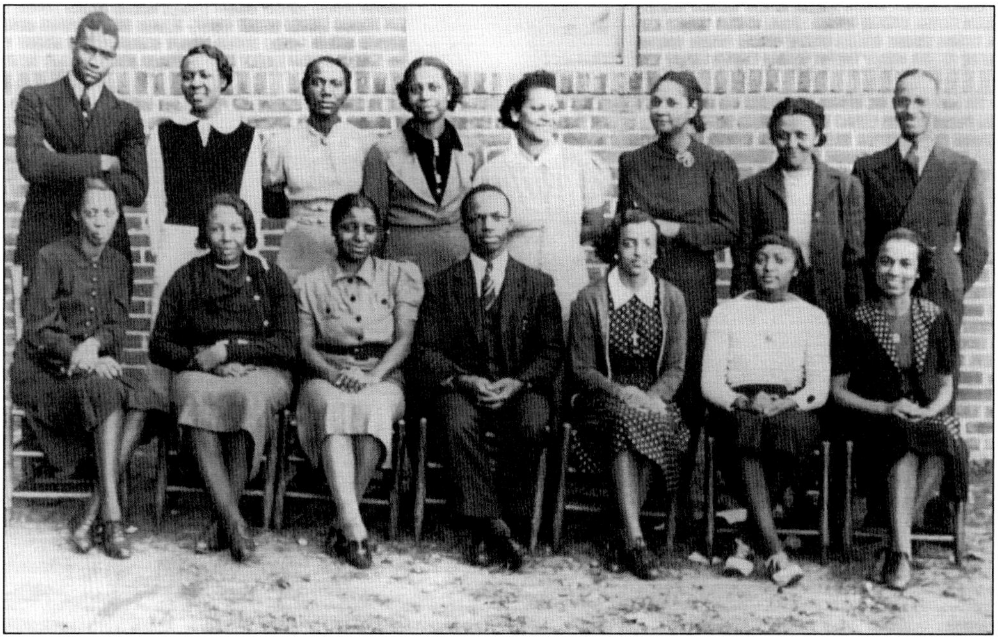

The 1939 faculty of the Clayton Negro School includes, from left to right, (first row) Thelma M. Penn, Matilda Ormond, Ernestine H. Wilson, Harry Edgar Payne, Pathenia Rowe, Flossie D. Lee, and Eleanor Jean Gray; (second row) Julius A. Holden, Pearl Elizabeth Thompson, Susie McIntosh, Irene Draper Spaulding, Flossie Davidson Cannady, Grace Whitley Kennedy, Lola Clarke, and principal Nixon L. Cannady. Other teachers that year were Cora A. Boyd and Olympia Perry.

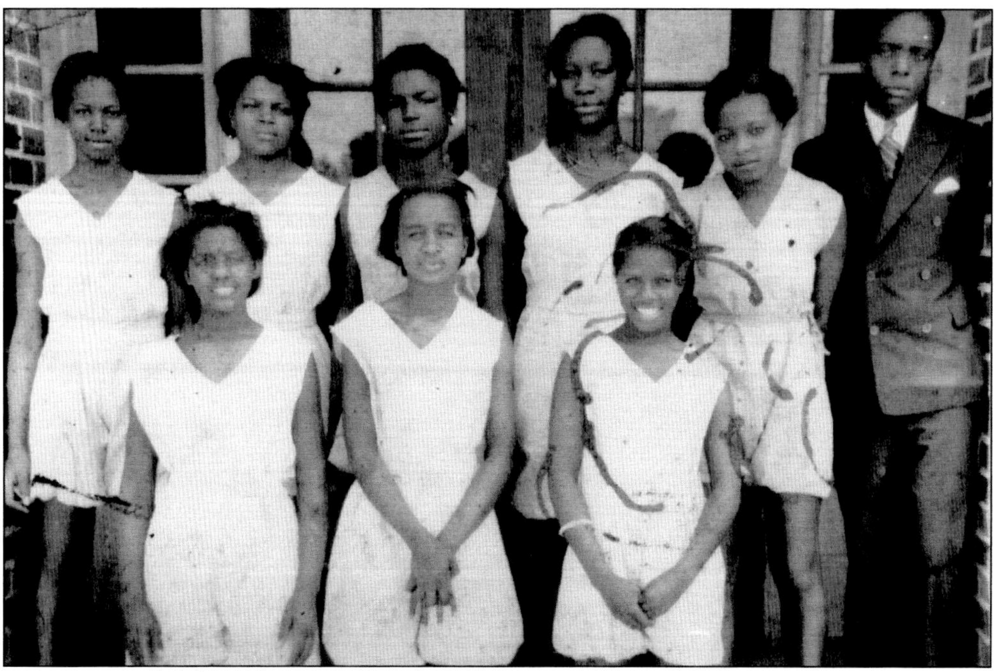

This photograph shows Harry Payne, assistant principal and English and French teacher at Cooper High School, with a girls' gymnastics class, probably in the late 1930s or early 1940s.

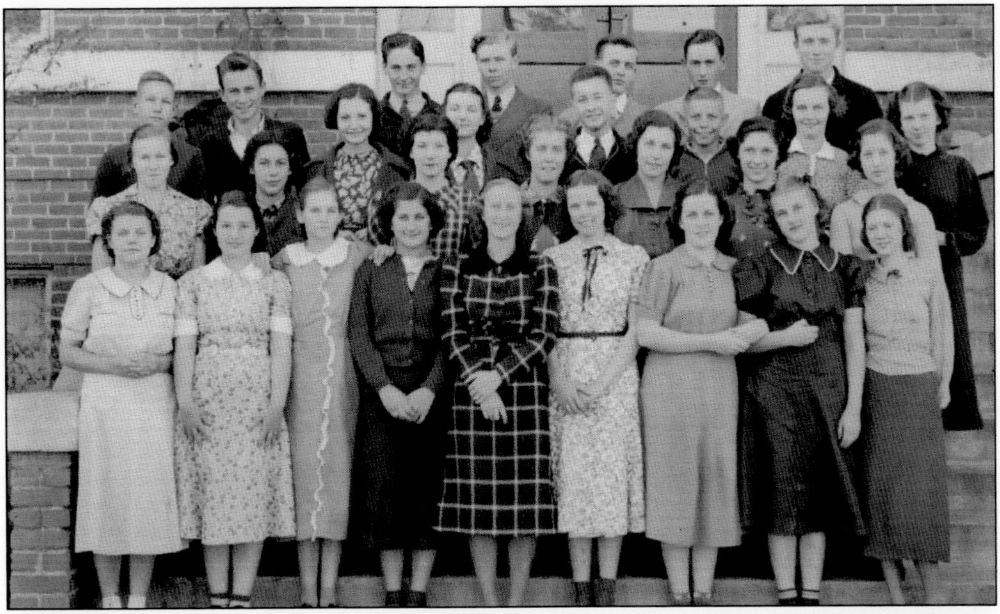

Clayton High's senior class of 1938 includes, from left to right, (first row) Elizabeth Harrell, Blonnie Johnson, Eloise Holmes, Merle Sasser, Grace Maynard, Christine Ellis, Martha Gattis, Frances Ellis, and Virginia Satterfield; (second row) Maxine Ellis, Bessie Bunn, Audrey Hinton, Eloise Parrish, Nadine Hinton, Betty Barbour, and Doris Talton; (third row) Minter Payne, Coy Ellis, Beatrice Smith, Aldine Lancaster, Luther Hinton, Angus Turner, Virginia Harris, and Betty White; (fourth row) James Harris, DeVan Boone, James Hatcher, Linwood Raines, and James Johnson.

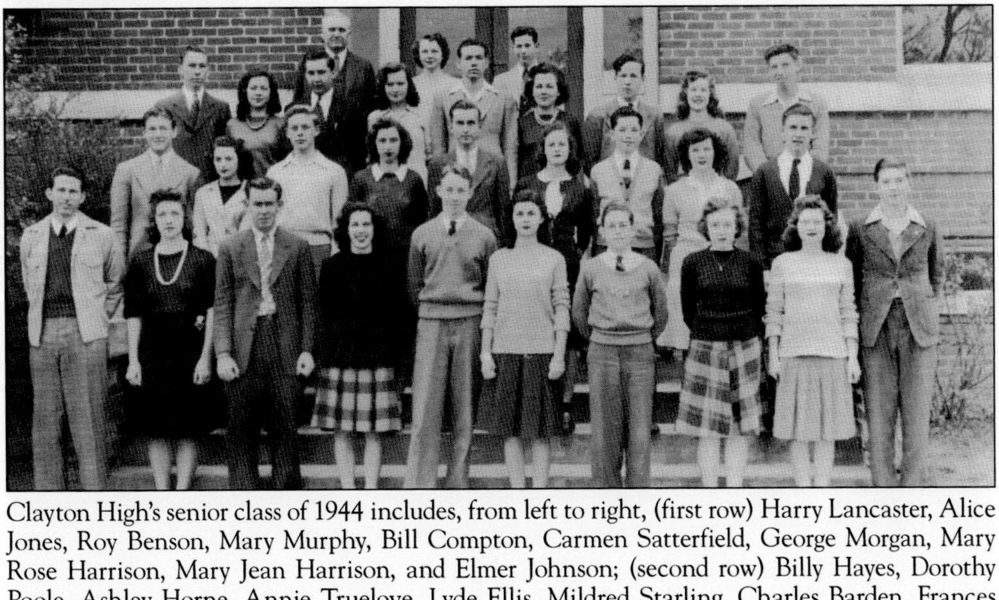

Clayton High's senior class of 1944 includes, from left to right, (first row) Harry Lancaster, Alice Jones, Roy Benson, Mary Murphy, Bill Compton, Carmen Satterfield, George Morgan, Mary Rose Harrison, Mary Jean Harrison, and Elmer Johnson; (second row) Billy Hayes, Dorothy Poole, Ashley Horne, Annie Truelove, Lyde Ellis, Mildred Starling, Charles Barden, Frances Hollingsworth, and Brooks Beddingfield; (third row) Jackson Allen, Honey Lou Harrison, David Blinson, Ellen Jones, Battle Duncan, Mary Helen Vinson, Jimmie McCarthy, Beatrice Hughes, and William Jones; (fourth row) O. B. Welch (principal), Elizabeth Strickland (teacher), and Gattis Lee.

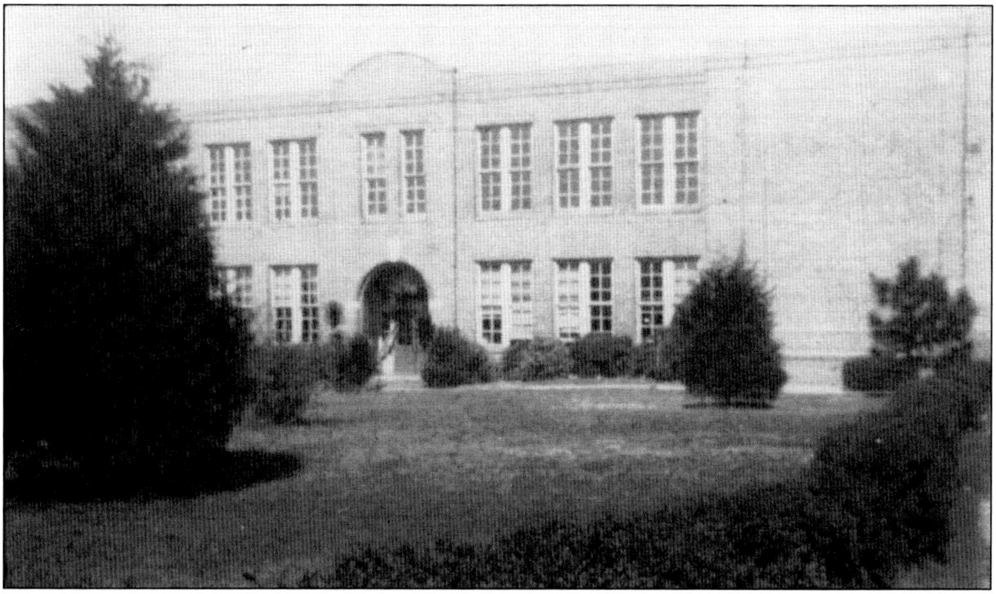

This 1945 photograph shows the main classroom building of the Cooper High School. It was constructed in 1924 and partially financed by the Julius Rosenwald Fund for Negro Schools. The Rosenwald fund helped many communities in the South build schools for African American students by offering matching funds. The county paid for most of the building expenses, and local citizens also had fund-raising projects and made personal contributions to build this school.

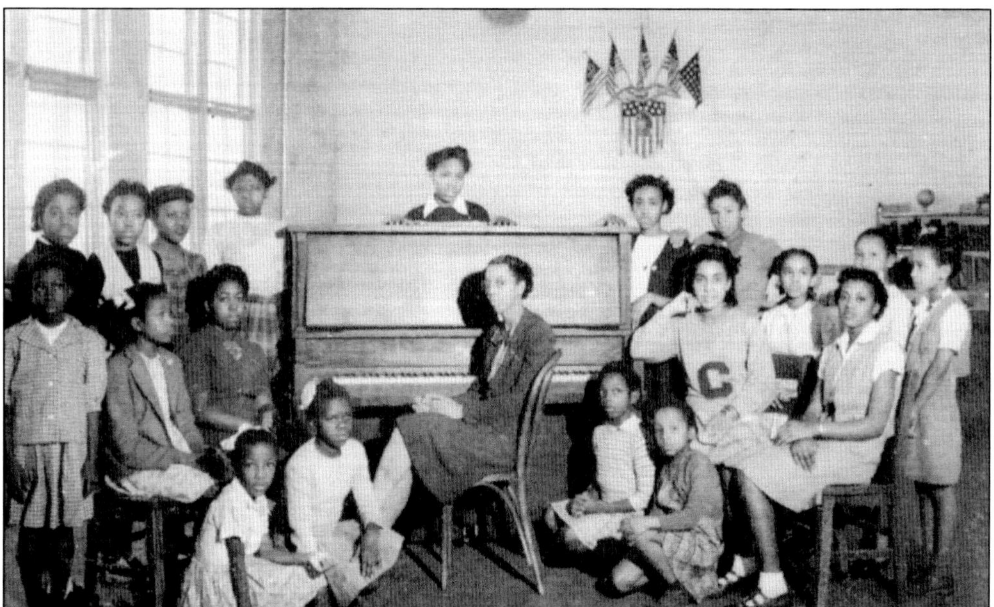

Music teacher Thelma Penn is shown with her piano students at the Cooper High School about 1945.

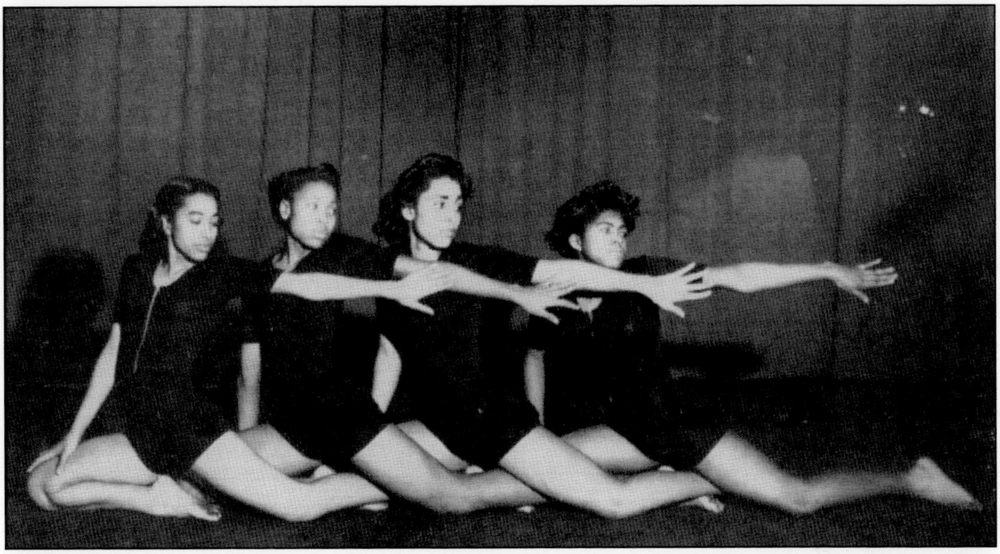

Teacher Flossie Lee Holden's creative dancers are pictured in 1945–1946 as they perform "Daydream." Shown from left to right are thought to be Grace Toole, Gwendolyn Smith, Harriet Goodson, and Lucille Moore.

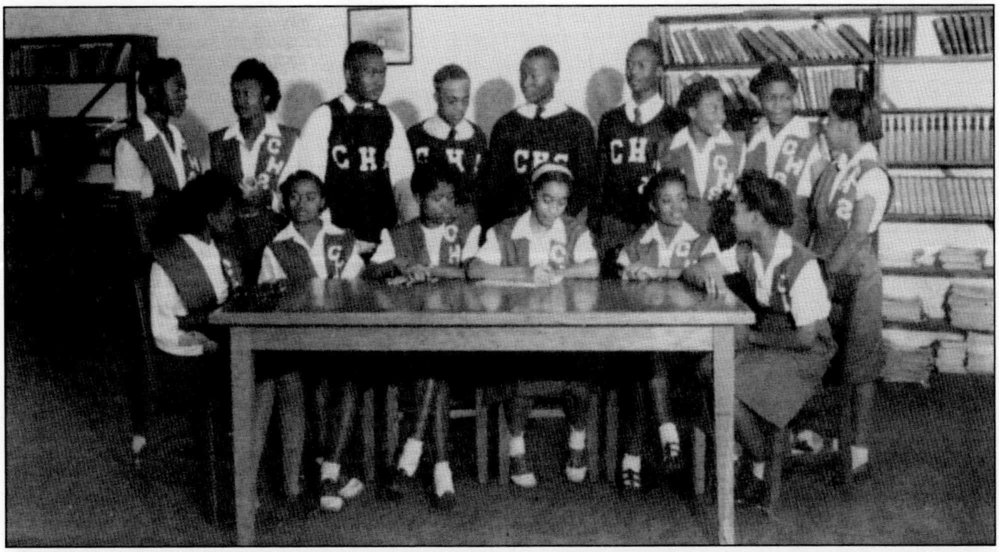

The Cooper High School had a student patrol system in place by 1945–1946, when this photograph was taken. Participants, not listed in order, include, Jessie Byrd, Ruth Clarke, Grace Toole, Ve Ella Jenkins, Elsieline Whitley, Ruby Fowler, Charlie Sanders, Ervin Davis, Edward Penny, Grover Sanders, Elizabeth Tomlinson, Bertha Line Sanders, Rosa McNeil, Lois Tomlinson, and Louise Everette.

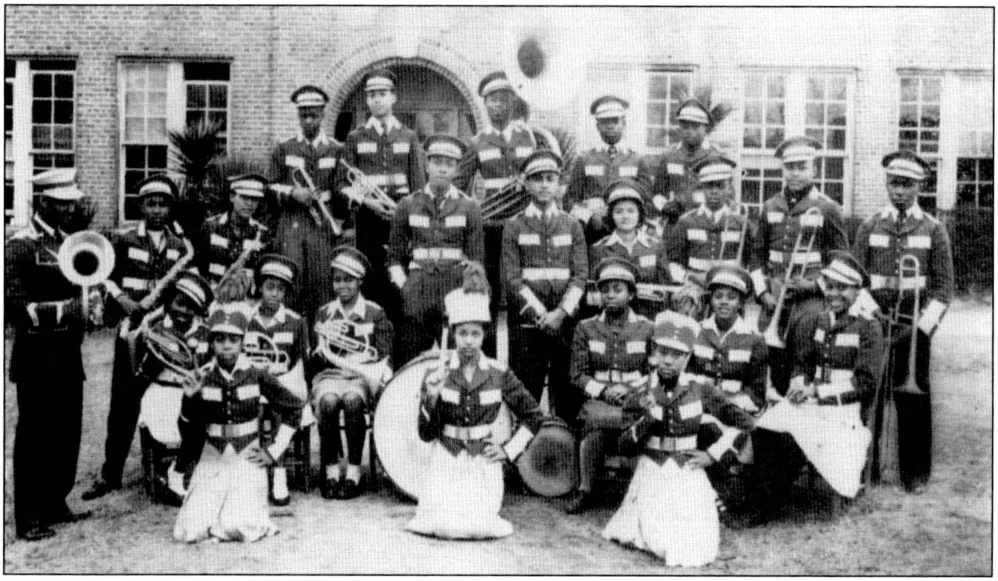

The Cooper High School band is shown here in 1945–1946 with director Julius A. Holden Jr. Majorettes are Rose Marie McNeil, Ann Ruth Bryant, and Evelyn Dodd. Band members (in no particular order) are Ethel Sanders, Earnest Lambert, John Whitley, Gordon Hinton, Royestine Rand, Harriet Goodson, Hazel Morgan, Gwendolyn Smith, Lois Tomlinson, Rayford Earp, Henry Goodson, Grover Sanders, Helen Peacock, Parthenia Hood, Elizabeth Tomlinson, David Price, Lee Earl Horton, and Frank Emory.

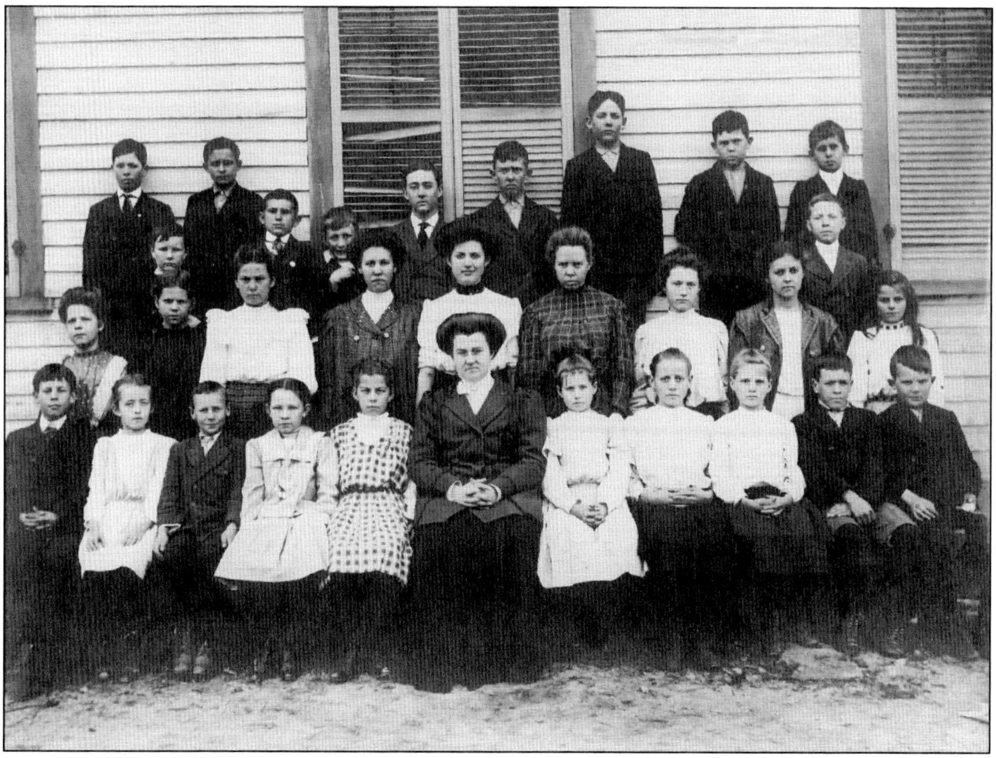

Elementary students at Clayton High School posed for this photograph about 1910.

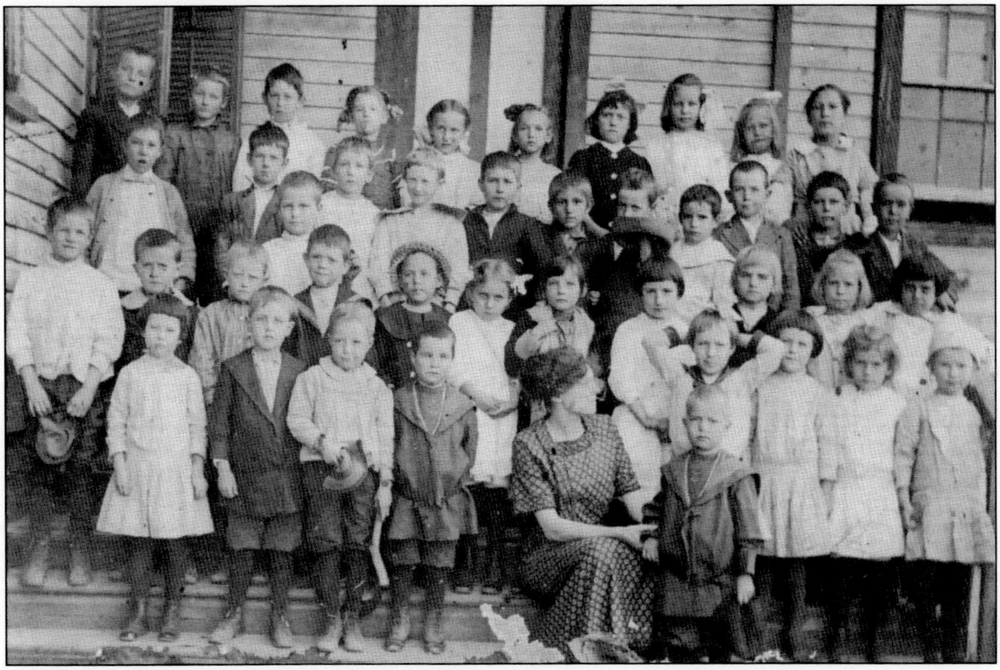

A group of primary students learning their alphabet at Clayton High School are shown in 1912.

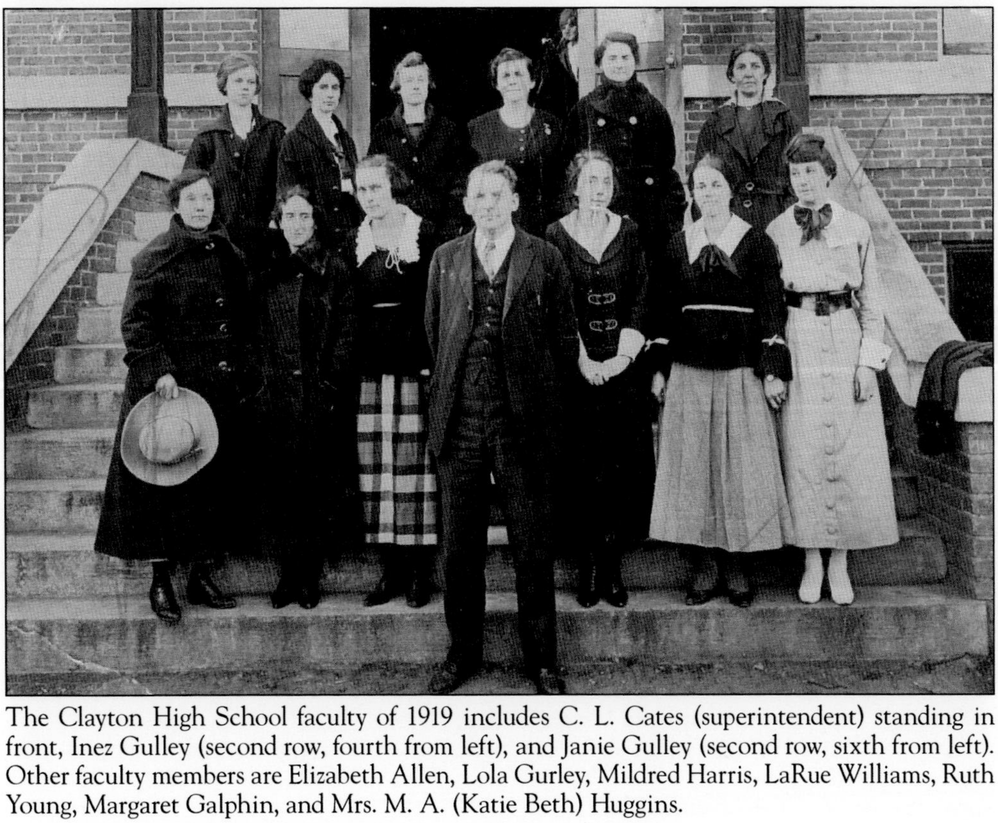

The Clayton High School faculty of 1919 includes C. L. Cates (superintendent) standing in front, Inez Gulley (second row, fourth from left), and Janie Gulley (second row, sixth from left). Other faculty members are Elizabeth Allen, Lola Gurley, Mildred Harris, LaRue Williams, Ruth Young, Margaret Galphin, and Mrs. M. A. (Katie Beth) Huggins.

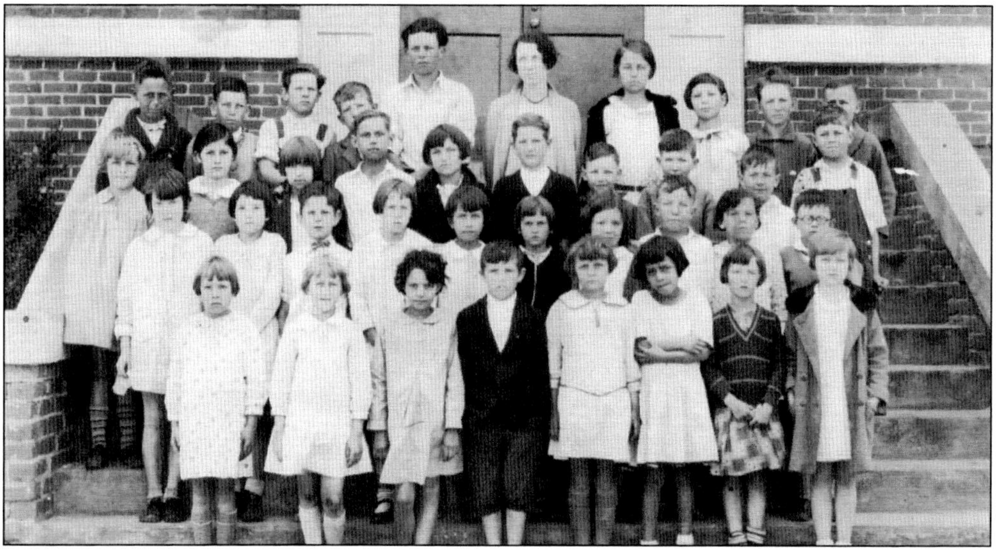

Clayton's third graders of 1930 are, from left to right, (first row) Victoria Worlds, Grace Maynard, Doris Ellis, Brantley Jones, Bernice Reaves, Lillian Sealey, Frances Ferrell, and Jane Lewis; (second row) Betty White, Audrey Hinton, Dick Barbour, Maxine Ellis, Snowden Pleasant, Eloise Holmes, Frances Elkes, Rudolph Hill, Sarah Barbour, and Dick Lee; (third row) Frances Ellis, Betty Barbour, ? Duncan, Ray Bailey, Aldine Lancaster, Noah Hardee, Joseph Wall, Burton Honeycutt, Luther Hinton, and ? Barbour; (fourth row) Earl Truelove, Cleveland Parrish, James Pounds, Joseph Nichols, Roland Pounds, Lilla Sitterson, Christine Johnson, Agnes Parrish, ? Durham, and Ervin Wall. (Courtesy of Jackie Smith.)

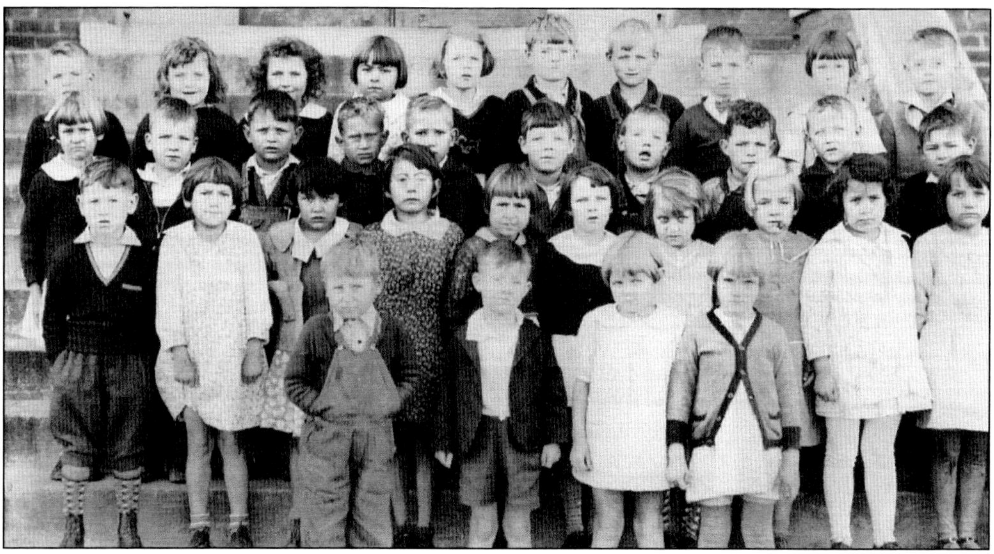

Clayton's second graders of 1935 are, from left to right, (first row) unidentified, Jack Forbes, unidentified, and Hilda Johnson; (second row) Russell Ellis, Florence Pulley, unidentified, Maude Sealy, Helen Ellis, Ruth Morgan, Almelia Lee, ? Norris, Nannie Penny, and Faye Garris; (third row) Lillian Lyles, two unidentified, Joseph Walker, Harold Worrells, three unidentified, Louie Reaves, and Ruperd Hogg; (fourth row) Randolph Parrish, Doris Vinson, Joyce Vinson, Ada Duncan, Martha Davis, unidentified, James Phillips, Turner Vinson, unidentified, and Dayton Poole. (Courtesy of Turner Vinson Jr.)

Five

Everyday Life and Leisure

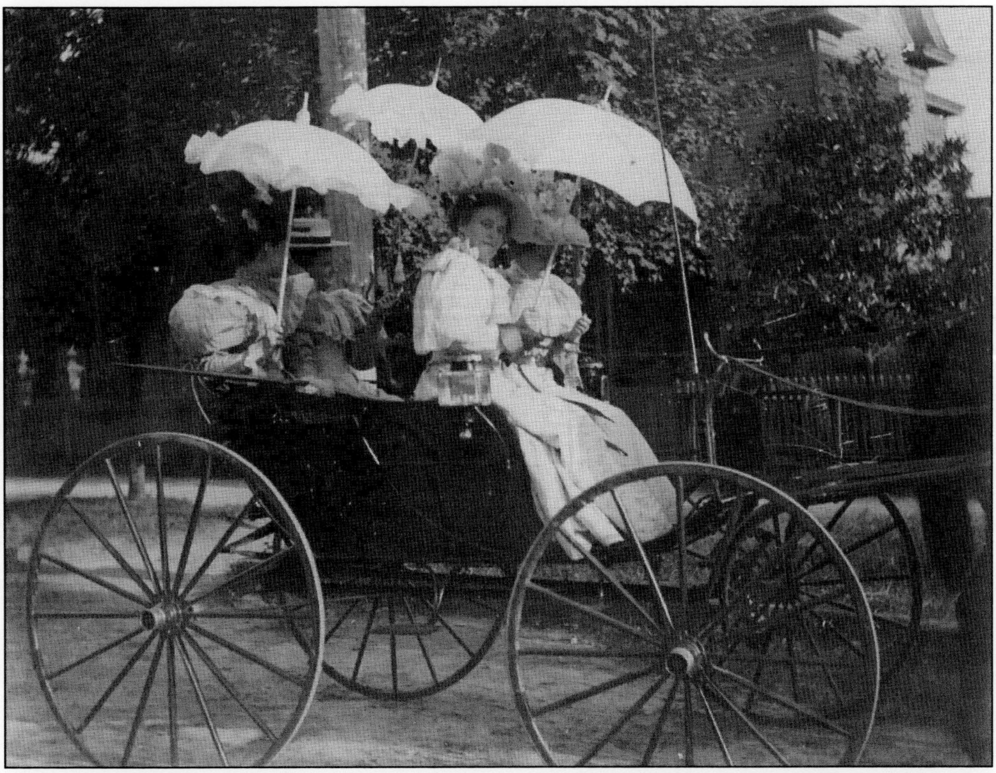

This unidentified group of ladies enjoys a ride in a four-seat phaeton in the 1880s or 1890s.

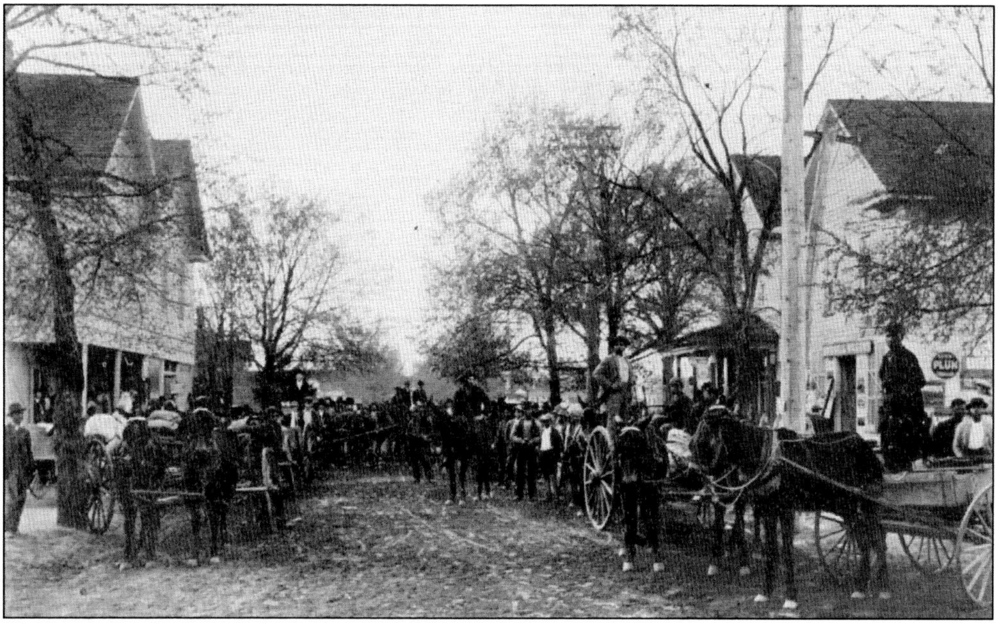

This corner of Main and Lombard Streets was a busy place on a Saturday afternoon. Shown in this 1904–1905 view are the Ashley Horne and Son store (left) and J. G. Barbour and Sons (right).

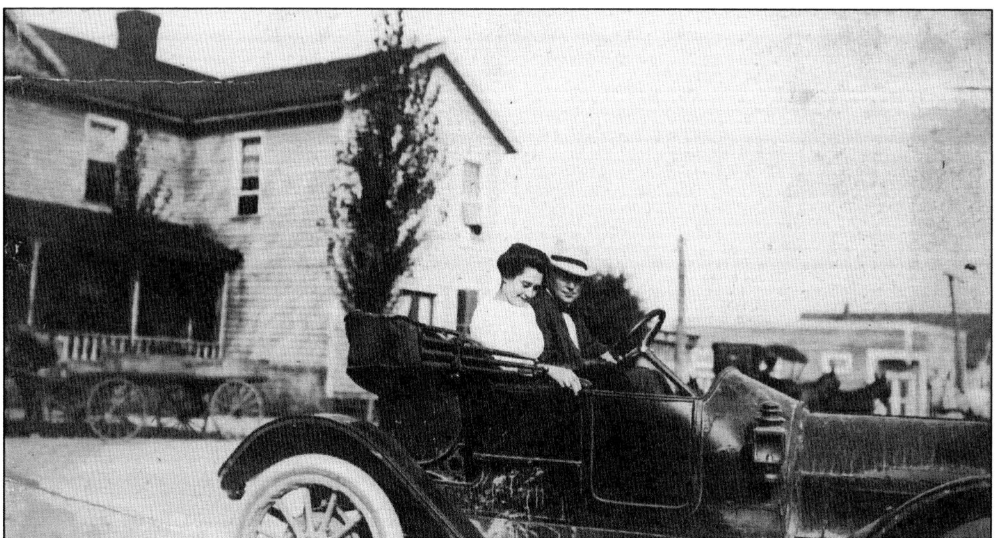

Dr. B. A. Hocutt and his wife, Lucile, are pictured in front of the Creech boardinghouse on First Street about 1910. At that time, automobiles were still rare in Clayton.

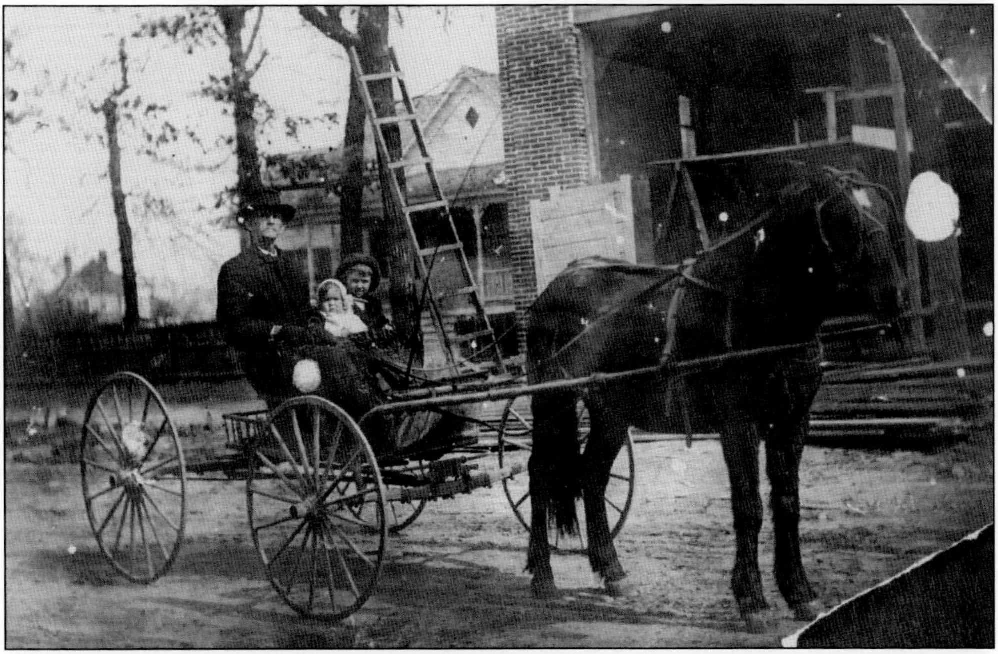

Mark Gulley is shown entertaining grandchildren Riley and Frances Gulley with a buggy ride down Main Street shortly before his death in 1913. The son of the area's first postmaster, Gulley was a justice of the peace, tax lister and assessor, and county commissioner. He operated Gulley and Gulley, a clothing store, with his son Charles G. Gulley and cousin Riley Gulley.

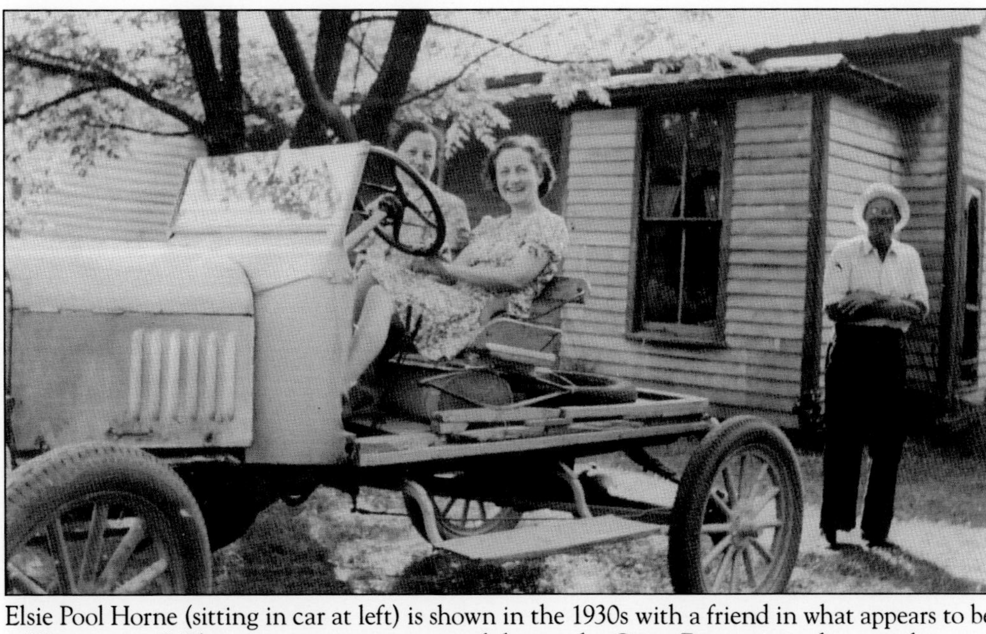

Elsie Pool Horne (sitting in car at left) is shown in the 1930s with a friend in what appears to be a "Hoover cart." This sarcastic name was used during the Great Depression when gasoline and tires were scarce and automobiles were converted into horse-drawn vehicles.

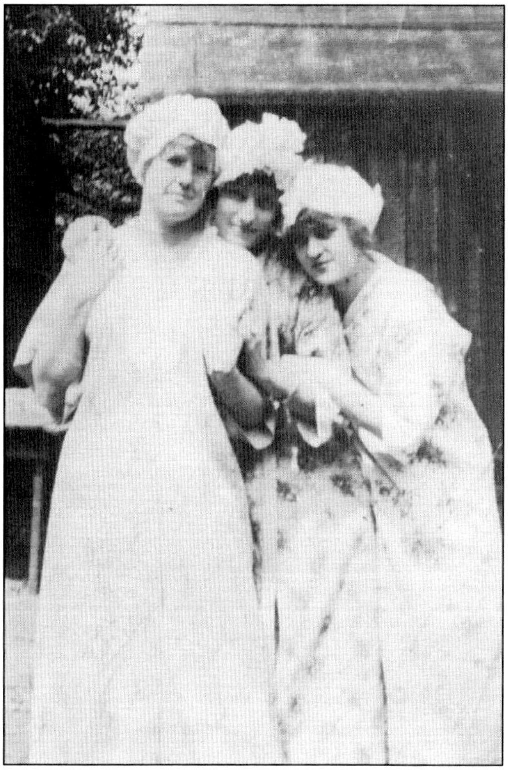

Mabel Hardee Ellis (left) and friends were photographed about 1919, apparently during a house party. (Courtesy of Jackie Smith.)

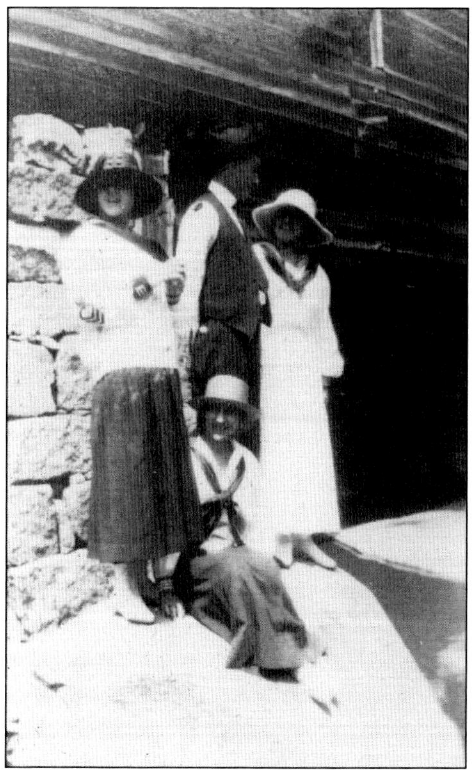

These unidentified young people, probably friends or relatives of the Horne family, were photographed enjoying an outing at a gristmill around 1920.

This unidentified employee of the Horne family was photographed about 1915 to 1920 with the family dog.

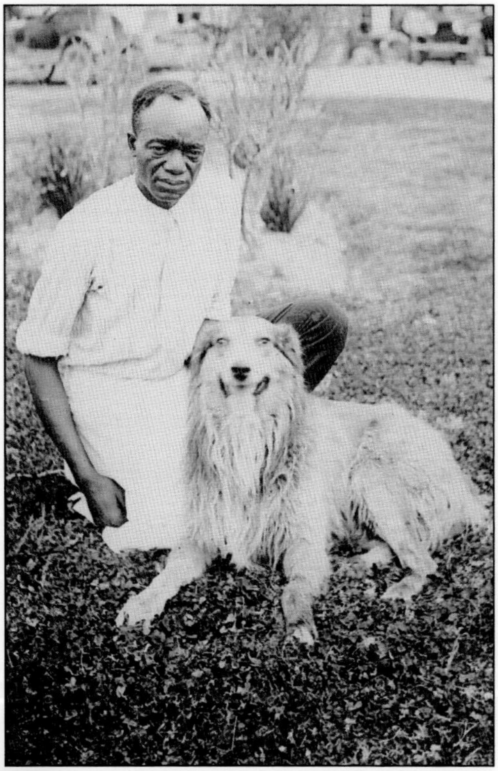

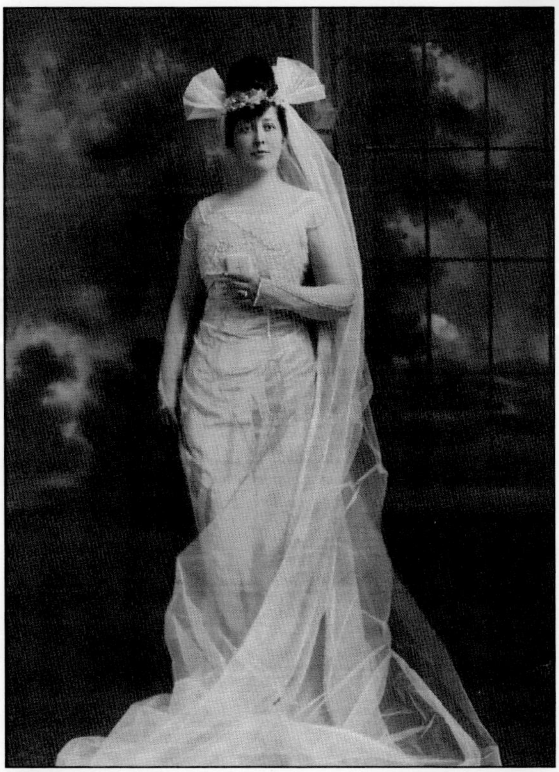

Melba McCullers, daughter of Dr. Herbert McCullers and his wife, Nellie, married John Jacob Misenhemier on June 26, 1918. The exquisite wedding gown was made of imported white brocade chiffon velvet, the bodice of duchess lace, and the sleeves of net embroidered with pearls. Her tulle veil was worn coronet style, fashioned with orange blossoms.

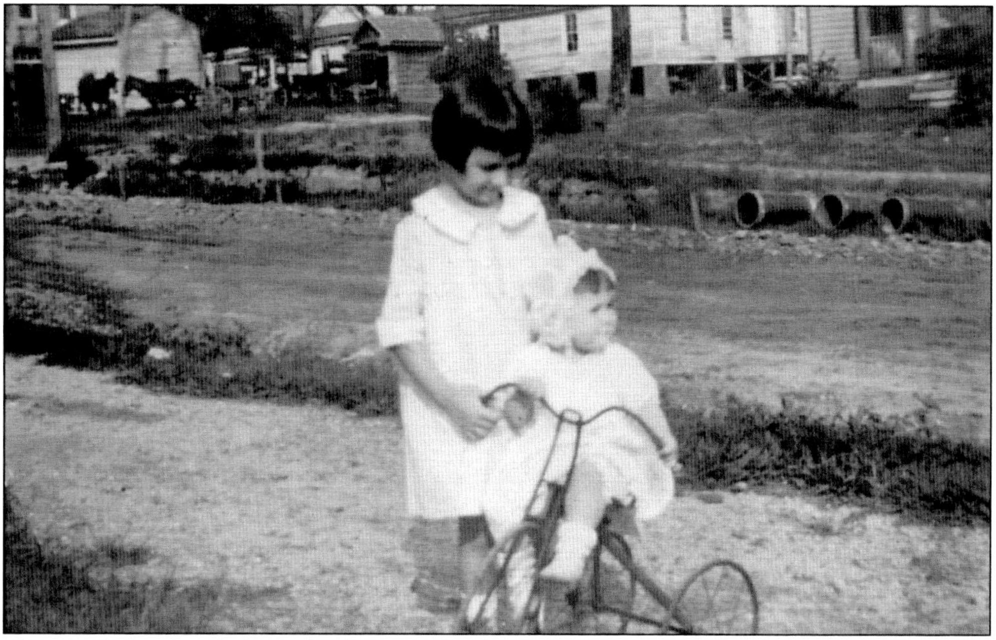

Alice Barbour was photographed on Lombard Street helping her younger sister Bettie on her tricycle in the early 1920s. The horses and wagons were parked behind the J. G. Barbour and Sons store. The long white building on the right was a warehouse for the Barbour company's supplies. (Courtesy of Carey Barbour.)

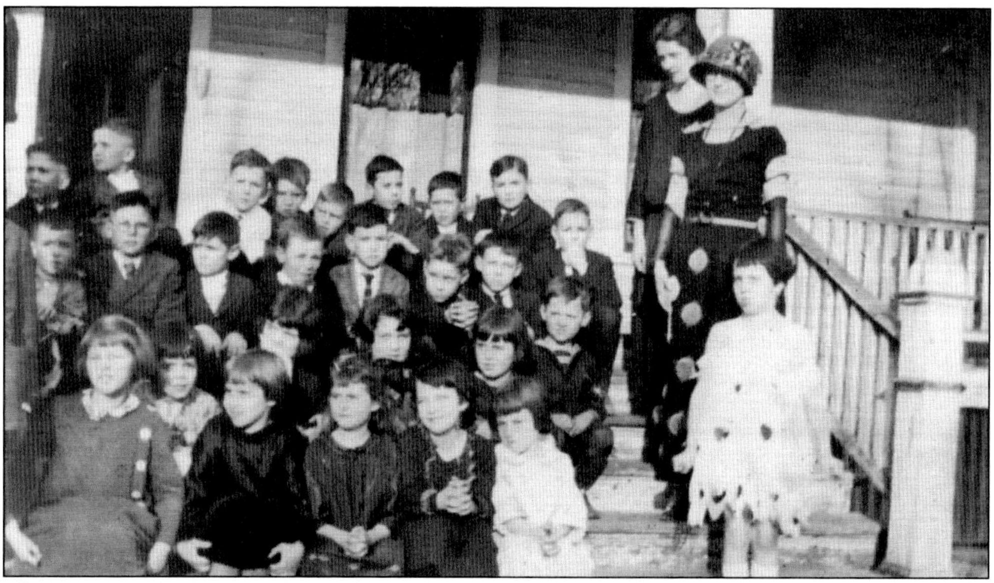

Thurman Smith's birthday party was attended by many local children in the early 1920s. Party guests are, from left to right, (first row) Jane Fort, Mildred Fort, Kathryn Ellis, Jane Gulley, Josephine Barnes, and Alice Barbour (standing); (second row) Patti Penn, Martha Gladys Wallace, Grace Talton, ? Stephenson, C. V. Stephenson, and unidentified; (third row) two unidentified, Carl Whitley, John I. Barnes, Mark Grady Gulley, Hugh Page, Preston Creech, and unidentified; (fourth row) four unidentified, D. G. Smith, Dick Hassell, Henry Price, Thurman Smith, and Norma Gulley Smith. (Courtesy of Carey Barbour.)

These unidentified employees of the Horne family were photographed about 1920.

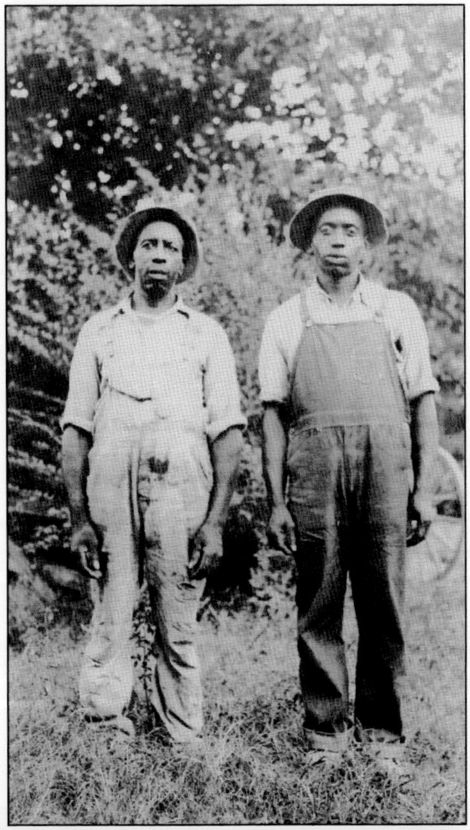

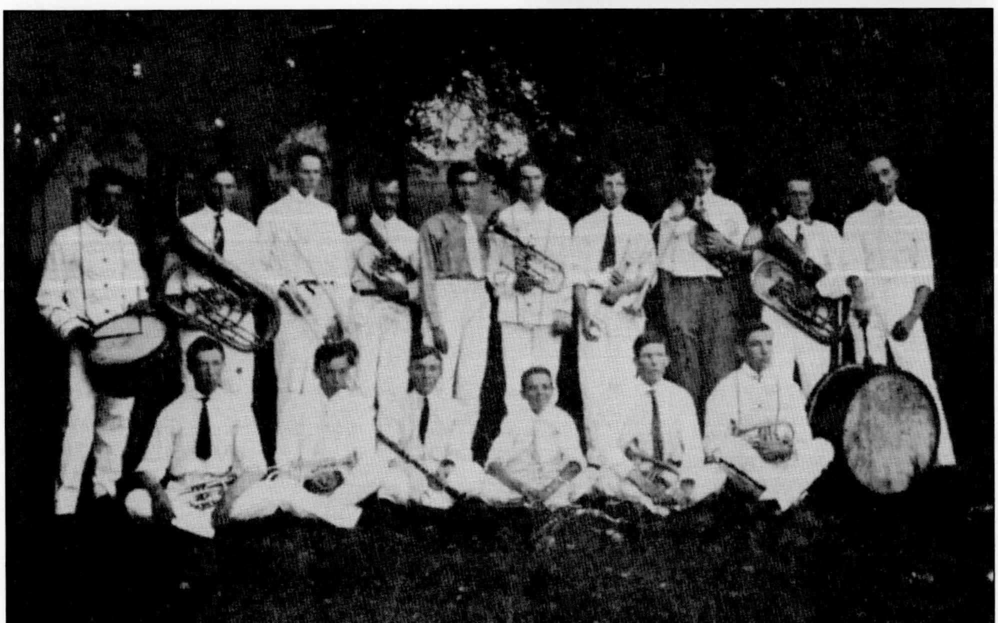

The Clayton High School band was organized in December 1908. This picture features the members and their instruments in 1909.

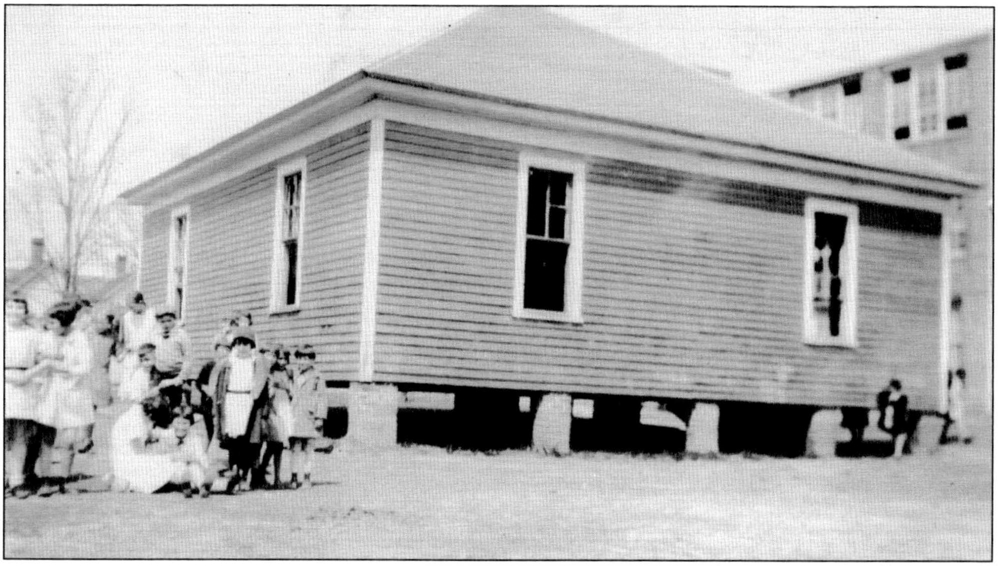

The 20th Century Mothers Club was organized in 1918 with 18 members. By 1920, the name was changed to the Woman's Club of Clayton. Members worked to promote the library, schools, art, and music. This auxiliary building was on the back of the school lot and was moved to its present location on Church Street in 1928. The building was remodeled to become the present-day home of the club. (Courtesy of the Woman's Club of Clayton.)

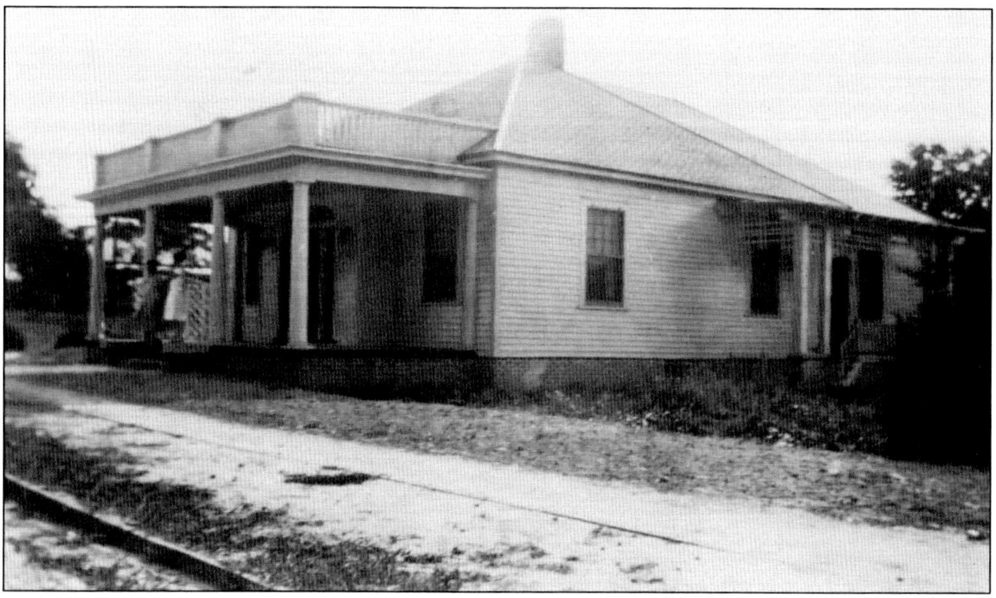

The Woman's Club of Clayton's building, moved and remodeled by 1930, is still used for community meetings, receptions, and other social events. Douglas Ellington (1886–1960), an internationally known architect, designed the renovations. Ellington was the brother of Lucile Ellington Hocutt, who was the club's president during this time. (Courtesy of the Woman's Club of Clayton.)

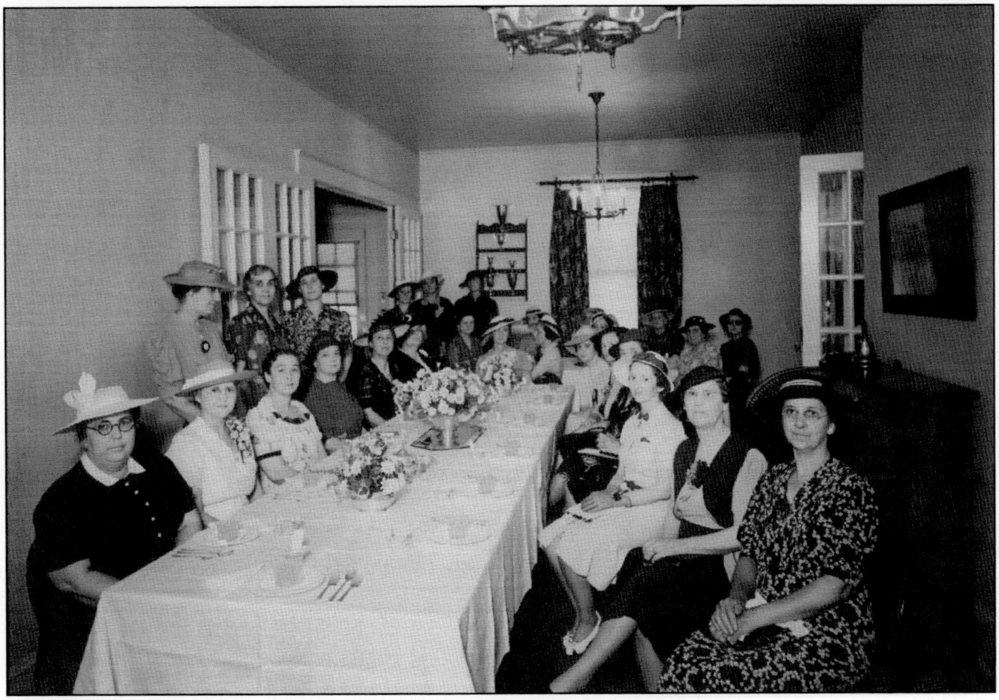

The Halcyon Club was organized in September 1912 as a literary club. The membership was limited to 16. Mrs. T. Arthur Griffin was the first president. This 1937 picture includes current and past members in recognition of the club's 25th anniversary. The Halcyon Club is the oldest established club in Clayton still meeting. (Courtesy of the Halcyon Club.)

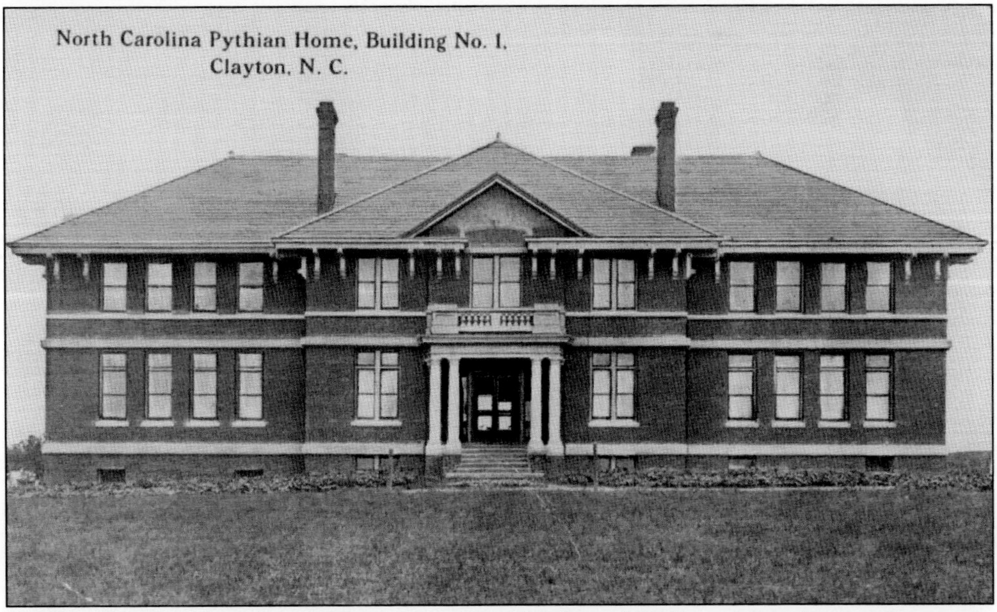

In 1911, the Grand Lodge of North Carolina, Knights of Pythias, opened an orphanage in this building, shown around 1915. The orphanage was located on a 177-acre tract of land near Clayton, acquired in part by purchase and in part by donation from brothers A. Julian and David W. Barbour. (Courtesy of the North Carolina Division of Archives and History.)

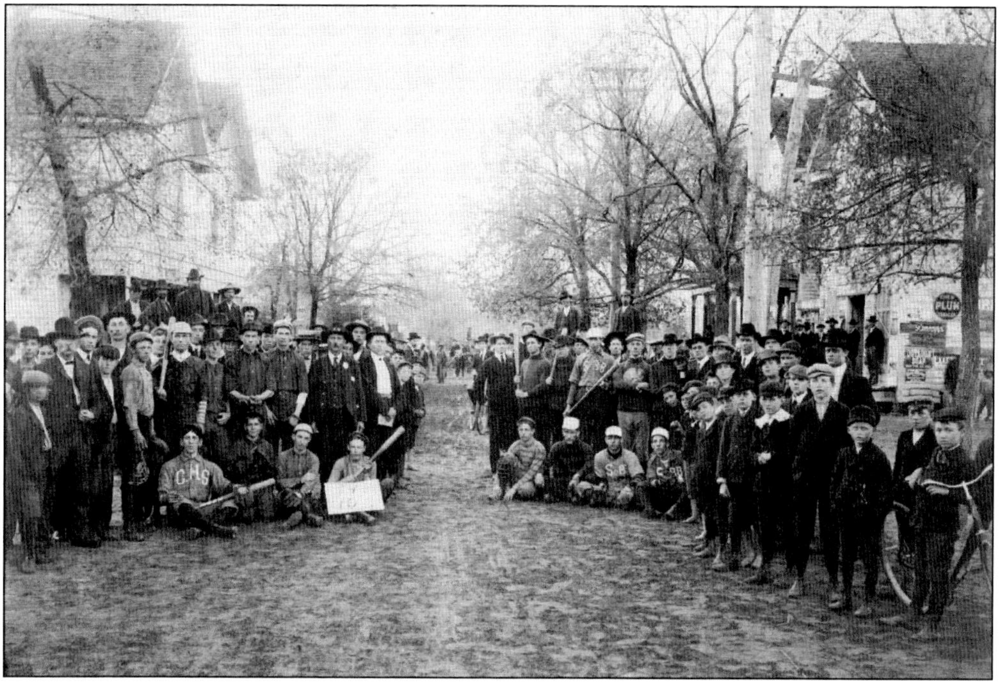

Baseball games were major highlights in a young boy's life in the late 19th century. The Clayton Red Stockings, pictured at left, pose with town elders and the visiting team on Main Street near Lombard Street. The local team was organized by 1883 and, by the early 1900s, was traveling in two-horse wagon and buggy caravans to compete across central North Carolina. Early players included unidentified, John Turley, Sam Honeycutt, and Duke Duncan (first row, seated).

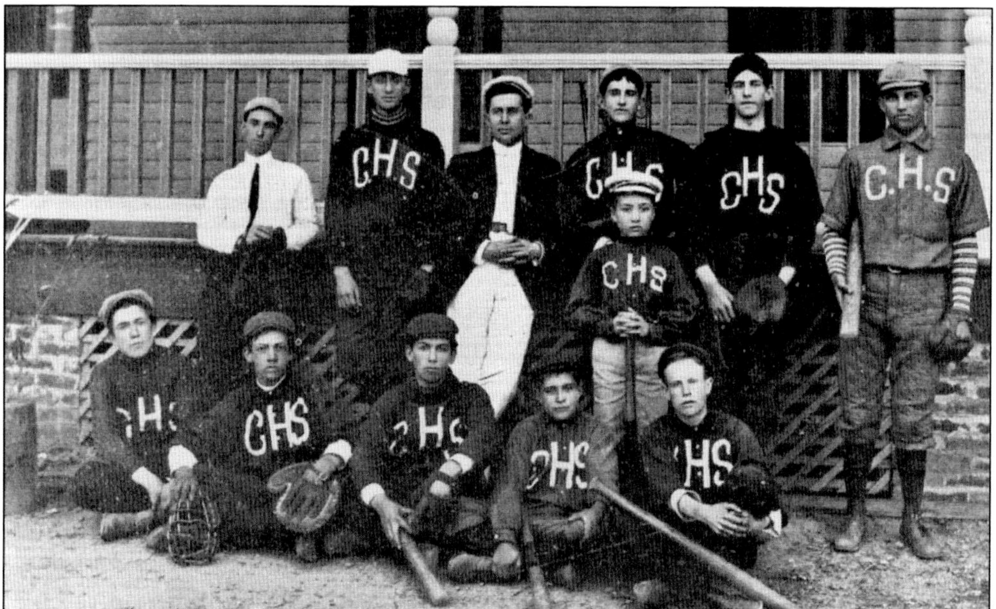

The Clayton High School baseball team members of 1904 pose in front of the school dormitory. Some members of the team were Duke Duncan, Ronnie Ellis, Saxe Barnes, Oscar Creech, Roy Robertson, Rudolph Barnes, and Clarence Cable.

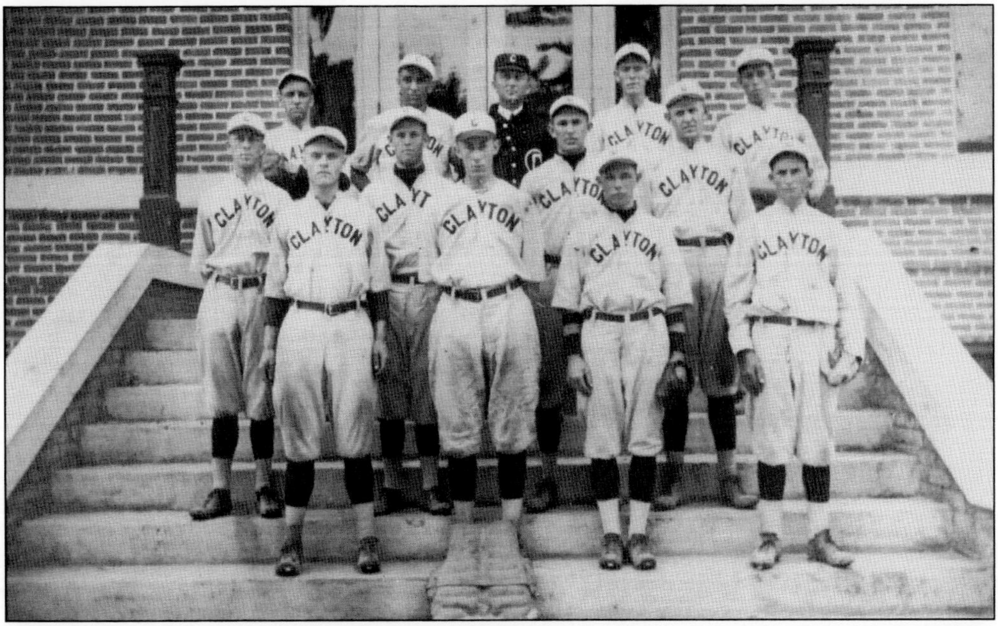

The Clayton High School baseball team of 1916 won the North Carolina state championship. From left to right are (first row) Dewey Davis, pitcher; Peg Poole, catcher; Sudie Creech, second base; and Bill Ellis, outfield; (second row) Bennett Poole, outfield; Max Barbour, outfield; Herman Duncan, shortstop; and Darwin Kelly, centerfield; (third row) Aubrey Gattis, first base; Ekie Gattis, outfield; Jesse J. Ellis, coach; Weisner Farmer, outfield; and Hume Creech, third base.

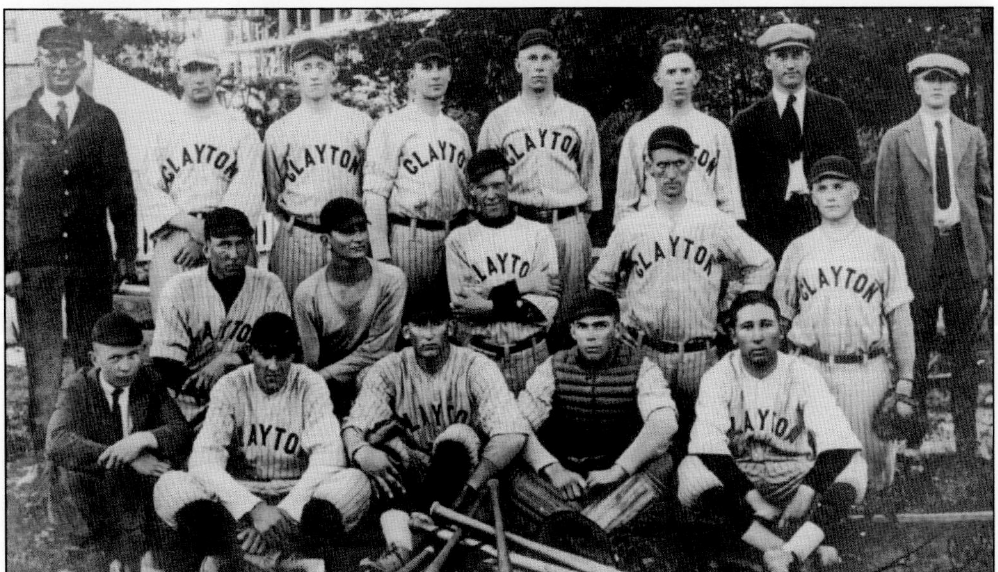

Clayton's second state championship was won by the Clayton High School baseball team of 1922. Clayton team members from left to right are (first row) John B. Robertson (mascot), Jake Hagwood, Vic Sorrell, Forest Broughton, and Loomis Truelove; (second row) Dwight Johnson, Hever Buckner, Algie Young, Ikie Matthews, and Walton Sherron; (third row) coach Jessie Ellis, Pat Massey, Joe Gulley, Bill Massey, John Baucom, Ernest Pete Hinton, Prof. J. W. Nichols, and manager ? Mangum.

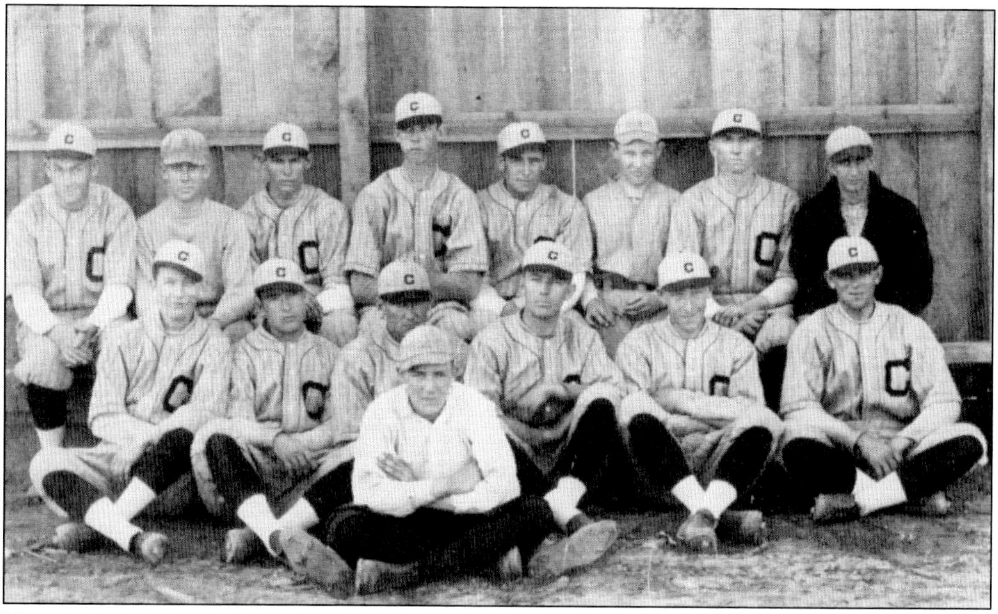

Victory came again in 1926, when the Clayton High School team took another state championship. Team players are, from left to right, (first row) Howard Hassell; (second row) John Battle Robertson, Millard Parrish, Dan Barnes, Ralph Williams, Ayden Lassiter, and Eugene Walters; (third row) Thel Allen, Doc Thurston, Tyler Dewar, Joe Young, Joe Turner Barnes, George Conner, William Clark, and Vann Stringfield (coach). (Courtesy of Sam Robertson.)

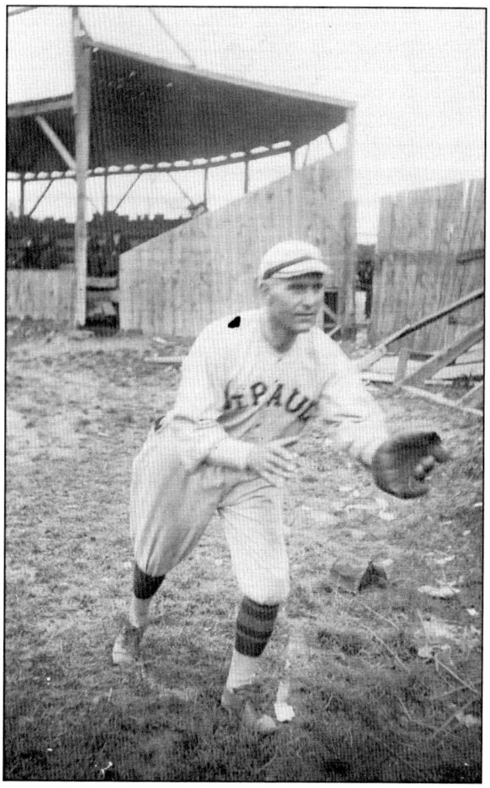

Vern Duke Duncan (1890–1954) played baseball with local teams from 1903 to 1907. He played with the University of North Carolina in 1909 and 1910. Duke played with professional teams from Columbia, Philadelphia, Montreal, Baltimore, and Raleigh before signing with St. Paul. He played with St. Paul from 1916 until 1921, except for one year when he was in the army. (Courtesy of the Rasor family.)

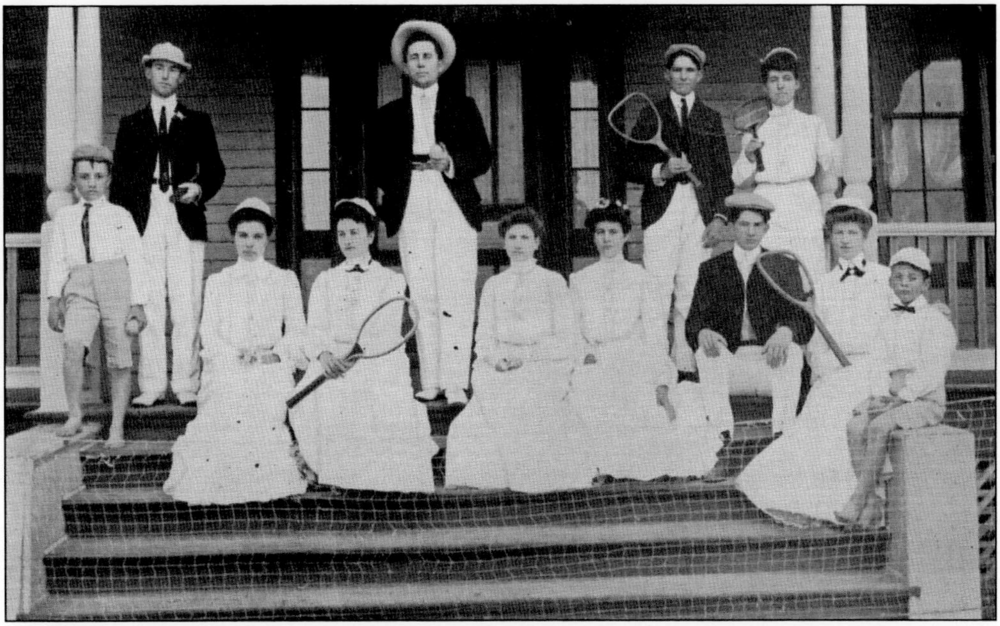

In 1897, Dr. J. J. Young was recognized for giving an "elegant tennis set" to the young ladies of Clayton. This game apparently had become popular among both sexes by 1904, when a tennis club at Clayton High School posed for this photograph.

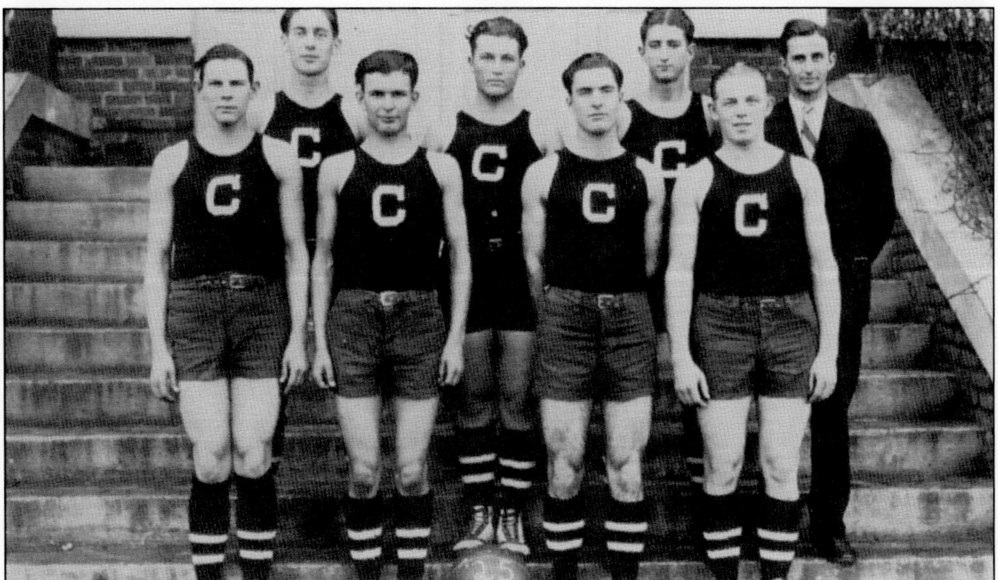

Clayton High School boys' basketball team members of 1925 are, from left to right, (first row) Tyler Dewar, Ralph Williams, Millard Parrish, and Eugene Walters; (second row) Laynelle Johnson, Latrelle Parrish, Steven Judson Wall, and coach Vann B. Stringfield. Other members of the team not pictured are John B. Robertson and Ayden Lassiter.

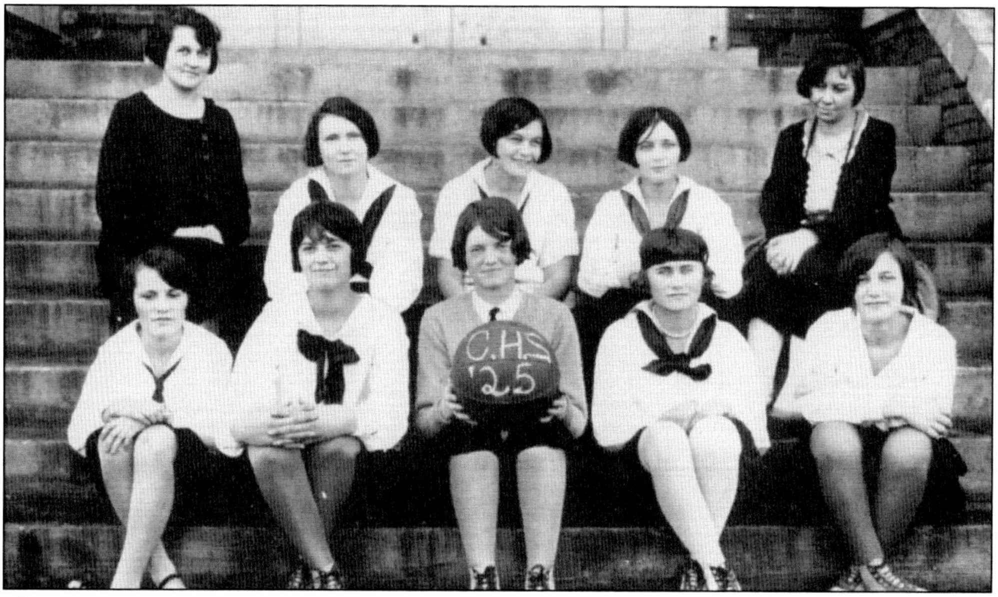

The 1925 Clayton High School girls' basketball team members are, from left to right, (first row) Hocutt Wall, Pauline Smith, Lucille Young, Kiva Coates, and Helen Austin; (second row) ? Wilson (coach), Estelle Clark, Bernice Turley, Florence Wilder, and Helen Askew (coach).

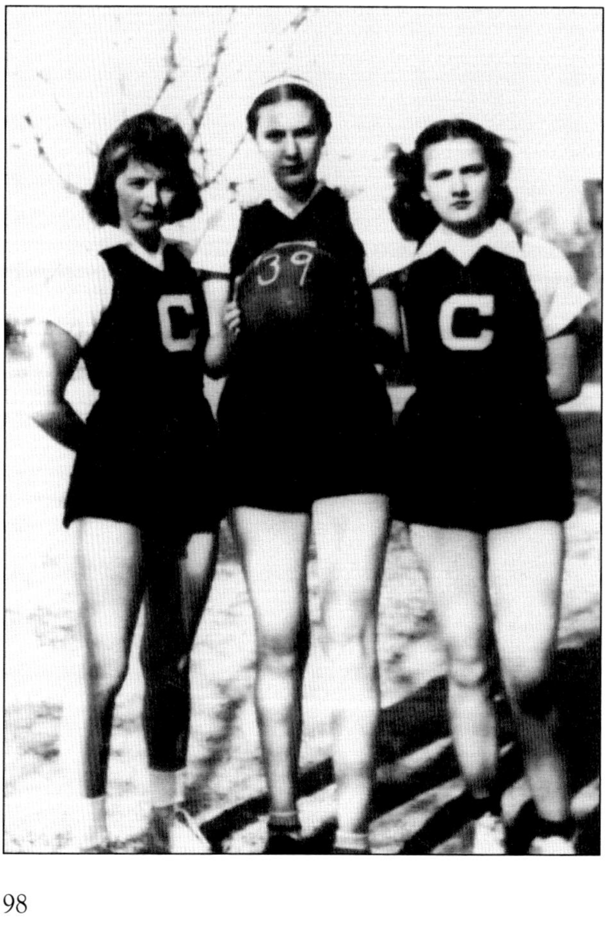

Among the members of the 1939 Clayton High School girls' basketball team are, from left to right, Ann Hinton, Dorothy Hill, and Betty Lambert. Other members were Josephine Bunn, Virginia Warren, Gertude Liles, Ethelene Holloway, Helen Whitley, Edith Weeks, and Louise Holland.

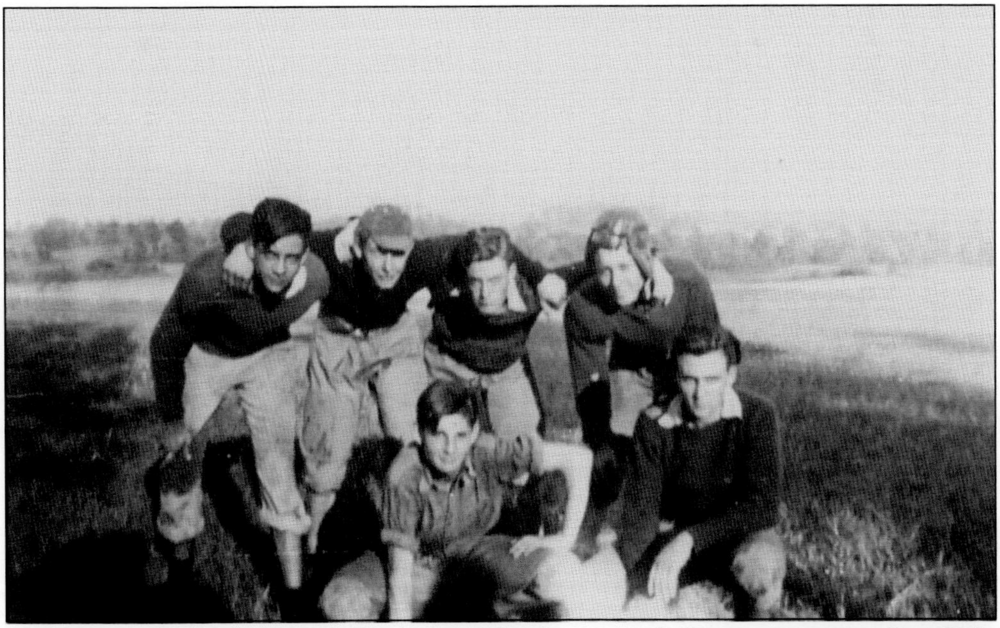

The Clayton High School football team poses for this picture before a game against Four Oaks around 1940. Members are, from left to right, (first row) Ransom Averitt and John Arch Vinson; (second row) Colin Hamilton, John "Pickle" Holland, David Stewart, and Cooper Starling.

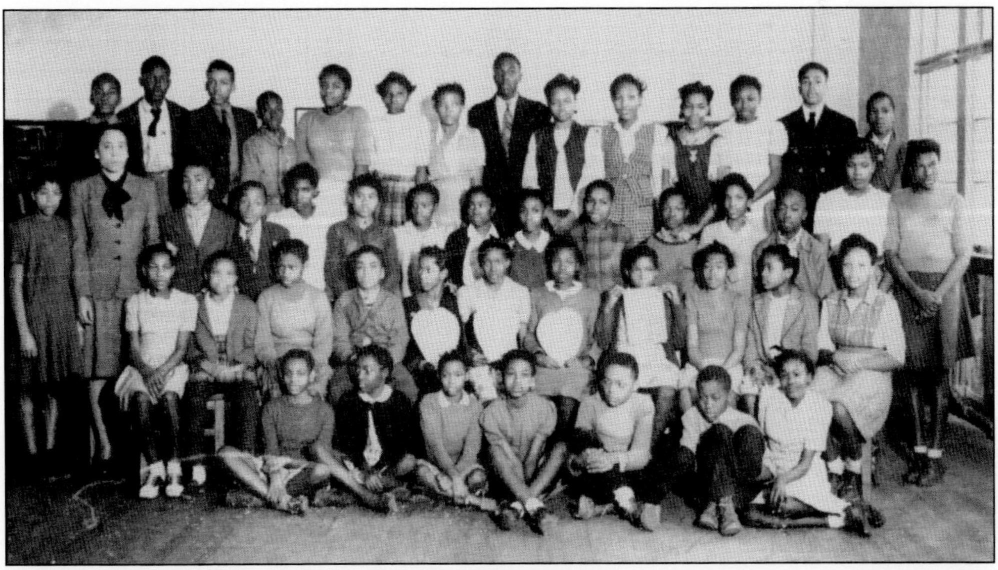

Members of the Cooper High School 4-H Club posed for this photograph about 1945. Leaders of the group were teachers Ethel D. Jones and Josephine Saunders, Johnston County farm agent Leroy R. Johnson, and home agent Lucy Hicks Toole (DeLaine).

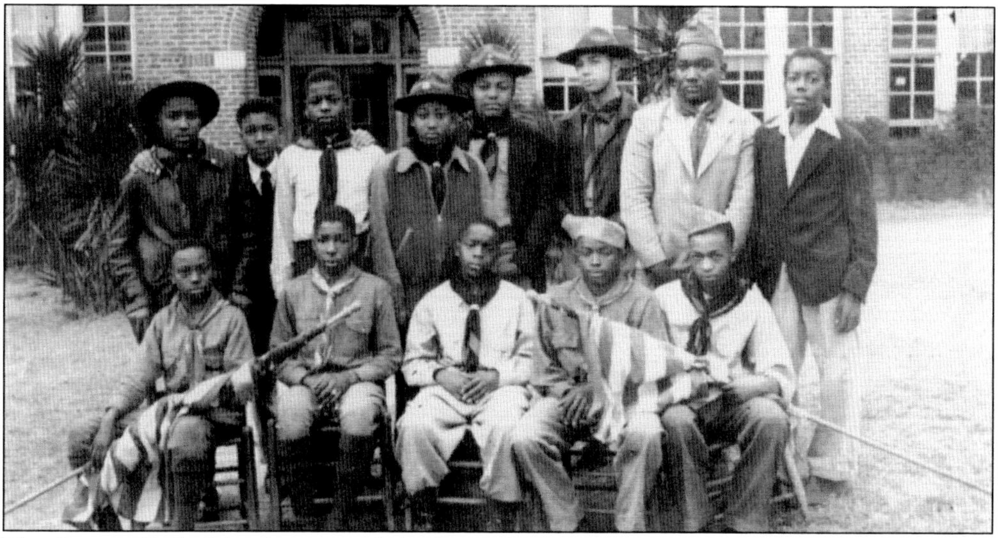

The Cooper High School sponsored the first African American Boy Scout troop in Johnston County. Troop members shown here in 1946 include, from left to right, (first row) Fred Stallings, Hubert Horton Jr., Edgar B. Blackmon, Roosevelt Sanders, and Gordon Hinton; (second row) Royestine Rand, Needham Lewis, John Whitley, Lewis Smith, Lee Earl Horton, Ernest Lambert, Charlie Sanders, and Jessie Vinson.

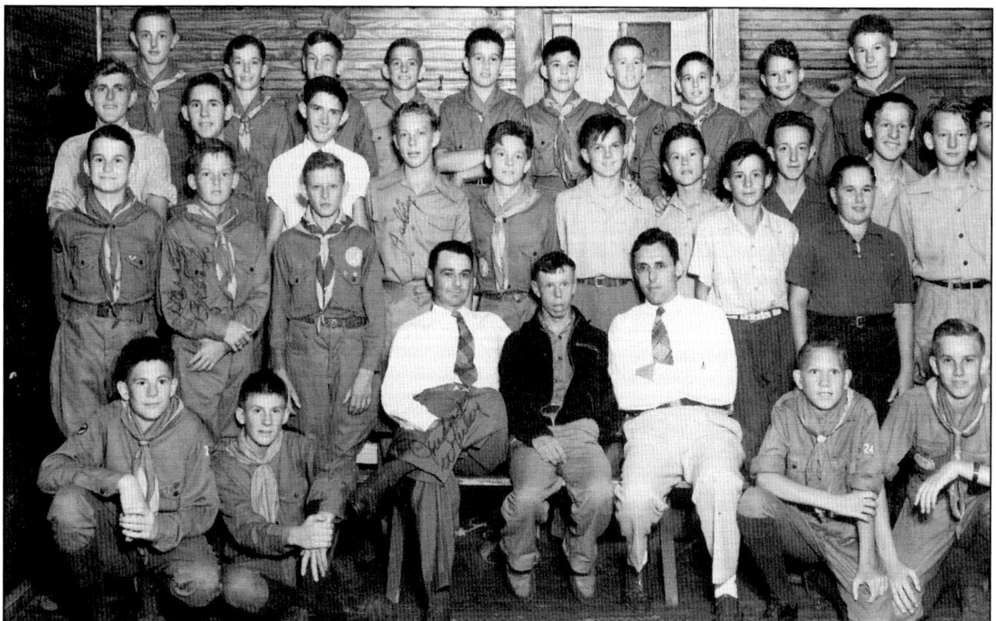

Clayton Boy Scouts and leaders in 1942 include, from left to right, (first row) Billy Massey, Brooks Beddingfield, Judson Whitley, Herbert Guy, Paul Keller, Harold Worlds, and Billy Wall; (second row) Douglas Bain Jr., James Allen, and Bruce Carroll; (third row) John Holland, John Payne, Alvin Britt, Ashley Horne, Harry Brooks Jr., Edward Lambert, Rudolph Allen, Bobby Davis, Edward Smith, Lawrence Smith, Jimmy McCarthy, Wallace Wall, and Fred Talton; (fourth row) Charles Lee, Charles Barden, Turner Vinson Jr., Bobby Davis, Lacy Smith, Glenn Austin, Jack Forbes, George Morgan, Jesse Austin Jr., and Russell Ellis.

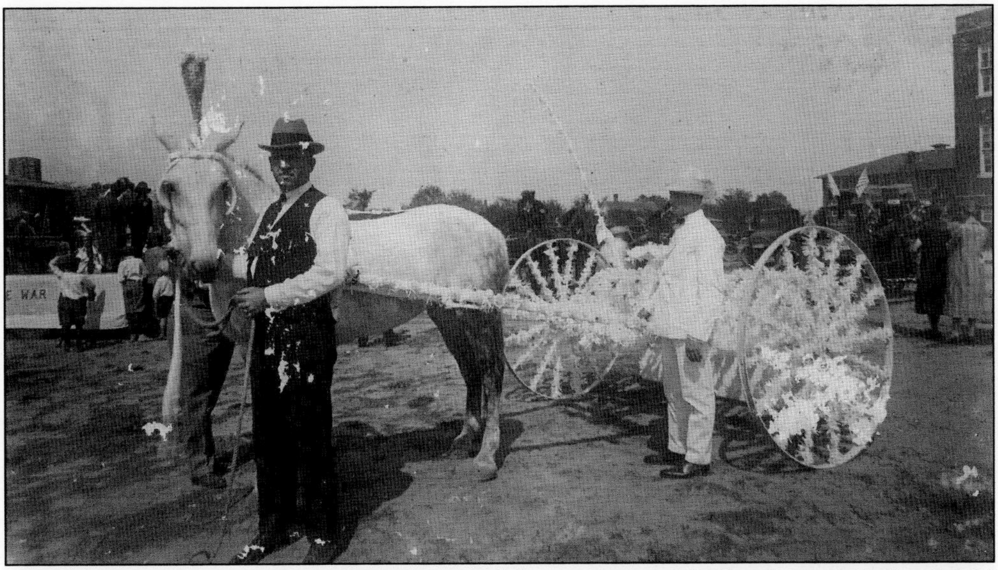

Clayton merchant J. Dwight Barbour, shown at left, was photographed in front of the Smithfield High School in the 1920s as he prepared his parade float. The event is thought to be part of Johnston County's celebration of the 150th anniversary of America's independence, on July 4, 1926.

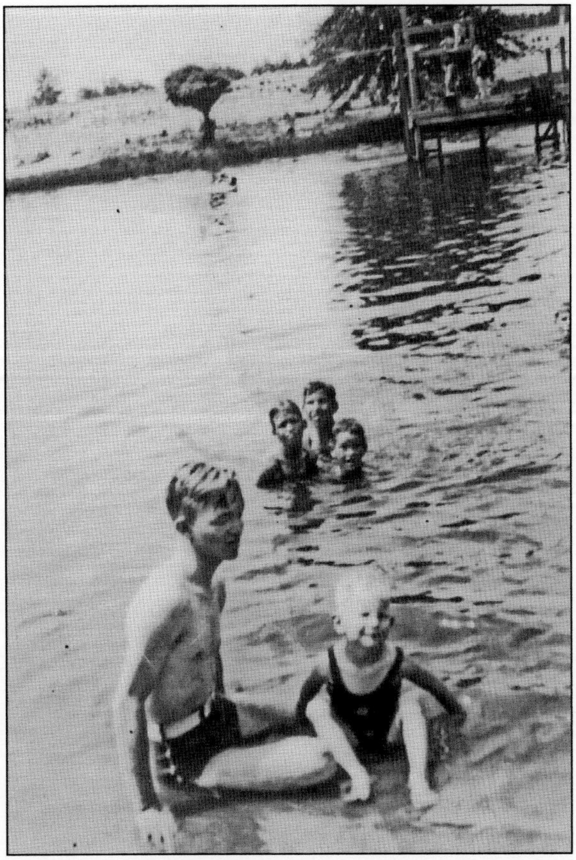

Wilbur Barnes's pond was a popular recreation spot in the 1930s and 1940s. The pond was located off Covered Bridge Road just past the Neuse River. One could swim in the cool waters that rose from the numerous springs that filled the pond. A dock and bathhouses were provided. Paul Williams (first row, left) and his younger brother, Lawrence, are shown in this 1934 photograph. The other swimmers are unidentified. (Courtesy of Lawrence Williams.)

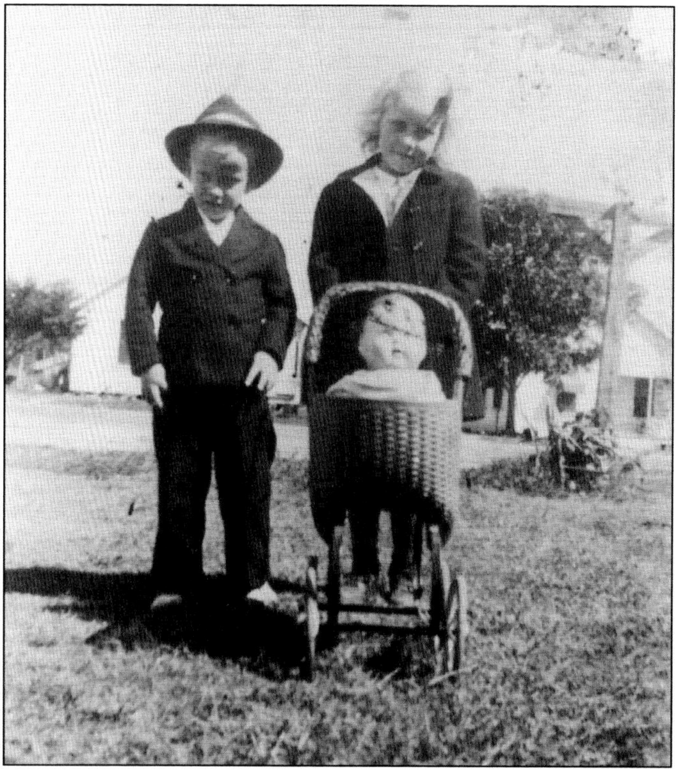

Waylon Spence and his sister Margaret are pictured in 1944 as they enjoy an afternoon of play. (Courtesy of Sherrill and Margaret S. Canady.)

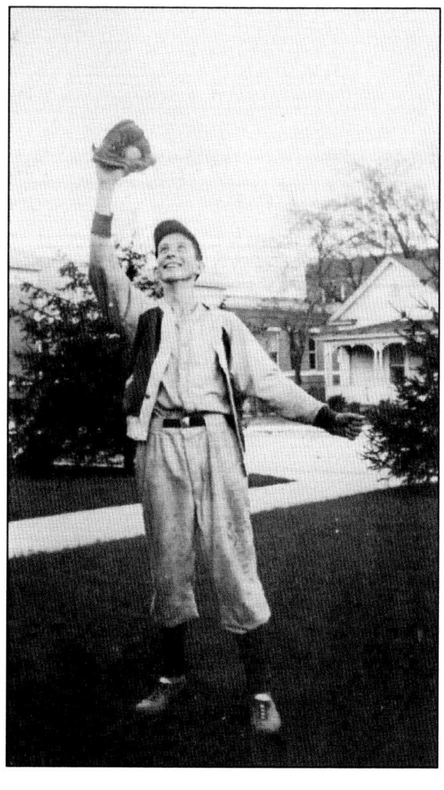

Where there was a sporting event, one could usually find Cooper Starling, pictured in the late 1930s. Although he remembers many good times, one particularly sad event stands out. As a caravan of Clayton High School basketball players and fans prepared to depart for a basketball game in Benson in January 1941, he and his buddy John Arch Vinson found themselves competing for the same seat. They decided to settle the matter with a coin toss. John Arch won the seat but soon lost his life when the car collided with a train in Benson. Also killed were Lilburn Barnes, Yvonne Whitley, and Bud Satterfield. The only survivor was David Grey Satterfield.

Racially segregated schools did not stop boys of both races from playing football together on school grounds, as shown in this late 1930s photograph from a Satterfield family photo album.

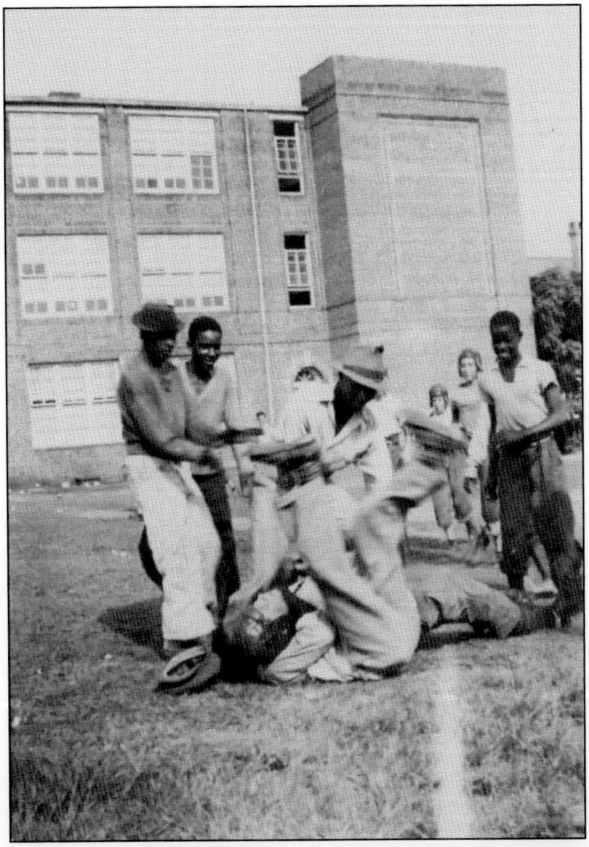

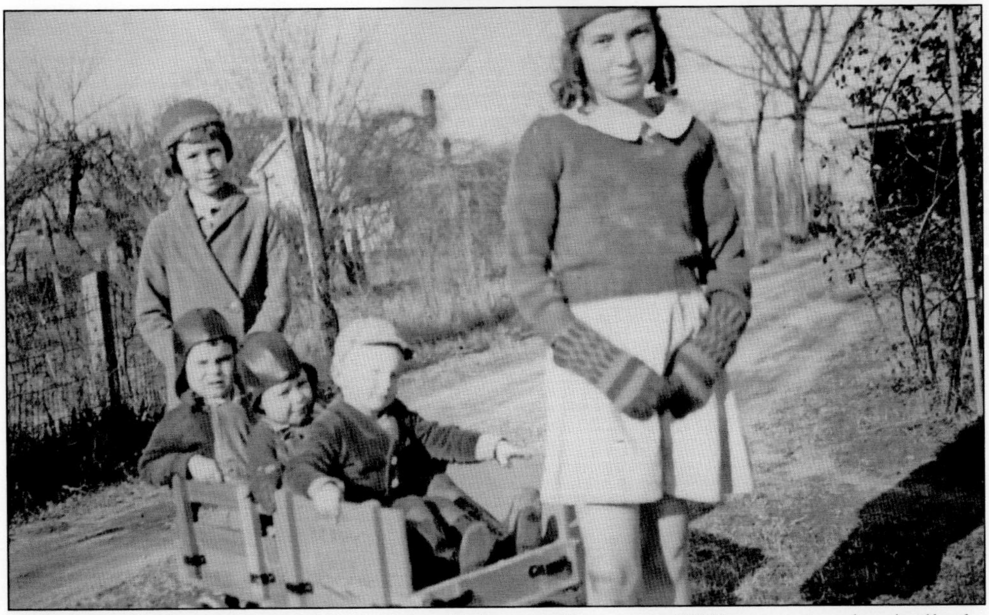

From left to right, Herman Vinson, Jerry Gulley, and Lawrence Williams enjoy the thrill of a wagon ride in the late 1930s. Anna Ruth Barbour (far left) and Ella Sue Vinson (far right) were apparently the ones responsible for propelling the vehicle. (Courtesy of Lawrence Williams.)

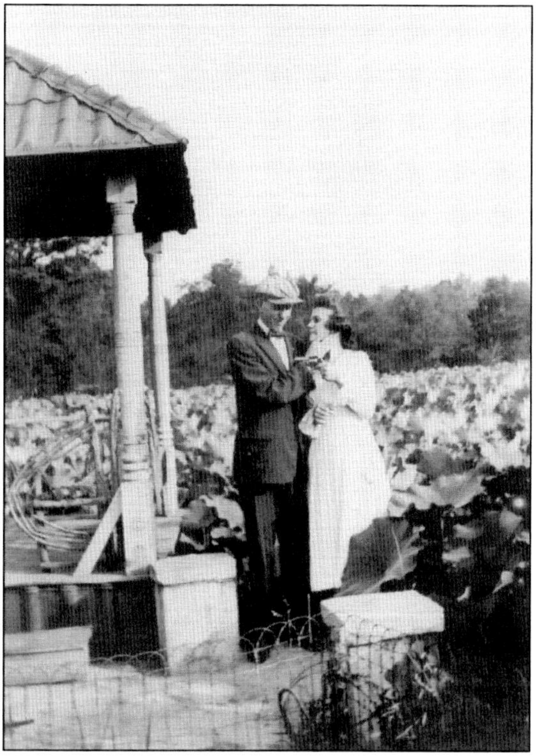

This courting couple was caught on camera in the 1920s, and the image was preserved in a Horne family photograph album.

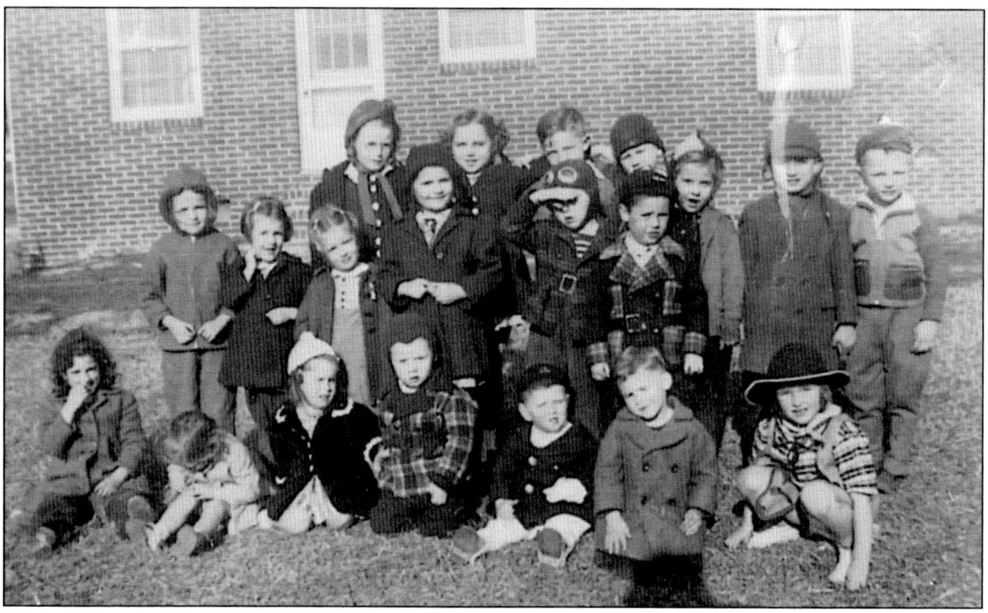

Jackie Yates, the daughter of Dr. Percy Yates and his wife, Mary, is shown here about 1940 with her birthday party friends. Pictured from left to right are (first row) Jackie Yates, Sybil Atkinson, Betty Bain, Robert Adams, Butch Beard, unidentified, and Ann Ellis; (second row) Emily Barden two unidentified, Helen Austin, Bucky Coats, unidentified, Sue Cavanaugh, Jimmy Moore, and Bat Robertson; (third row) Mamie Davis, Julia Ann Knott, Ed Hollingsworth, and Dan Knott. (Courtesy of Helen Ellerbe.)

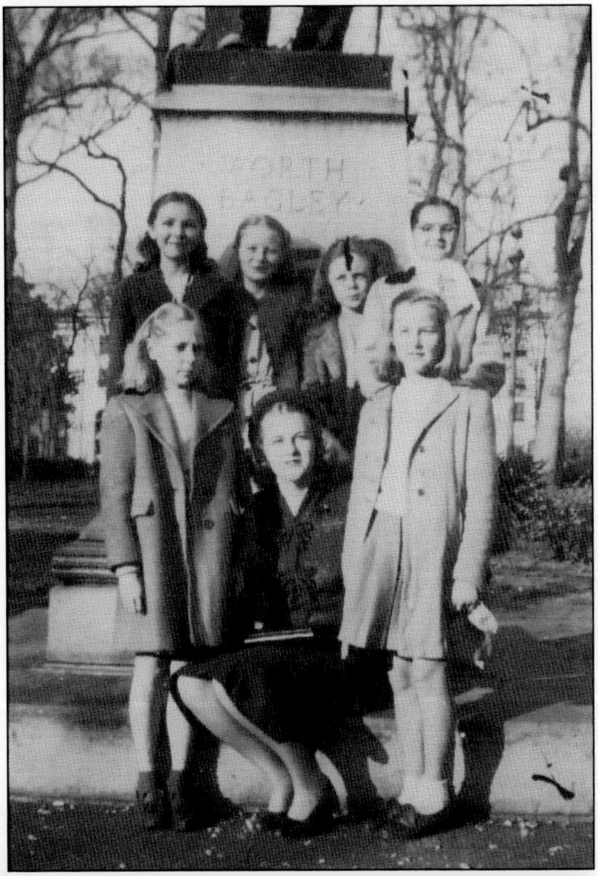

This First Baptist Church Sunday school class took a trip to Raleigh to visit the state capital in December 1946. Pictured from left to right are (first row) Betsy Moore, Francis Ellis, and Jean Wheeler; (second row) Janice Crumpler, Vera Mouser, Marilyn Blinson, and Helen Austin. (Courtesy of Helen Ellerbe.)

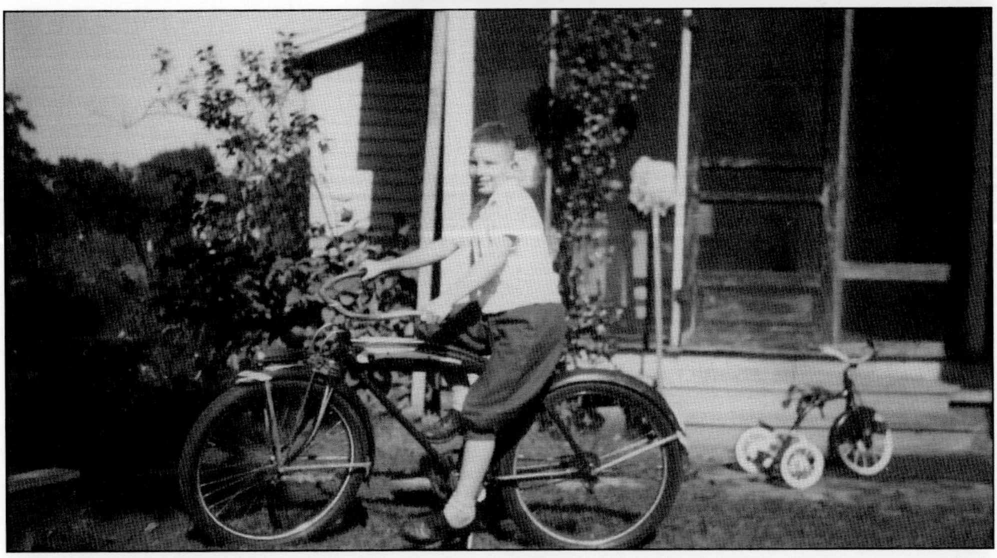

Paul Williams ordered this red-and-white bicycle from Sears for his son, Lawrence, in 1940. It was to be shipped on the freight train to Clayton. Lawrence went to the train station every day for many days in anticipation of finding that special bicycle delivered. (Courtesy of Lawrence Williams.)

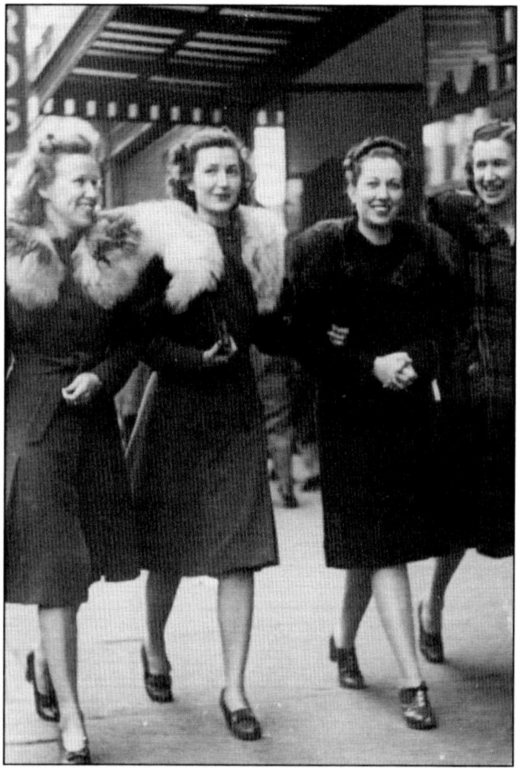

Shopping sprees in Raleigh were major outings for young women in the years before World War II. Pictured here about 1940 are, from left to right, Maxine Ellis, Aldine Lancaster, Helen Lancaster, and Mary Ellen Ellis, all dressed up and proudly strolling in front of the Boylan-Pearce Department Store on Fayetteville Street. (Courtesy of Jackie Smith.)

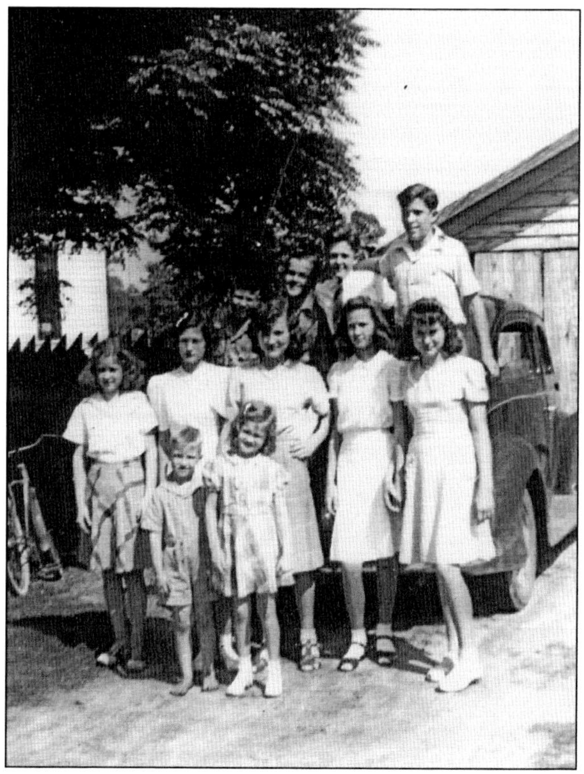

Neighborhood friends gathered for Sunday evening fun, visiting each others' homes, singing around the piano, playing games, and eating special refreshments prepared by their mothers. Friends in this 1943 photograph are, from left to right, (first row) Jimmy and Mary Moore; (second row) Ann Moore, Marie Averitt, Joyce Vinson, Maxine Dodd, and Doris Vinson; (third row) Glenn Austin, Ed Lambert, Harry Brooks, and Fred Talton. (Courtesy of Joyce Lipscomb Canady.)

Six

WARTIME

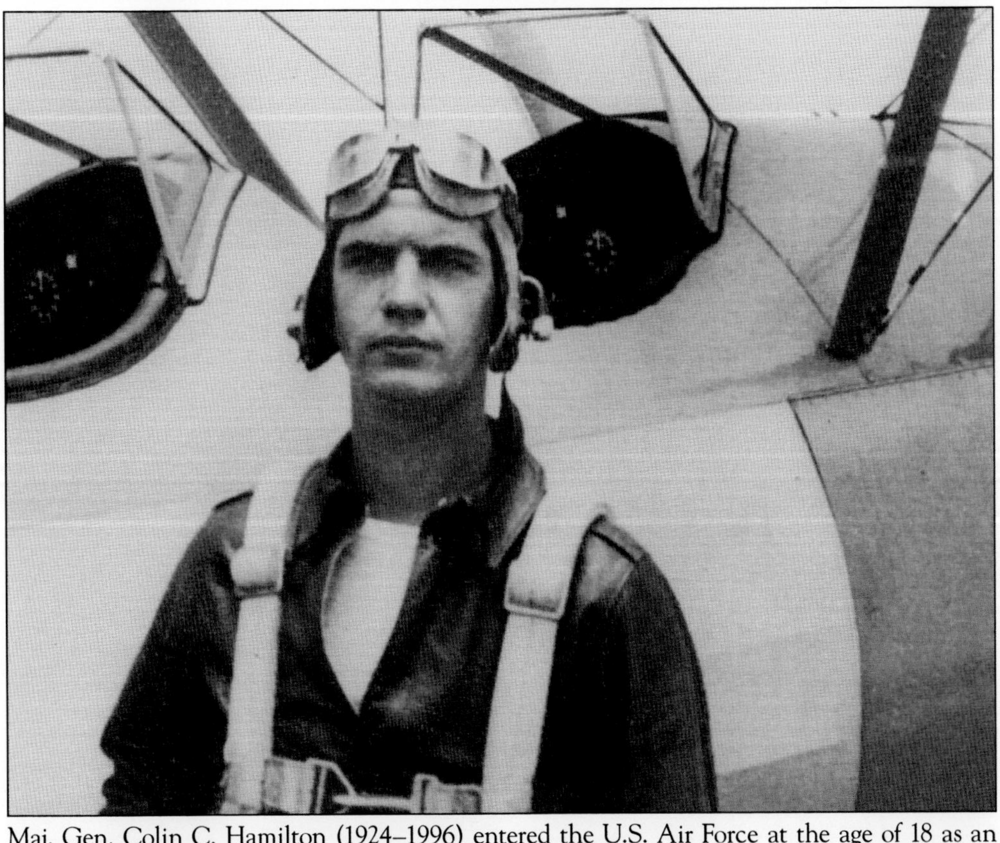

Maj. Gen. Colin C. Hamilton (1924–1996) entered the U.S. Air Force at the age of 18 as an aviation cadet, as shown here in 1942. He was the youngest B-24 bomber pilot in the European theater and flew 50 bombing missions during World War II. Hamilton retired after a 35-year military career, approximately 10,500 flying hours, and numerous awards and decorations. (Courtesy of the Hamilton family.)

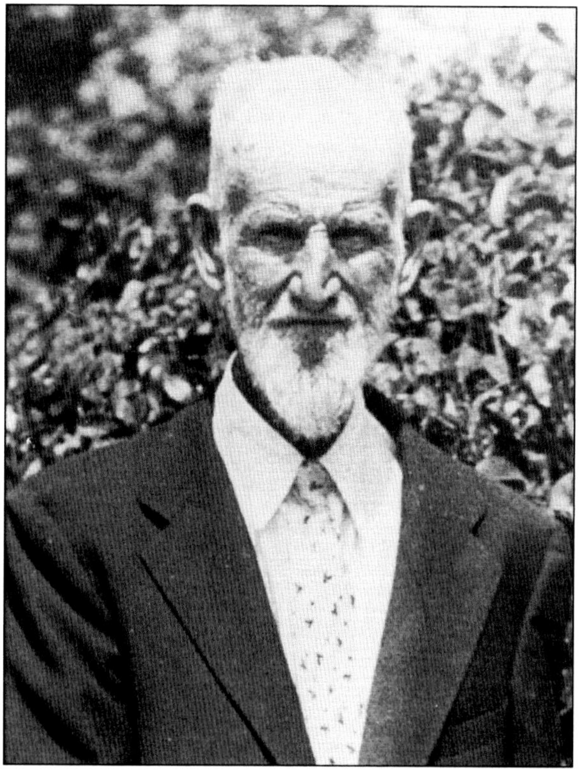

Andrew Jackson Ellis (1847–1944) enlisted in the North Carolina Second Junior Reserves Troops in 1864. On April 12, 1865, while at home recovering from measles, he heard the gunshots and cannon fire of a skirmish near his home between Union infantry forces and retreating Confederate cavalry. Ellis was a commander in chief of the North Carolina United Confederate Veterans and was Johnston County's last living Confederate veteran.

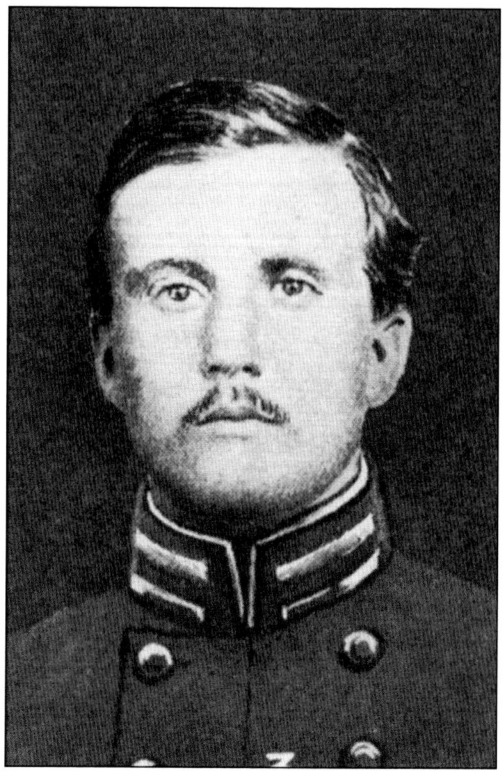

Jesse T. Ellington (1840–1910) served in the 50th North Carolina Regiment during the Civil War. The unit fought at the Battle of Bentonville and marched through Clayton in early April 1865 just prior to Gen. Joseph E. Johnston's surrender to Gen. William T. Sherman near Durham. (Courtesy of Walter Clark's *Histories of the Several Regiments and Battalions from north Carolina in the Great War, 1861–1865*, 1901.)

Joseph C. Ellington (1842–1905) served in the 50th North Carolina Regiment during the Civil War along with his brother, Jesse T. Ellington. Joseph was the state librarian in the 1890s. (Courtesy of Walter Clark's *Histories of the Several Regiments and Battalions from north Carolina in the Great War, 1861–1865*, 1901.)

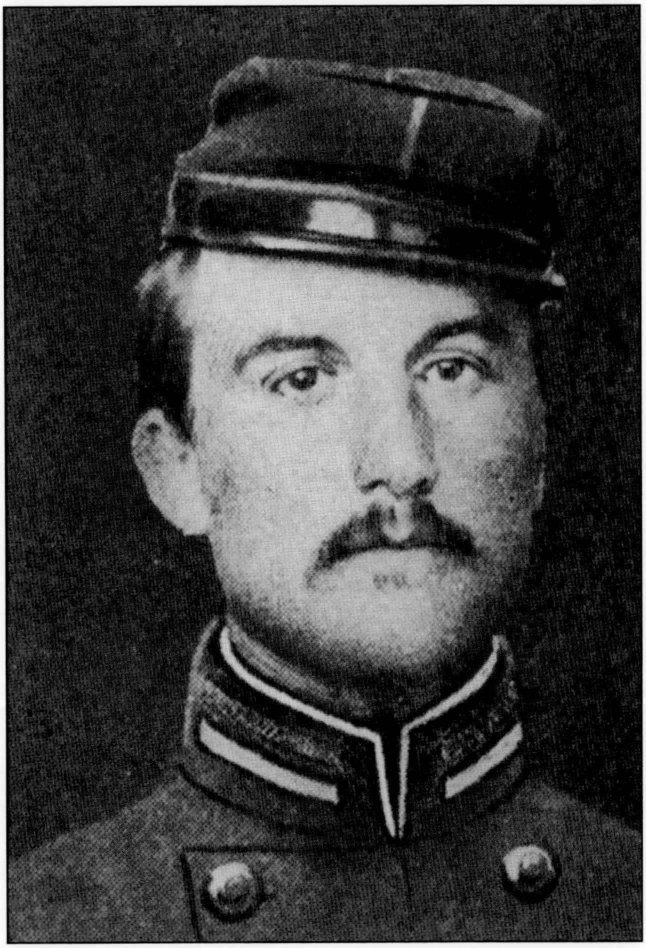

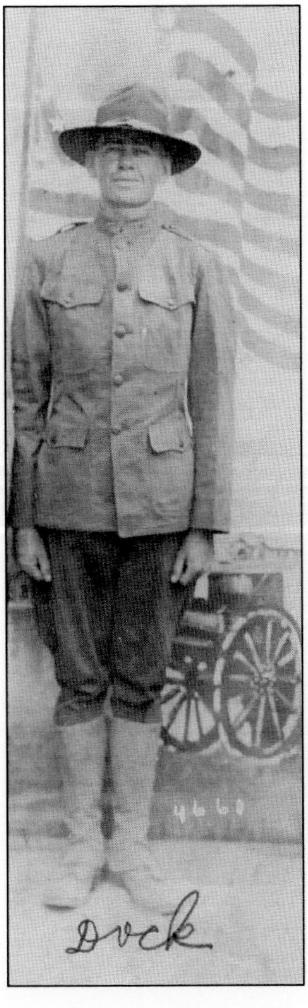

Doctor "Dock" Hubert Austin (1893–1933) was the first soldier from Clayton wounded during World War I. Leonard Moore died on the battlefield of France and was the first Clayton-area soldier killed in World War I. Local veterans named the American Legion for Leonard Moore in 1919. The American Legion received its charter in 1920. (Courtesy of Lawrence Williams.)

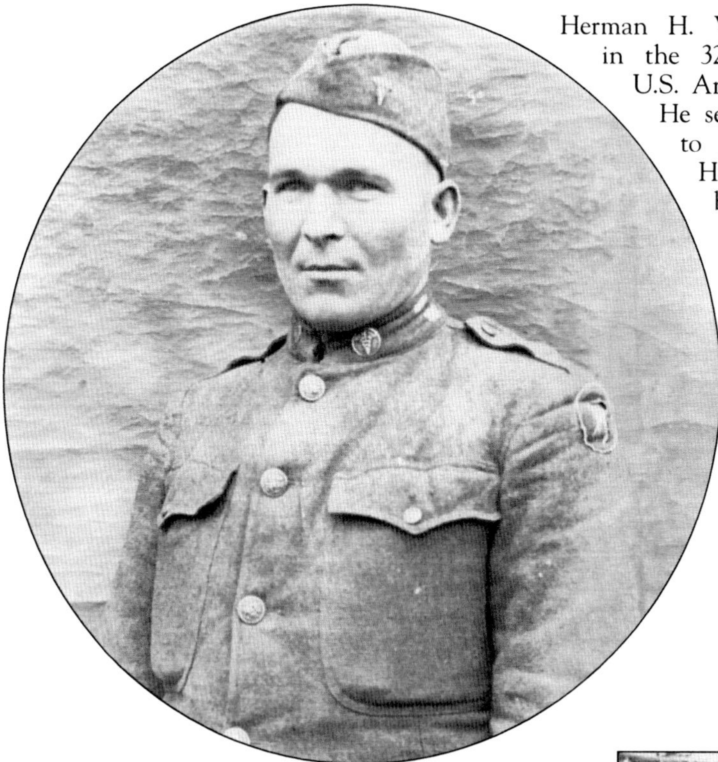

Herman H. Vinson (1895–1946) was in the 322nd Infantry with the U.S. Army during World War I. He served from October 1917 to June 1919 as a medic. He received a Victory badge and one Bronze Star. (Courtesy of Joyce Lipscomb Canady.)

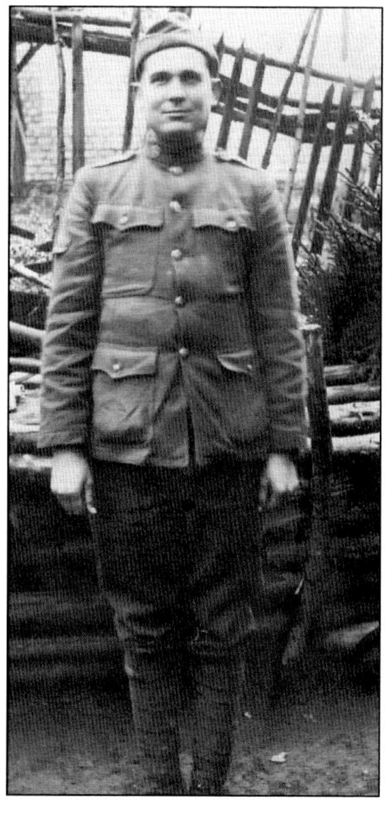

Turner Vinson (1895–1962) was in the infantry during World War I and served 13 months in Europe. During World War II, he served as chairman of the Johnston County Rationing Board. He was a farmer, lumber dealer, merchant, town commissioner, and was active in church and civic organizations, especially the Rotary Club. (Courtesy of Herman Vinson.)

Ralph Austin (1894–1976) was the son of Victor and Dora Austin. He served in the 322nd Infantry and was wounded in France on November 10, 1918, during the last battle. Austin was the second Clayton-area soldier wounded during World War I. (Courtesy of Helen Ellerbe.)

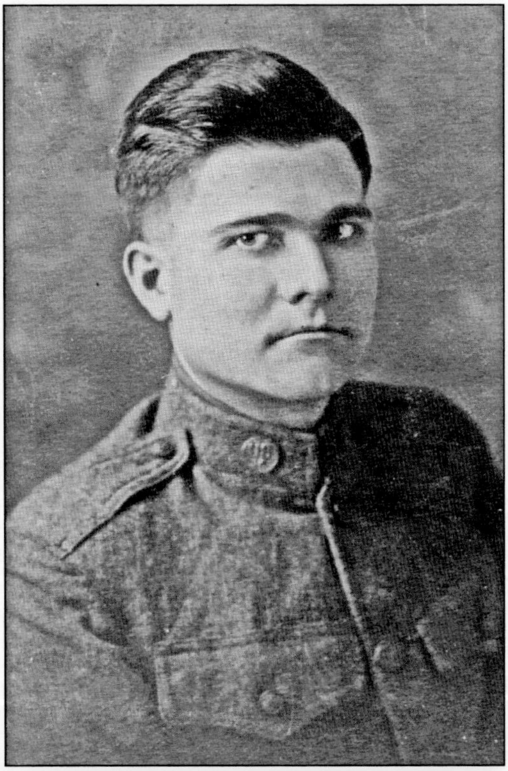

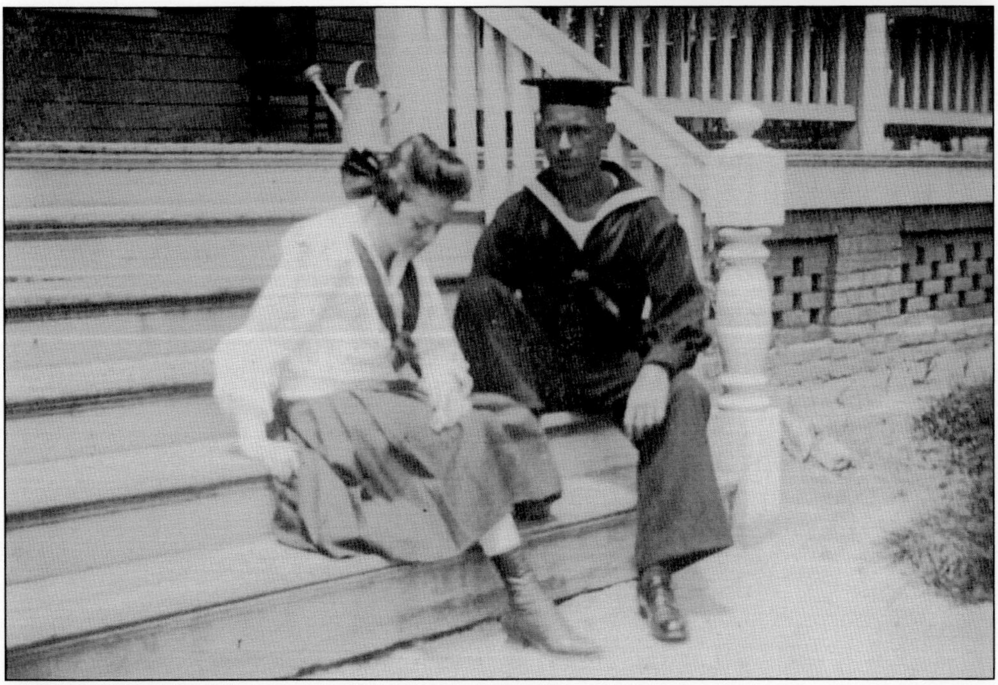

A uniformed Swade Barbour is shown with sister Winnie around 1917 at the family home on Main Street. Barbour served in the Naval Aviation Corps during World War I. (Courtesy of Joyce T. Barbour.)

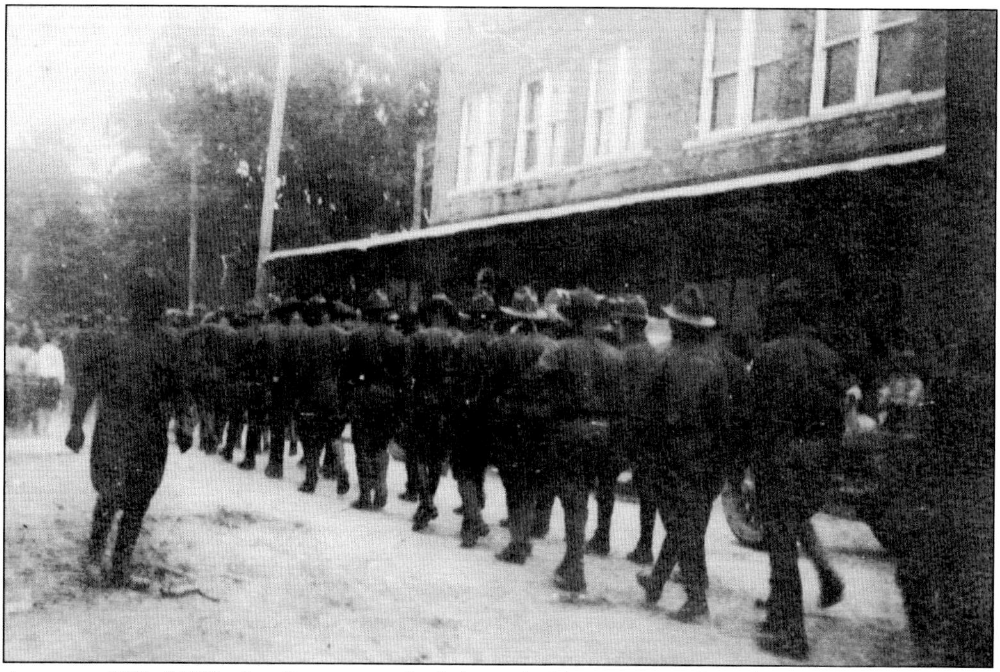

A group of World War I enlistees marched through Clayton in 1917 and were photographed in front of the Ashley Horne and Son building at the corner of Main and Lombard Streets.

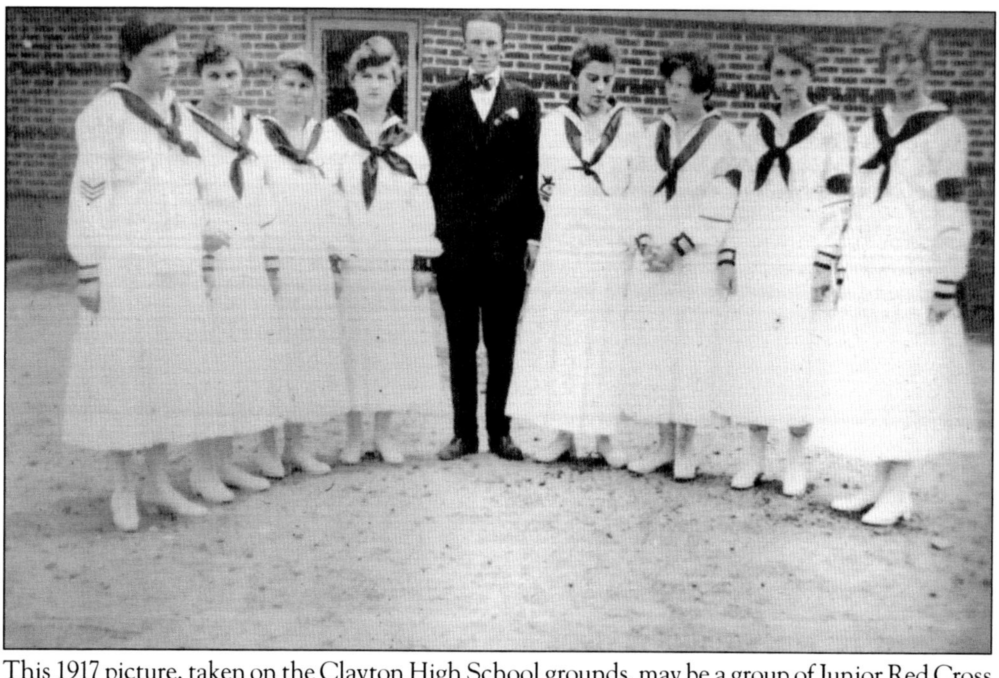

This 1917 picture, taken on the Clayton High School grounds, may be a group of Junior Red Cross members. The Red Cross was organized in June 1917. The junior members met every Saturday. They performed plays and musical programs to raise money. Admission was 15¢ or 25¢. Winnie Barbour is the first girl on the left. The others are unidentified. (Courtesy of Joyce T. Barbour.)

Paul A. Williams Jr. (1915–1989) was a U.S. Army veteran of World War II. Williams is shown about 1945, standing behind the family's 1935 Chevrolet. (Courtesy of Lawrence Williams.)

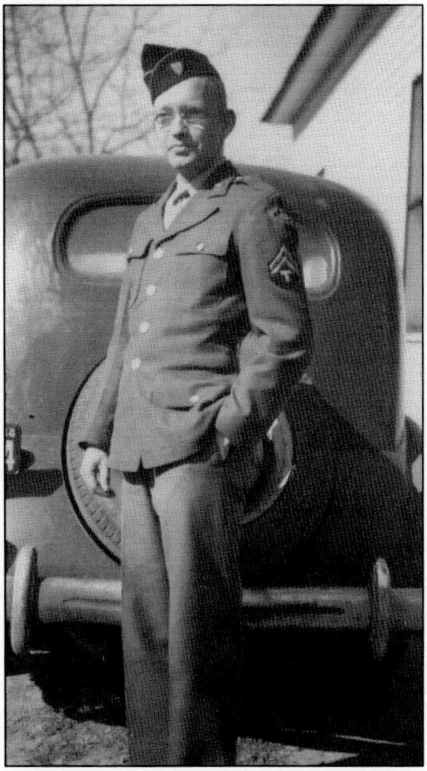

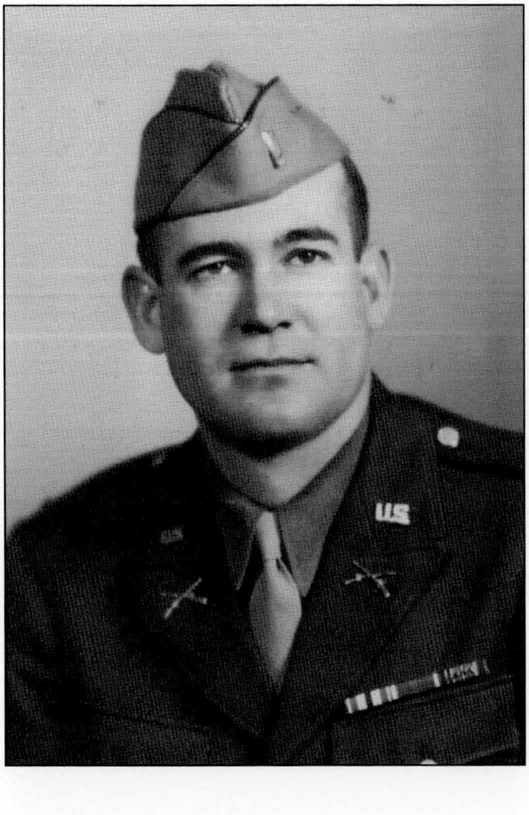

A graduate of Duke University, Capt. Battle Wilson Champion (1915–1981) served as a reconnaissance officer in the 9th Division, 60th Infantry under Gen. Omar Bradley. He took part in the landings in North Africa, Sicily, and the invasion of Europe, and received the Silver Star and the Purple Heart medals. (Courtesy of Sybil T. Champion.)

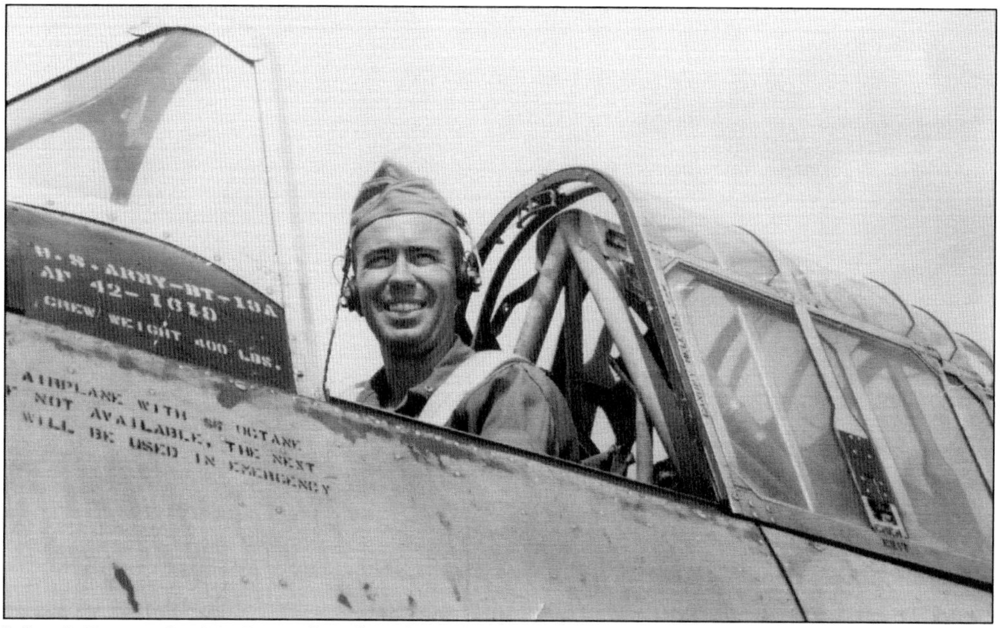

John I. Barnes Jr. (1916–1986) enlisted in the U.S. Army Air Corps in August 1942 and, by November 1943, was a pilot in charge of flying gunnery students at Buckingham Field in Florida. Toward the war's end, he was transferred to Kadena Field, Okinawa, B-29 (VH). He was assigned to Crew 115 of the 435th Bomb Squadron, 333rd Bomb Group, 316th Bomb Wing. (Courtesy of the Barnes family.)

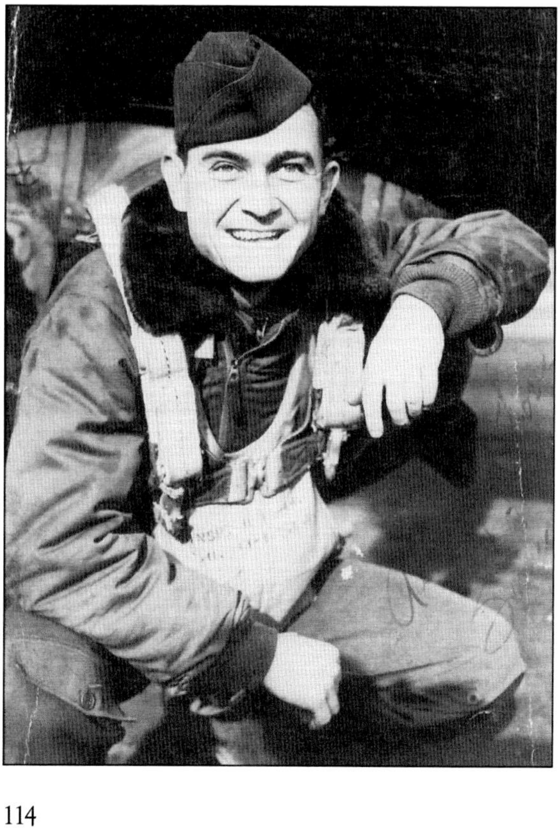

Sam E. Robertson was a staff sergeant with the U.S. Army Air Corp, 390th Bomb Group, 570th Squadron during World War II. Stationed at Parham, Suffolk, England, in 1945, he flew on 20 missions as the ball turret gunner of a B-17 Flying Fortress. (Courtesy of Sam Robertson.)

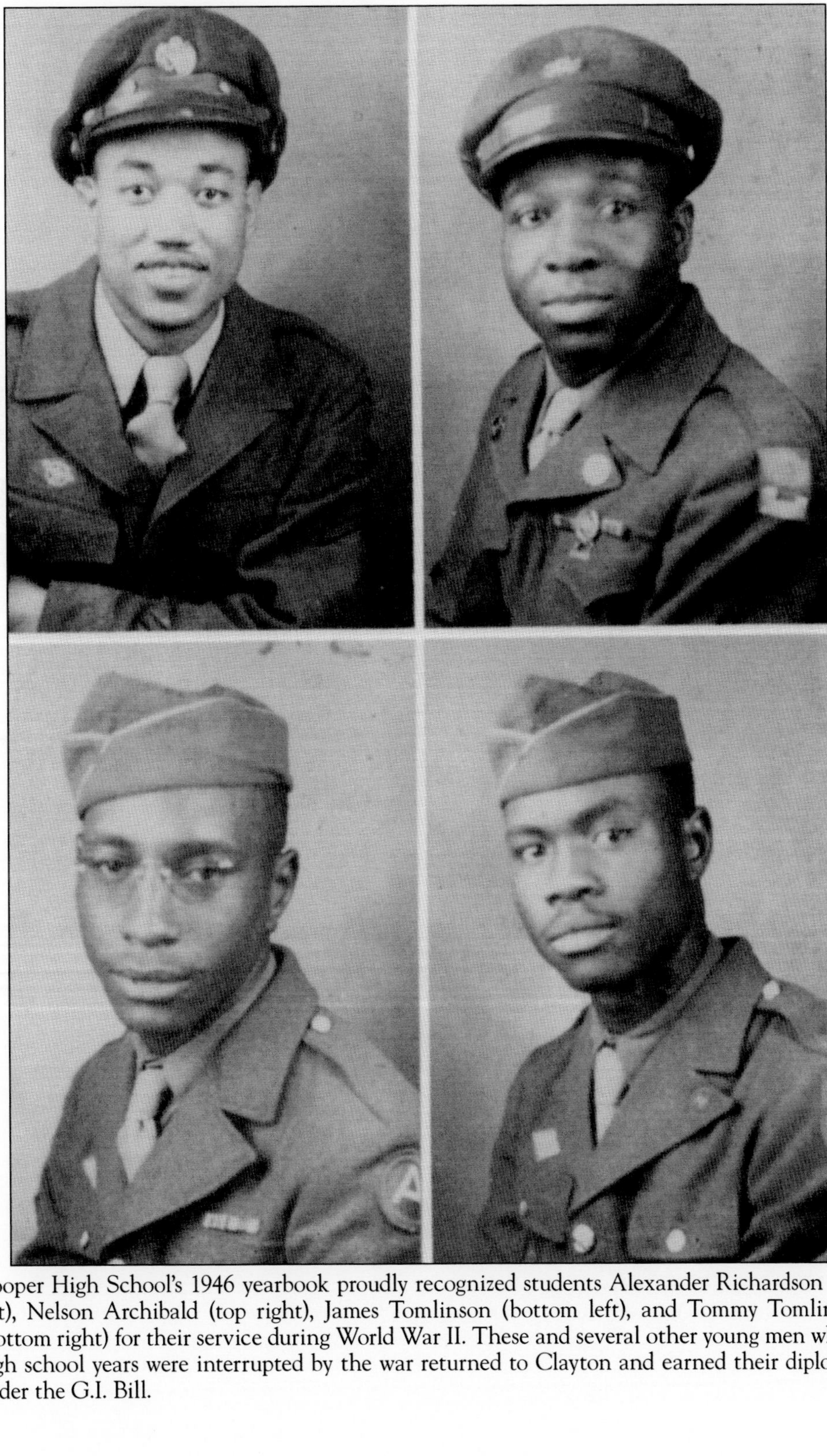

Cooper High School's 1946 yearbook proudly recognized students Alexander Richardson (top left), Nelson Archibald (top right), James Tomlinson (bottom left), and Tommy Tomlinson (bottom right) for their service during World War II. These and several other young men whose high school years were interrupted by the war returned to Clayton and earned their diplomas under the G.I. Bill.

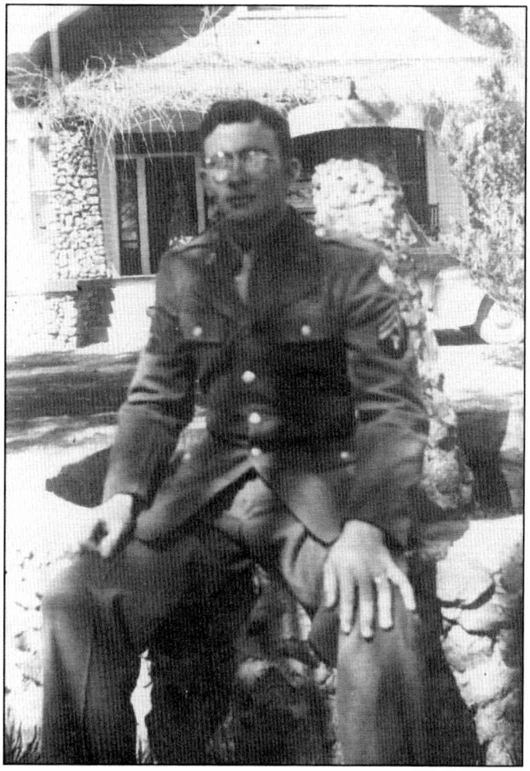

Richard R. Lee (1922–2006) was assigned to an infantry battalion in the U.S. Army during World War II. He was a decoder for the army and had to deliver the messages to the front. (Courtesy of the Julius Lee family.)

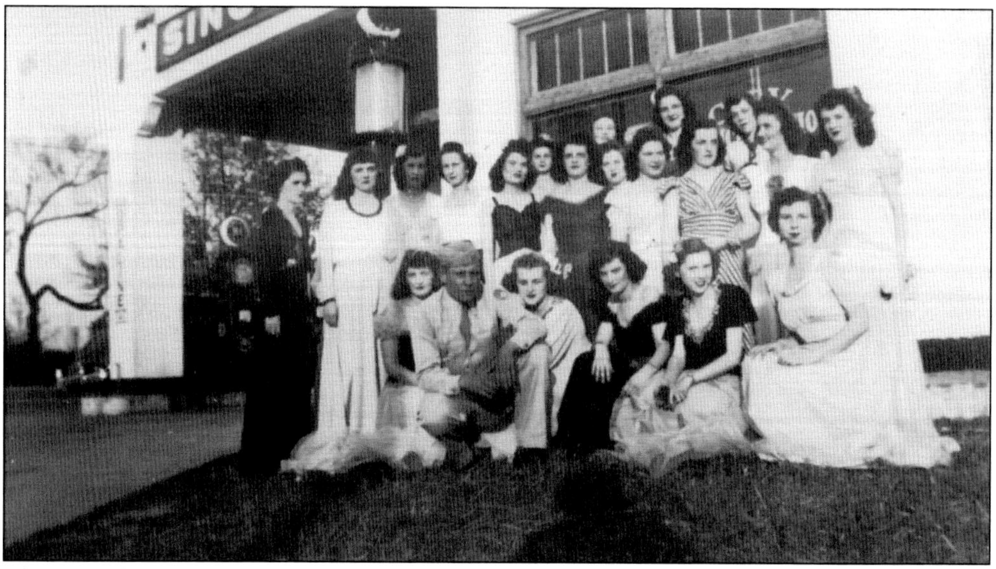

Clayton girls wore evening dresses on Friday nights during World War II to attend many USO dances at the Seymour Johnson Air Force Base. Gathered at the Sinclair's filling station for the bus ride in 1942 are, from left to right, (first row) Ann Hardee, the unidentified bus driver, Frances Ellis, Doris Ellis, Virginia Satterfield, and Maxine Barbour; (second row) Carmine Satterfield, Betty Lambert, Larue Stephenson, Rachel Peele, Dorothy Young, Rebecca Gattis, Peggy Gower, Martha Gattis, Jane Young, and Foy Durham; (third row) Tut Satterfield, Ernestine Dodd, Joyce Talton, Doris Talton, and Virginia Stephenson. (Courtesy of Joyce T. Barbour.)

Seven

Rural Communities

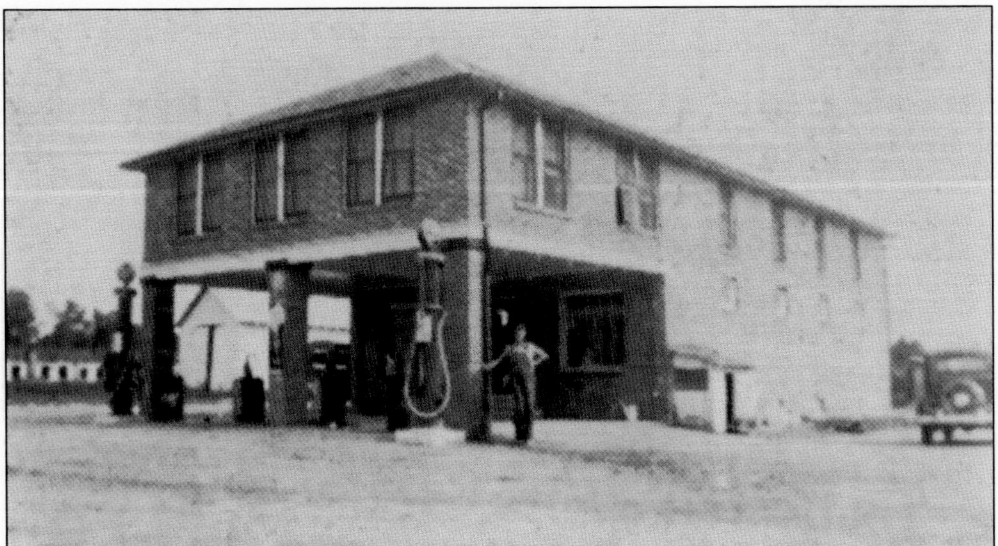

The Percy Flowers Store, shown in 1936, was a popular stopping place for travelers between Clayton and Wilson, and was a gathering place for Archer Lodge residents.

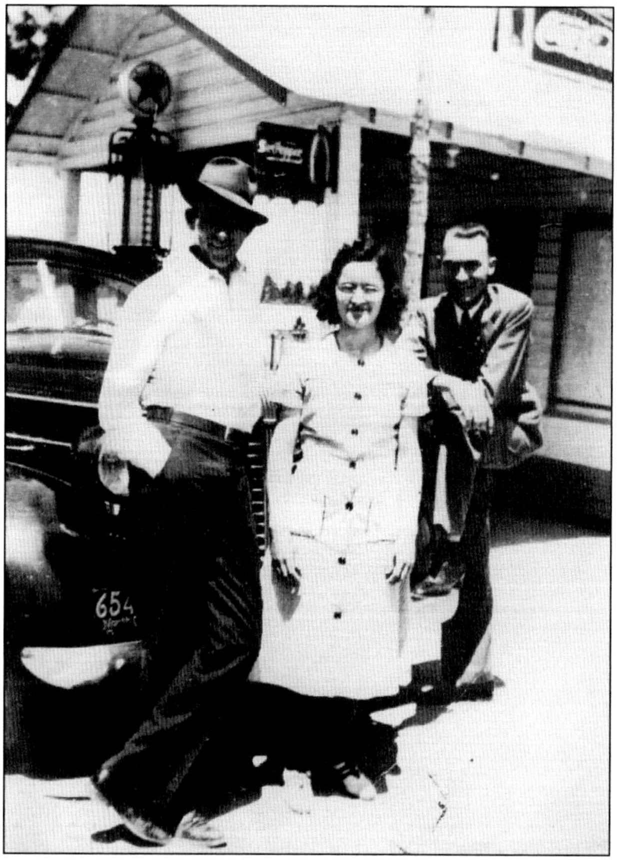

T. R. Lee's Grocery store operated from 1936 to 1950 on Shotwell Road. Pictured in front of the store around 1938 are, from left to right, T. R. Lee, his wife, Lena, and Kenneth Lee. (Courtesy of the Percy Lee family.)

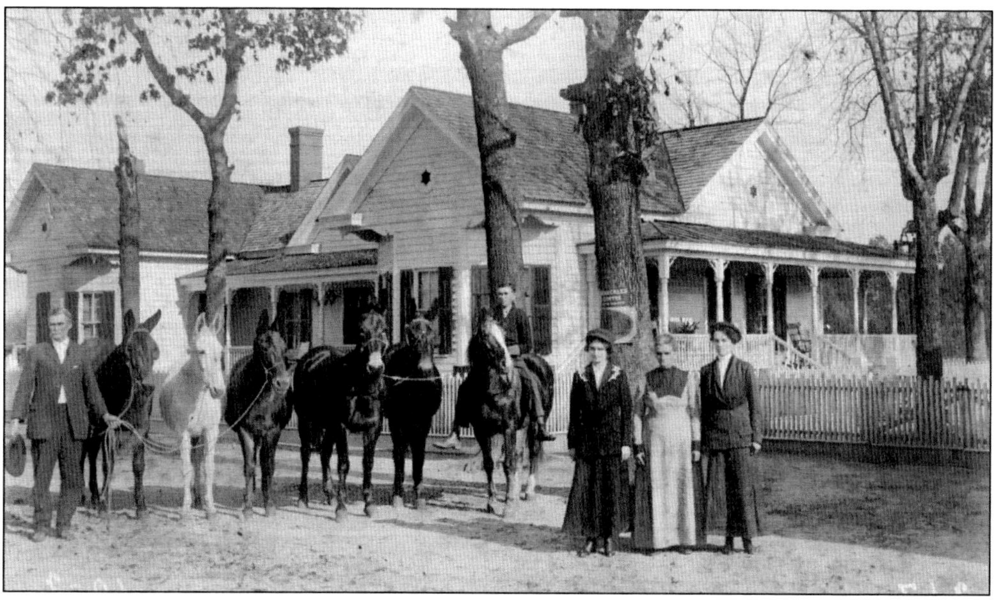

Sylvester V. Smith was no one-horse farmer, as evidenced in this photograph of the Smith family about 1900. The house, located across from the Bethesda Baptist Church, had a general store attached and a well that passersby and church folk often used.

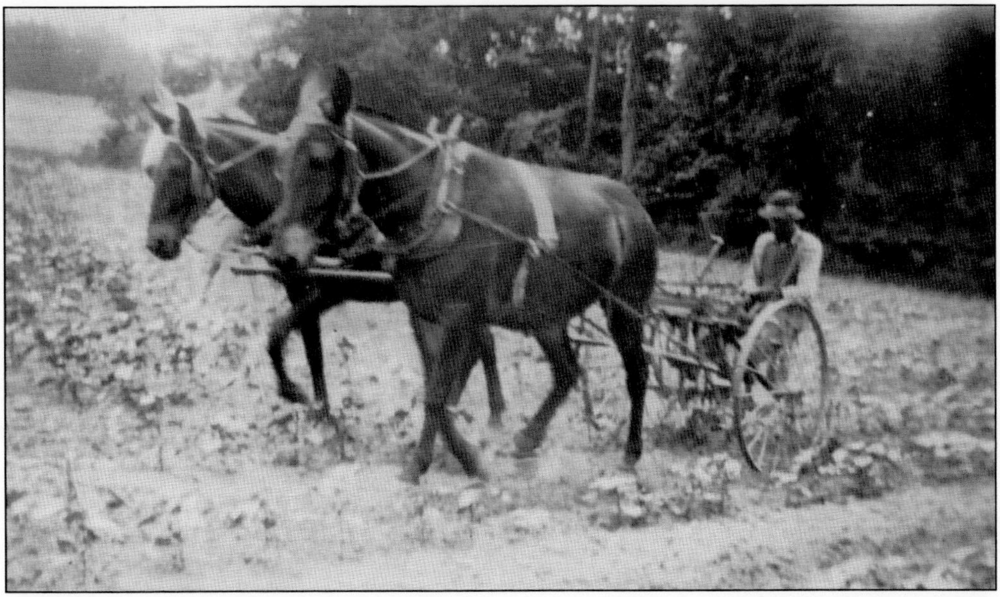

This plowman from about 1920 is thought to have been working on one of the Barbour family farms near Clayton. (Courtesy of Carey Barbour.)

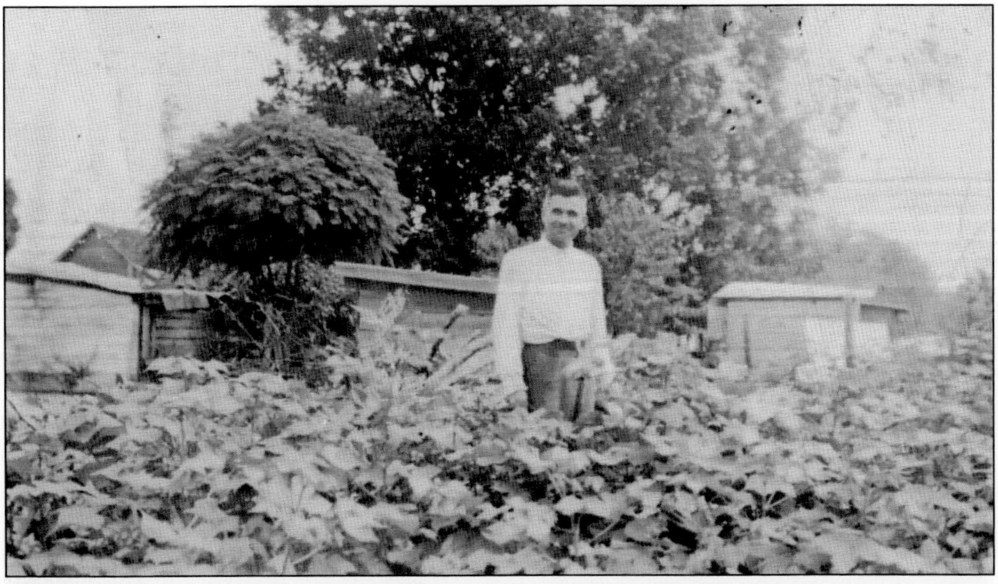

Ralph Austin was photographed in 1939 as he admired his cotton field. This postcard was sent to Austin from J. G. Barbour and Sons. Farming has always been important to the Clayton area. In the early 1900s, some farmers made as much as two bales of cotton, 75 bushels of corn, or 35 bushels of wheat an acre. Major crops in the 1930s were small grains, cotton, corn, potatoes, and tobacco. (Courtesy of Helen Ellerbe.)

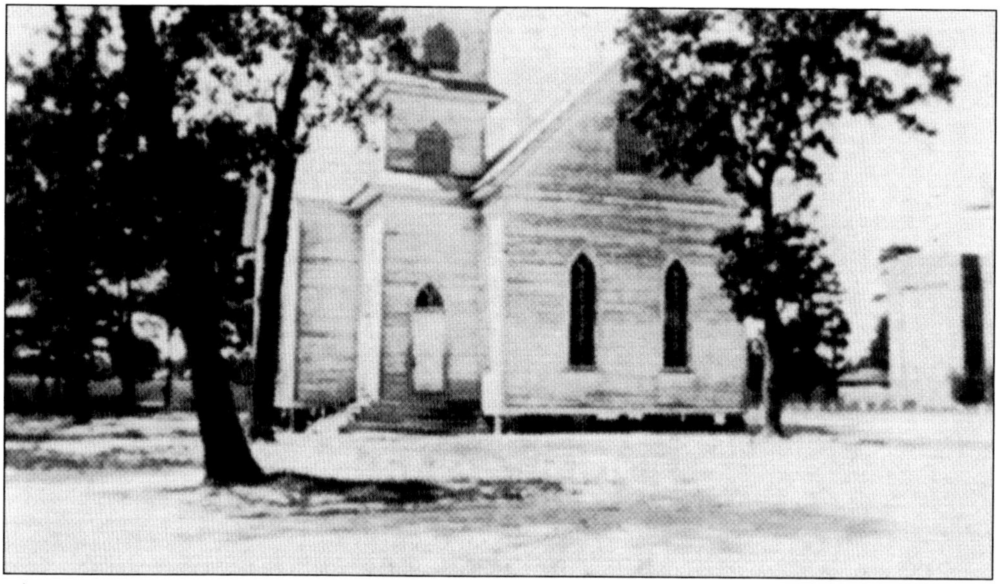

The Archer Lodge Baptist Church was organized on September 20, 1859, with 43 members. The church first met in the community's Masonic Lodge building. A new church building was built in 1883 on property deeded to the church by Elias G. Barnes. The name of the church was changed to White Oak Baptist Church that same year.

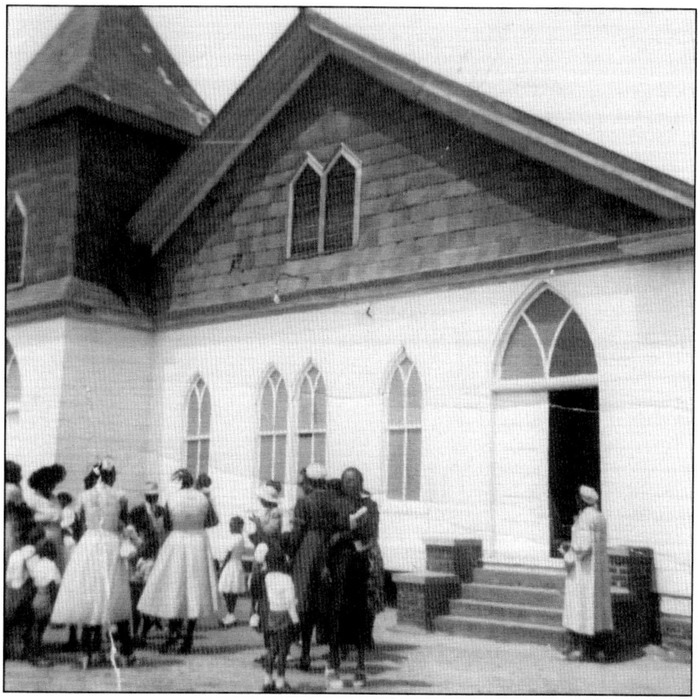

The congregation of the Red Hill Christian Church, founded in 1885, has worshipped in the building shown here since 1923. It was constructed under the leadership of pastor E. L. Sellars and has since undergone two renovations. In 1934, the church became affiliated with the Congregational Christian denomination and is now Red Hill United Church of Christ. (Courtesy of Eula Watson Carter.)

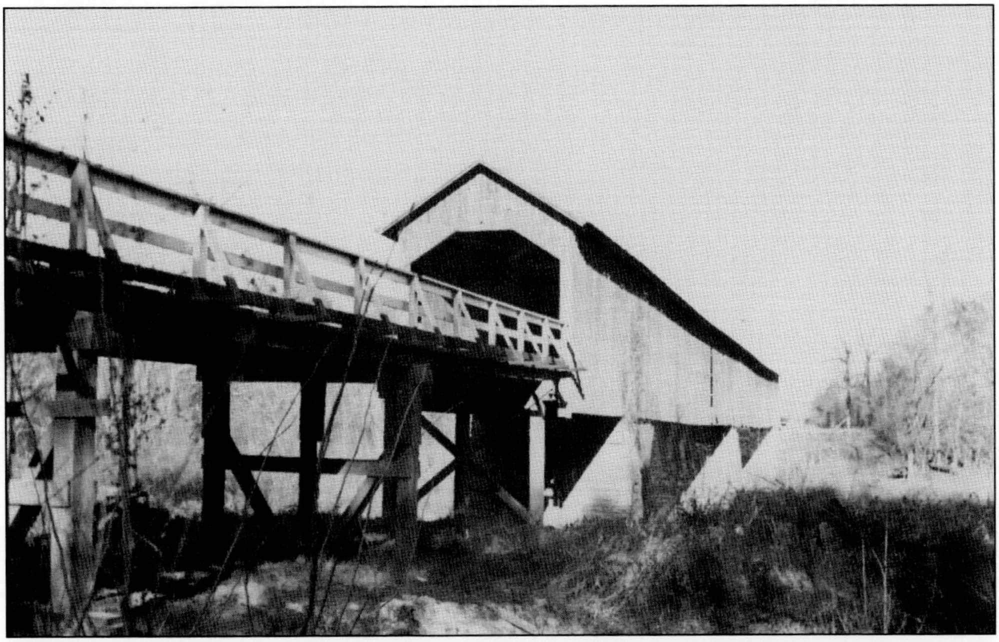

The last covered bridge over the Neuse River was built in 1883. This bridge was located on Covered Bridge Road between Clayton and Archer Lodge. The bridge was replaced in July 1940.

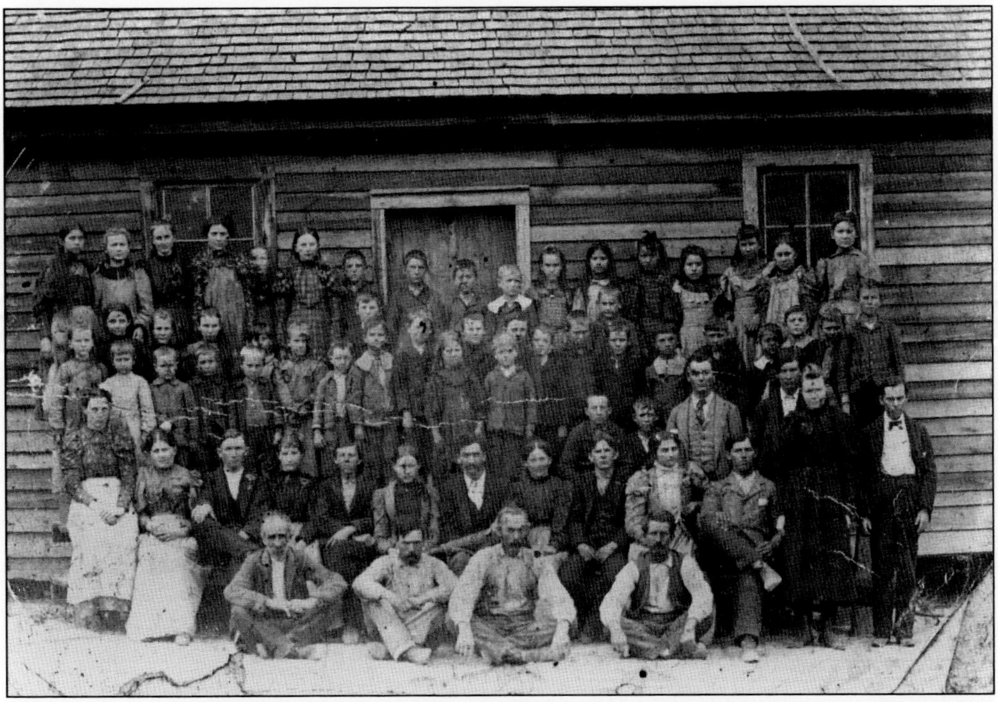

The Archer Lodge School, built about 1890, was replaced by a brick building in the 1920s. L. H. Champion was the principal when this photograph was taken in 1902. There were two schools at Archer Lodge in 1905, the Archer Academy and Barnes' Schoolhouse.

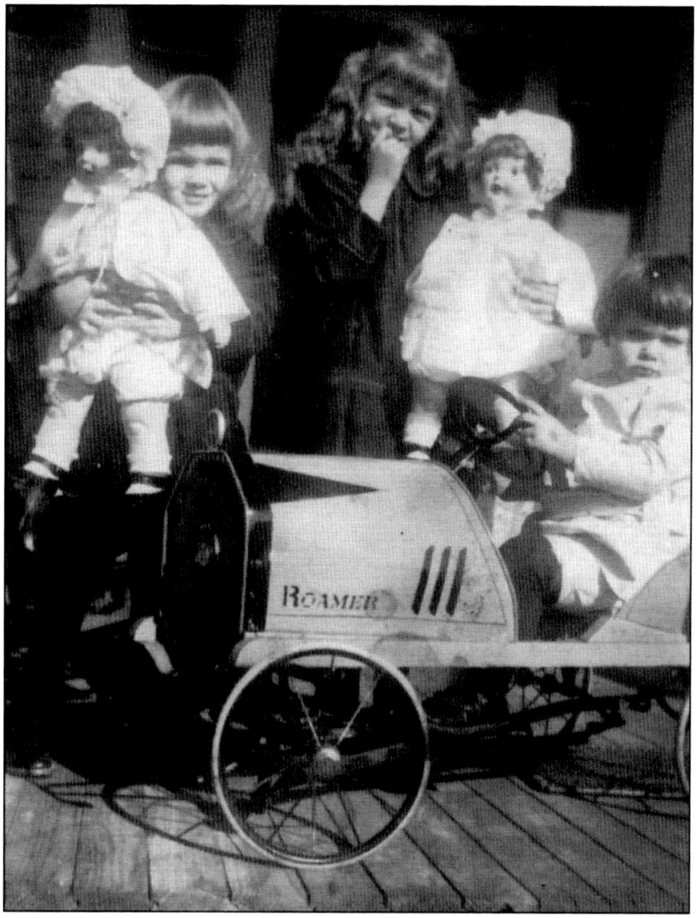

Lucille (left) and Lillian Lee watch little brother Dick as he sputters around in his highly prized toy automobile about 1925 while they play with their dolls. Their parents, Julius and Nellie Lee, operated a dairy and a country store in the Baptist Center area. (Courtesy of the Julius Lee family.)

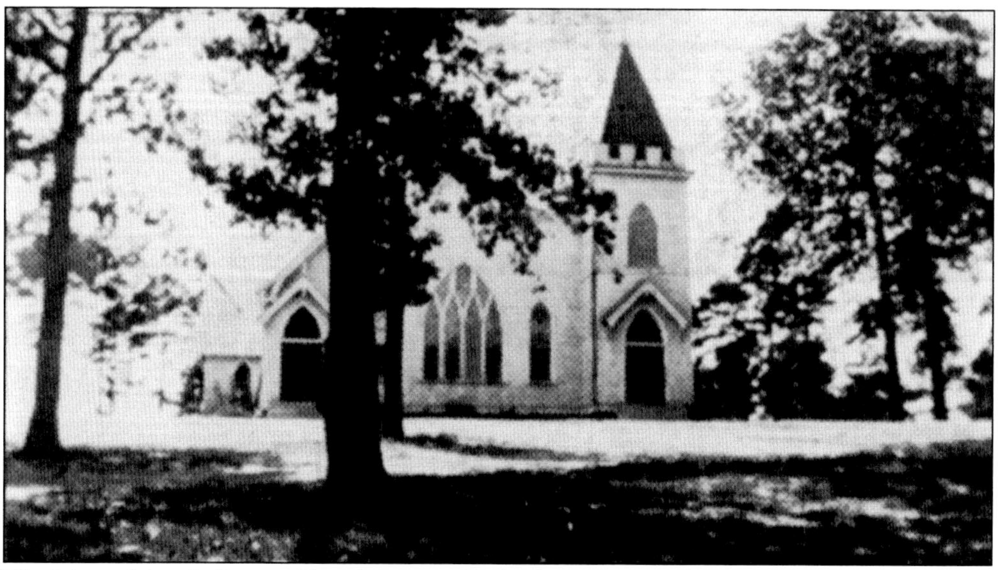

The Mount Moriah Baptist Church was established in 1834. Total membership in 1840 was 76. This view of the church was taken in 1936.

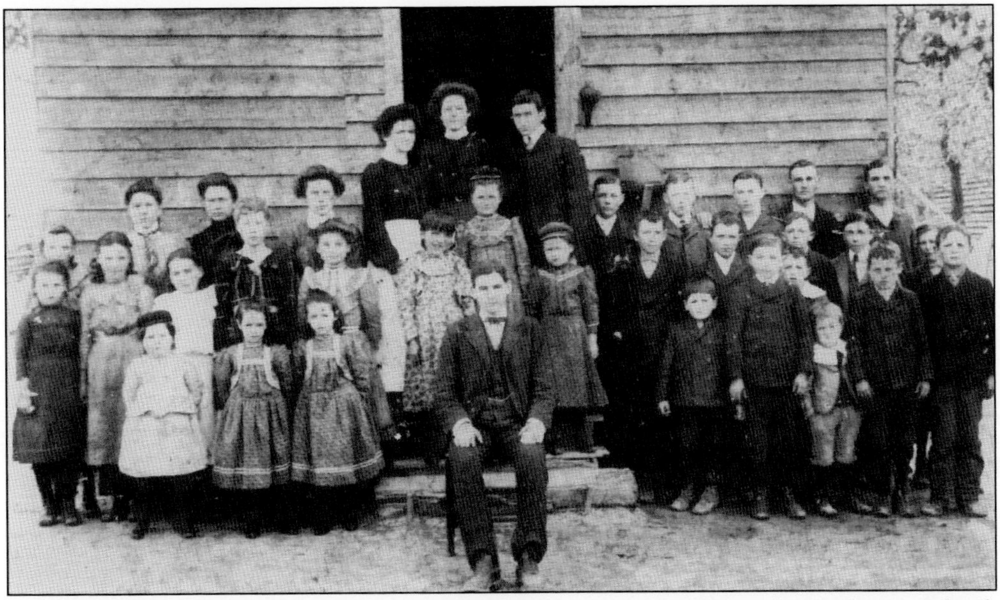

L. H. Champion (seated) is pictured with his students around 1897 at the Powhatan School. The Powhatan Free Will Baptist Church was founded in January 1888 and was moved to the Powhatan School property in 1922. A Powhatan post office had operated in the area from 1900 to 1912 with Isaac Jones as postmaster. (Courtesy of Sybil Champion.)

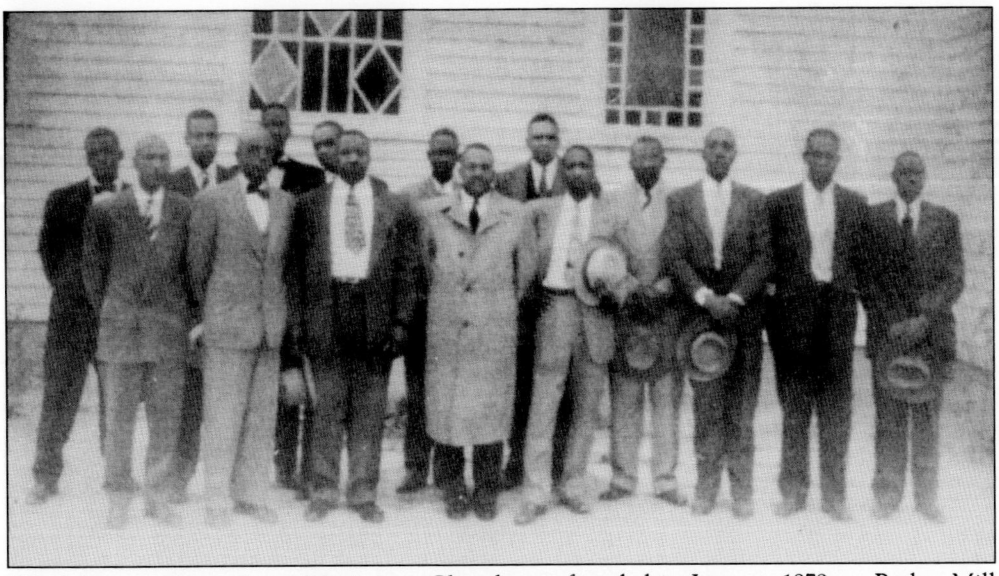

The Johnston Piney Grove Missionary Church was founded in January 1879 on Barber Mill Road. Men of the church are shown in this picture, taken about 1940.

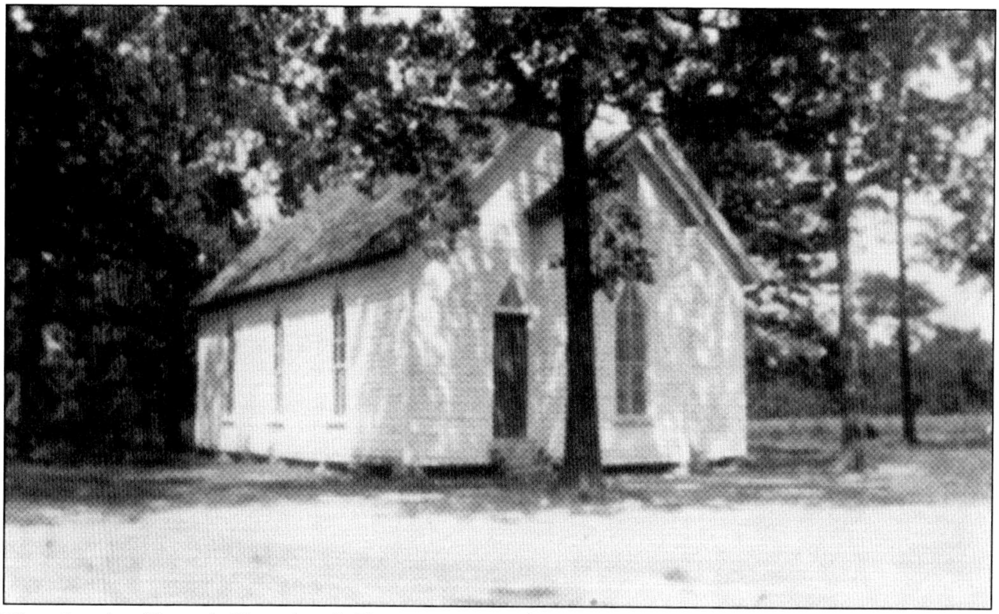

The Amelia United Church of Christ, organized in 1887, was named for its oldest charter member, Amelia Austin. J. A. Jones was the first pastor, with a salary of $15 a year. The church originally met in a small schoolhouse across the road. The church was constructed at its present location around the beginning of the 20th century.

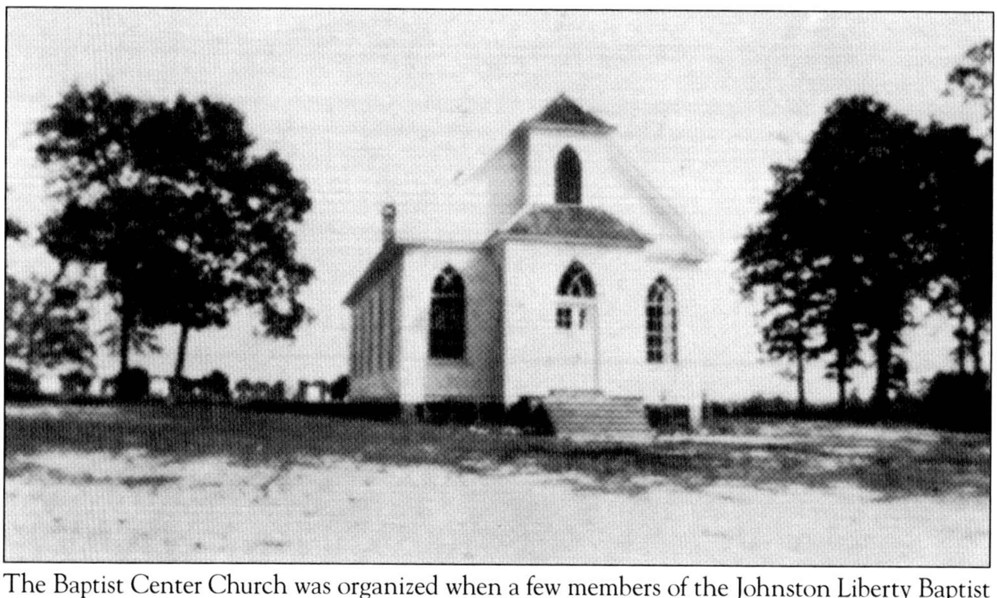

The Baptist Center Church was organized when a few members of the Johnston Liberty Baptist Church, Shiloh, Mount Moriah, and Bethesda asked for dismissals to form a new church in their neighborhood in 1871. Family names of these members were Austin, Yelvington, Massengill, Barber, Boon, Jones, Eatman, Vinson, and Turner. The church was built on property deeded to it by Sabrina Duncan, J. H. Duncan, and his wife, Sarah.

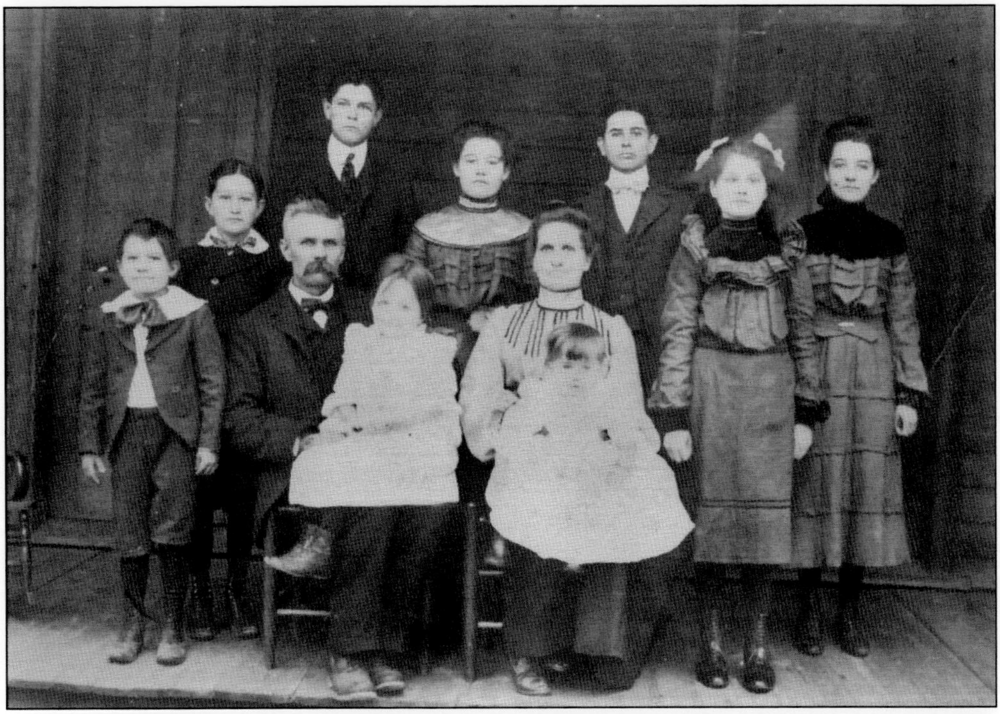

The Victor and Dora Austin family members in 1903 are, from left to right, (first row) Ralph, Victor, Agnes, Dora, Veta, and Pearl; (second row) Herbert, Clifford, Sophia, Ernest, and Myrtie. Dora (1862–1938) was the daughter of Henry and Sophia Mitchiner Austin. (Courtesy of Helen Ellerbe.)

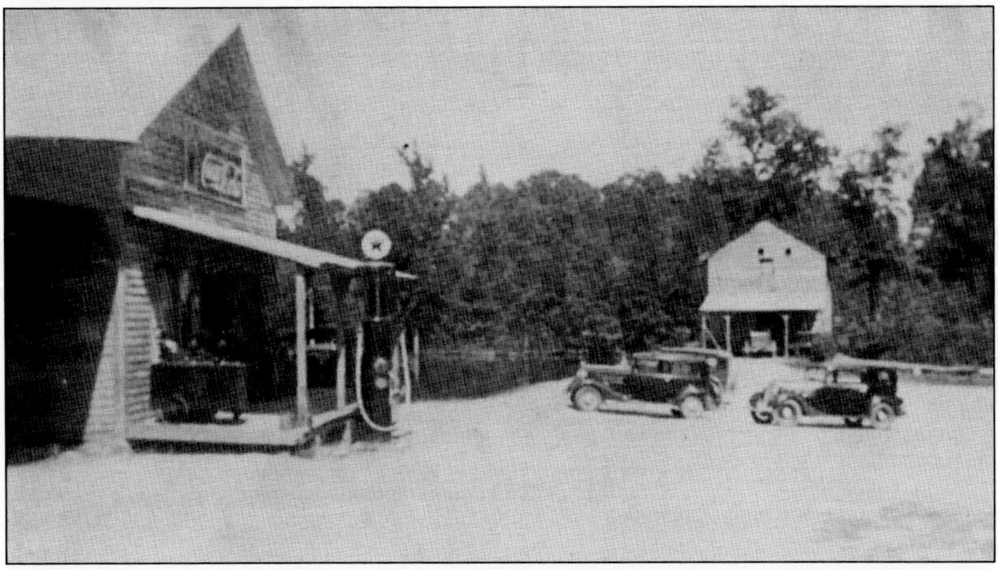

Rand's Mill, pictured in 1936, was the site of picnics, barbecue dinners, fishing, and boating. A 1935 *Clayton News* article stated that an enormous amount of meal was being manufactured around Clayton and hundreds of bags were hauled daily. Among the manufacturers and their products were Jesse Austin's Pappy, Millard Duncan's Blue Ribbon, and Wade Tippett's Water Ground Meal.

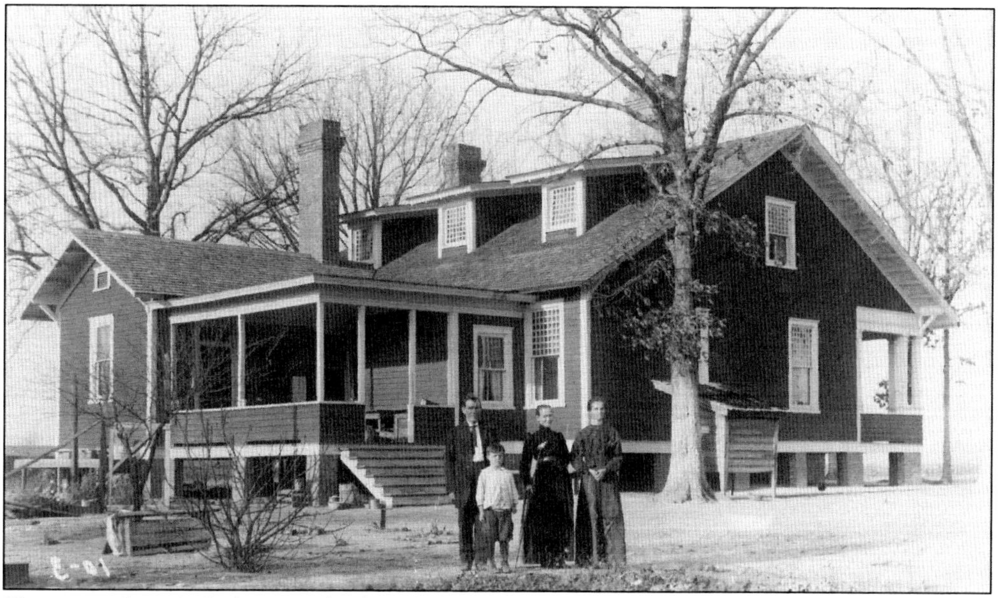

Shown in this 1915 photograph, from left to right, are Joe Turner Jeffreys, Nicholas Jeffreys, Octavia Hocutt, and her daughter Octavia Hocutt Jeffreys. Octavia Hocutt was the wife of Irvin W. Hocutt and also the mother of Dr. B. A. Hocutt.

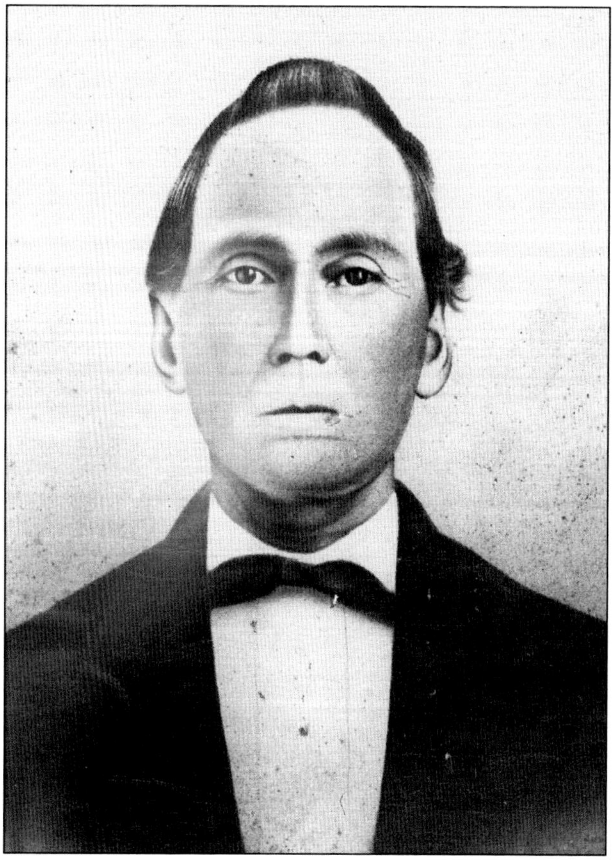

Rev. John F. Ellington was a well-known Baptist minister and farmer in the Clayton area from the antebellum period until his death in 1892. He was particularly remembered for his many years leading the flock at either Johnston Liberty Baptist Church (the First Baptist Church) or Bethesda Baptist Church. He walked several miles to and from preaching engagements and often received chickens and other goods in lieu of money for his services.

John T. Talton (1880–1964) was regarded as a local historian. He researched and compiled three books titled *Illustrated Handbook of Clayton North Carolina and Vicinity* for the years 1909, 1936, and 1961. These treasured books continue to educate with their historical pictures and information. In 1911, he married Ruth Barnes, and they had eight children. Talton worked with Clayton Banking from 1906 to 1930 and started an insurance company that he retained until 1959. He was active in business, civic, and social clubs. (Courtesy of Joyce T. Barbour.)

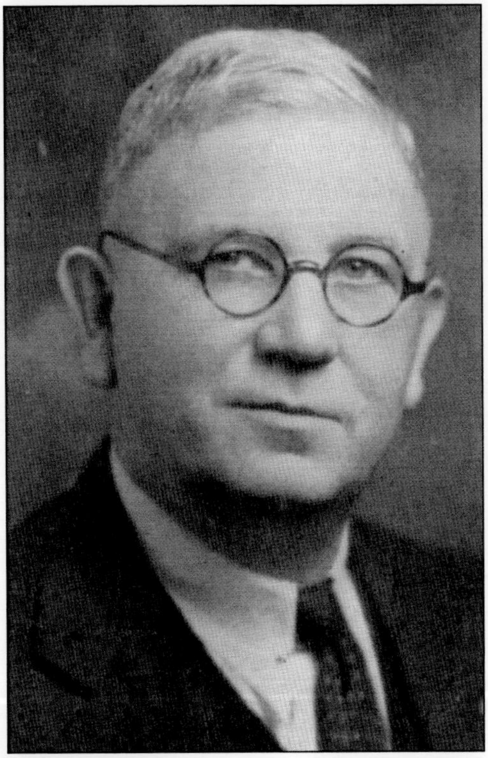

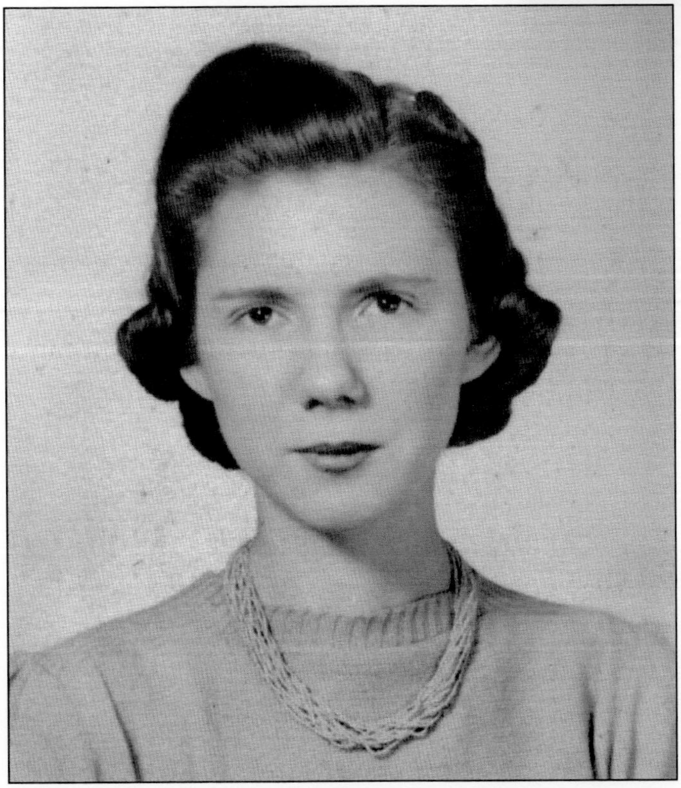

Virginia Lee Satterfield (1921–2003) devoted much of her life to collecting and preserving Clayton's history. She was a charter member of the Johnston County Historical Society in 1955 and became particularly interested in Clayton's history following the town's centennial celebration in 1969. In December 2007, she was memorialized in the naming of the Virginia Lee Satterfield History Room in the Hocutt-Ellington Memorial Library, in recognition of her voluminous work.

Consistent with our mission to preserve history on a local level, this book was printed in South Carolina on American-made paper and manufactured entirely in the United States. Products carrying the accredited Forest Stewardship Council (FSC) label are printed on 100 percent FSC-certified paper.

MADE IN THE USA